SELF-SCIENCE:
The Subject Is Me

This book is part of the Goodyear Series in Education,
Sandra N. Kaplan, Sheila K. Madsen, and Bette T. Gould, Editors.

OTHER GOODYEAR BOOKS IN GENERAL METHODS & CENTERS

AH HAH! The Inquiry Process of Generating and Testing Knowledge
John McCollum

A CALENDAR OF HOME/SCHOOL ACTIVITIES
Jo Anne Patricia Brosnahan and Barbara Walters Milne

CHANGE FOR CHILDREN Ideas and Activities for Individualizing Learning
Sandra N. Kaplan, Jo Ann B. Kaplan, Sheila K. Madsen, Bette K. Taylor

CREATING A LEARNING ENVIRONMENT A Learning Center Handbook
Ethel Breyfogle, Susan Nelson, Carol Pitts, Pamela Santich

THE LEARNING CENTER BOOK An Integrated Approach
Tom Davidson, Phyllis Fountain, Rachel Grogan, Verl Short, Judy Steely, Katherine Freeman

ONE AT A TIME ALL AT ONCE The Creative Teacher's Guide to Individualized Instruction Without Anarchy
Jack E. Blackburn and W. Conrad Powell

OPEN SESAME A Primer in Open Education
Evelyn M. Carswell and Darrell L. Roubinek

THE OTHER SIDE OF THE REPORT CARD A How-to-Do-It Program for Affective Education
Larry Chase

THE TEACHER'S CHOICE Ideas and Activities for Teaching Basic Skills
Sandra N. Kaplan, Sheila K. Madsen, Bette T. Gould

TEACHING FOR LEARNING Applying Educational Psychology in the Classroom
Myron H. Dembo

OTHER WAYS, OTHER MEANS Altered Awareness Activities for Receptive Learning
Alton Harrison and Diann Musial

WILL THE REAL TEACHER PLEASE STAND UP? A Primer in Humanistic Education, 2nd edition
Mary Greer and Bonnie Rubinstein

A YOUNG CHILD EXPERIENCES Activities for Teaching and Learning
Sandra N. Kaplan, Jo Ann B. Kaplan, Sheila K. Madsen, Bette T. Gould

For information about these, or Goodyear books in Language Arts, Reading, Science, Math, and Social Studies, write to
Janet Jackson
Goodyear Publishing Company
1640 Fifth Street
Santa Monica, CA 90401
(213) 393-6731

SELF-SCIENCE: The Subject Is Me

Karen F. Stone, M.A.
Harold Q. Dillehunt, Ph.D.
Nueva Learning Center

Goodyear Publishing Company, Inc.
SANTA MONICA, CALIFORNIA

Library of Congress Cataloging in Publication Data

Stone, Karen F
  Self-science.

    1. Self-perception—Study and teaching (Elementary).
I. Dillehunt, Harold Q., joint author. II. Title.
BF697.S84   372.1'1'2   78-4545
ISBN 0-87620-833-2
ISBN 0-87620-832-4 pbk.

ISBN: 0-87620-832-4 (p)   Y-8324-9 (p)
       0-87620-833-2 (c)   Y-8332-2 (c)

Current Printing (last digit):
10 9 8 7 6 5 4 3 2 1

Printed in the United States of America

To the children at Nueva Learning Center

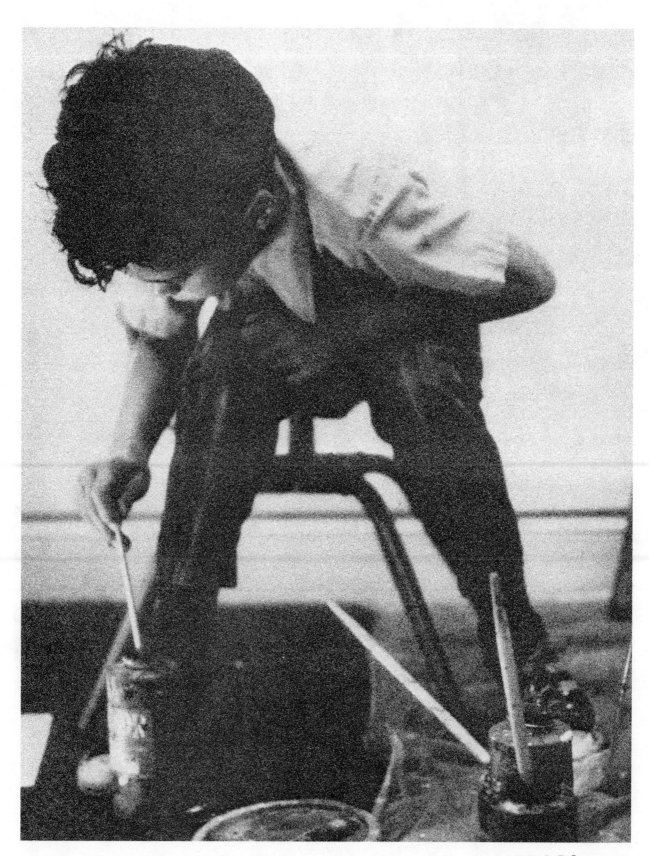

Acknowledgments

We would like to express our gratitude to friends and colleagues whose help and support made *Self-Science* a reality rather than a dream. We wish in particular to thank the children at the Nueva Learning Center who, through their participation, involvement, and evaluation, helped us in the development of this program, and the staff, parents, and board of directors who supported and encouraged the project.

We are also indebted to the following people, who provided guidance, assistance, and direction:

- **Gerald Weinstein,** professor of education at the University of Massachusetts, Amherst, for his work as principal investigator on a three-year Ford Foundation Project in Humanistic Education, which resulted in the creation of the trumpet process and in the initial development of self-science. We have relied heavily on the work of Weinstein and his colleagues as a basis for this curriculum.
- **James L. Olivero,** director of the Nueva Learning Center, for his enthusiastic support during the entire project; his invaluable assistance in the preparation, writing, and editing of the manuscript; his availability in times of need; his patience; and his confidence in our ability to produce the final manuscript.
- **Alan Gartner and Frank Riessman** for providing direction and assistance in the organization of the material.
- **Jackie Rienach** for technical assistance.
- **Jan Cook** for typing and more typing.

Contents

Preface

For five years we have been meeting at the Nueva Day School, just south of San Francisco. Once or twice a week, with small groups of children in grades two through six, we have been exploring what a school (or some other community group) can do to fulfill its promise to educate young human beings.

In college, we used to soul-search over terms such as "self-realization," "helping children reach their potential," and "educating for life." Out in the classroom, however, we saw Clarence sitting in the back row every day, totally uninvolved in what was going on; George laughing at everything, including history, grades, and girls; Rosemary always being the first to put her hand up; Virginia copying from others every chance she got. Teachers seemed weary: "All right, class, let's go over the facts again." There was day-after-day processing of information about the external world with seemingly little regard for the *person* who had to do the processing before learning could take place.

If a Martian were to look in on the situation (this is a fantasy technique we have learned to use successfully), he might observe that what is being taught and what is being learned are as far apart as the Earth and Mars, and that acquisition of survival skills such as those we need for working and loving is left entirely to chance! He might well ask, "Where do young people learn the techniques of survival? Where do they learn how to relate to themselves and others? To communicate? To solve problems? To take responsibility for their own learning?"

At Nueva we have been trying to answer the Martian by creating a separate course to be taught alongside the traditional three Rs. We call the course *Self-Science*.

Self-science is an affective program. Until recently, affect was the private preserve of poets, novelists, and musicians. Lately, it expanded to include psychiatrists and psychologists, who rarely enter the picture until after a child has demonstrated severe problems. It has certainly not been a concern of the schools. They have given little attention to the positive emotional development of children.

To develop our affective program, we have reached deeply into the world of humanistic educators, particularly the work of Gerald Weinstein and others at the University of Massachusetts. We have relied equally heavily on the methods and processes of modern science—the cognitive domain—which have been used extensively in the service of subject matter (schools often know a lot about the scientific method), but rarely in the study of self. We have explored ways to help children obtain the tools they need in order to combine the affective and cognitive processes.

We made these basic assumptions:

- There is no thinking without feeling and no feeling without thinking.
- Learning requires thinking *and* feeling and begins with experiencing.
- The more conscious one is of what one is experiencing, the more learning is possible.
- Experiencing one's self in a conscious manner—that is, gaining self-knowledge—is an integral part of learning.

When we put these assumptions to work at Nueva (not without a full share of gropings, meanderings, and mistakes), we were delighted to make the following observation: In the process (cognitive) of learning about self (affective), children acquire process tools relevant to dealing with personal concerns.

Slowly a curriculum emerged which we are now ready to share. It is by no means perfect, or a panacea, or meant for everyone. Any curriculum represents, at best, only one-third of a triangle. It is no more than a catalyst between student and teacher.

We believe in philosophical pluralism and realize that self-science may be appropriate for some schools (or even parts of some schools) and inappropriate for others. Likewise, we realize that not everyone should be a self-science leader. Some persons do not possess the requisite commitments to teach this curriculum. An honest self-search should be your first step toward an awareness of how to lead your students in developing the same kinds of decision-making abilities.

Section 1 of this handbook is an introduction to self-science. Section 2 covers what we think people want to know about self-science: how to teach it. Sections 3 and 4 contain sixty-four step-by-step lesson plans for the curriculum. Several appendixes offer suggestions concerning such matters as classroom management strategies, record keeping, and evaluation. The "Notes from Nueva" are extracts from our journals (with names changed in the spirit of the trust we advocate), offered in an effort to communicate some of the flavor and excitement of a self-science group in action. The real excitement, however, is experienced only by those who decide to risk themselves in this teaching-learning experience. We hope this book will help.

Karen Stone
Harold Dillehunt
The Authors

Section I
What is Self-Science?

I hear . . . and I forget.
I see . . . and I remember.
I do . . . and I understand.

—ANCIENT CHINESE PROVERB

GOAL GUIDELINES
First Half of Course
Goals 1-5

	AFFECTIVE EXPECTATIONS	**COGNITIVE EXPECTATIONS**
Approaching Goal 1: Legitimizing self-knowledge as valuable subject matter.	Choosing to take self-science. Participating in activities and discussions. Talking about one's self. Verbalizing what one is learning about one's self and how this knowledge is useful.	Understanding the scientific process. Understanding concepts of investigating, manipulating, organizing, quantifying, generalizing, inventorying. Understanding how scientists observe. There are many ways of looking at things. Understanding different ways of learning.
Approaching Goal 2: Developing a trusting attitude toward members of one's class.	Increasing willingness to utilize all members of the class as partners in exercises. Willingness to disclose personal feelings and concerns. Accepting and respecting the confidentiality of the class.	Realizing the importance of trust; keeping confidences; accepting; respecting. Using reading, writing, observing, classifying, and judgmental skills in understanding "trust." Learning ways of making decisions. Learning to classify by listening.
Approaching Goal 3: Becoming more aware of the many feelings one has.	Increasing ability to inventory one's thoughts and feelings. Increasing awareness of the relationship between one's emotions and physical states. Increasing acceptance and support of the thoughts and feelings of others in the class. Increasing awareness of the similarities and differences between one's responses and the responses of others.	Developing vocabulary for feelings. Understanding concepts for the process of feelings; labeling feelings. Understanding relevance of feelings to self, home, school. Understanding various modes of perceiving feelings. Accepting one's own feelings.
Approaching Goal 4: Developing communication skills for affective states.	Accepting new procedures for learning; such as gaming, fantasizing, role playing, and nonverbal communication. Improving listening skills and self-expression. Developing vocabulary. Relaxing and creating visual imagery.	Developing interpretation and inference skills. Distinguishing between fact and judgment. Learning the concept of negotiation in terms of negotiating problem situations. Developing listening skills. Understanding what communication is, i.e., sending and receiving.
Approaching Goal 5: Disclosing one's thoughts and feelings.	Increasing ability to disclose one's thoughts and feelings. Increasing ability to participate in self-disclosure exercises.	Classifying behavior into categories; seeing patterns. Understanding the connection between behavior and communication. Valuing open communication. Conducting and reporting on experiments. Improving listening and question-asking skills.

Winding Up Goals 1-5 Learning and experiencing the trumpet, an eight-step cognitive road map for charting affective processes.

Background

The imparting of traditional subject matter that emphasizes factual knowledge of the external world is called *cognitive education*. Studies that emphasize knowledge of one's own internal world in relation to one's self and others are called *affective* or *humanistic education*. Affective education programs now exist widely—primarily outside the school system—in the form of encounter groups, sensitivity training groups, and executive management groups. These groups share the premise that learning about self is an important and neglected part of education, and that directed experiences within a group setting facilitate such learning. These groups are made up largely of adults voluntarily seeking self-knowledge.

Few opportunities for affective learning are available to children, although the field of humanistic education is rich with data on experiential techniques. Here and there, some teachers do adapt techniques of affective education, such as simulation games for social studies, role playing in language arts, and experiential games in math. Others are experimenting with the teaching of values and values clarification. Ironically, however, the majority of affective education is taking place in remediation courses, as a means of reaching and teaching children after traditional techniques have failed.

A blending of affective and cognitive education may produce what is little more than a concept—*confluent education*, learning that emphasizes both the cognitive and affective elements in any learning situation. We believe that most, if not all, future learning environments will be of a confluent nature; but it will take time, patience, and understanding to synthesize the tenets of educational psychology, child development and learning, and communication theory into confluent curriculum programs, as well as to train teachers who will understand and enjoy teaching them. Self-science is such a program.

THE SELF-SCIENCE PROGRAM: SCOPE AND SEQUENCE

Self-science is an experience-based program designed for children from the second grade through the upper-elementary grades. Its aim is to equip children with affective and cognitive skills that can broaden their understanding and functioning in all learning and social situations. Students are taught to learn and to use scientific inquiry methods in studying themselves, within small-group "laboratory" situations. Special attention is given to helping students discover their own best learning styles and study habits. Frequent outside assignments provide students with opportunities to apply their self-science learning as they go.

The curriculum was field-tested at the Nueva Learning Center in Hillsborough, California, where self-science is offered as an open-ended course at each grade level from the second grade on up. The course may be taught over one school year (two lessons each week) or over two school years (one lesson each week). It may be offered as an elective or included as a mini-course within other curriculum areas, such as language arts, social studies, or health.

The program consists of sixty-four lessons grouped under ten goals. (See the Goal Guidelines.) The goals should be followed in sequence because the sequence itself exemplifies the inquiry process. Introductions to each goal include affective expectations, cognitive expectations, and discussions of the content and of group processes pertaining to that goal.

The term *approaching* (e.g., Approaching Goal 1), which is used throughout, is meant to convey to self-science teachers the idea that process learning is very much like seed planting. There may or may not be immediate evidence that learning is taking place, yet one can be confident, based on innumerable reports from teachers and students involved in humanistic education, that some growth is occurring. Accepting the idea of delayed reaction can help self-science teachers set realistic expectations and feel more comfortable with their role in the program. Evaluation techniques are provided periodically and their implications discussed.

GOAL GUIDELINES
Second Half of Course
Goals 6-10

	AFFECTIVE EXPECTATIONS	**COGNITIVE EXPECTATIONS**
Approaching Goal 6: Enhancing self-esteem in terms of awareness and acceptance of one's strengths.	Increasing ability to think and talk more positively about one's self. Increasing ability to laugh at one's self. Expressing pride in one's self. Describing accurately one's strengths and weaknesses.	Learning to make evaluations and judgments. Relating moral concepts to characters in fiction, myths, and folk tales. Reinforcing skills in classifying data.
Approaching Goal 7: Accepting responsibility for one's self.	Increasing acceptance of one's feelings, moods, conduct, and the consequences of one's own behavior. Increasing the ability to follow through on a commitment.	Understanding concepts of projection and avoidance. Applying evaluation skills to one's own study habits.
Approaching Goal 8: Becoming aware of one's major concerns.	Increasing the ability to state specific personal concerns and relate personally to the concerns of others.	Integrating and using the skills and concepts developed thus far.
Approaching Goal 9: Recognizing one's present behavioral patterns; learning about one's own learning styles.	Increasing the ability to identify and describe one's own behavioral patterns. Identifying one's own learning patterns. Increasing one's awareness of the consequences and functions of behavioral patterns.	Stating one's own learning patterns. Integrating and using the process tools learned thus far.
Approaching Goal 10: Experimenting with alternative behavioral patterns.	Increasing the ability to conceptualize alternatives. Increasing the ability to experiment with new behavior. Accepting one's limitations.	Understanding the processes for making changes.

Winding Up Goals 6-10	Understanding the tools now at one's command and sensing when the tools will be useful. Acquiring a sense of accomplishment and closure.

Rationale

There are, besides the gifts of the head, also those gifts of the heart, which are no whit less important, although they may be easily overlooked because in such cases the head is often the weaker organ.

—JUNG

The self-science curriculum is based on some very simple assumptions:

- The more conscious one is of experiencing, the greater the potential for self-knowledge.
- The more self-knowledge one gains, the more likely it is that one can respond positively to one's self and others.

While these assumptions are reasonably simple, they are based upon a careful and critical study of respected research in the area of affective education. Eclectic in origin, self-science draws principally from Maslow's hierarchy of needs; Kelly's psychology of personal constructs; child personality and development studies; Gestalt theory; role playing; and scientific methods of inquiry. (See Appendix E for a more detailed description of Kelly's and Maslow's theoretical positions.)

Affective education isn't new. However, there has been great resistance to affective programs in most educational circles. One reason for this resistance in recent times has been the difficulty of measuring the results of such a program. (Irrespective of this difficulty, one need not look too closely at current societal upheavals to find indications of less than total success in the areas of self-knowledge and interpersonal relationships.) Another obstacle has been our failure to ask relevant questions: "What is the effective value of a knowledge of externals if we lack an equally deep personal insight? Can there be wisdom even about the objective world around us in the absence of wisdom about the world within? Can there be any mature understanding of others without self-knowledge?"[1] The questions are obviously somewhat rhetorical. Following are statements by Kubie and Jung that we feel exemplify the foundation of self-science education. "Education without self-knowledge can never mean wisdom and maturity; but self-knowledge in depth is a process, like education itself, and is never finished. . . . It is relative and not absolute."[2] The exclusive aim of education should not be "to stuff the children's heads with knowledge, but rather to make them real men and women."[3]

The goal, then, is to educate the whole being, not just that portion of the anatomy from the neck up. Life-long learning is impossible if education is valued only in terms of intellectual prowess. We are more than our thoughts; we are also feelings and actions. Feelings and actions are as important in determining our self-esteem as is our intellectual development.

Clearly, the school, as a major socializing institution of childhood, plays a significant role in determining self-concept. The give-and-take associations of contemporaries intrinsic to that environment help develop self-esteem. A challenge to education is to define components that help children see themselves as valued and successful people.

Different scholars of affective education have different ideas about these components. Rogers suggests that an atmosphere which permits free expression of ideas and affect and does not resort to harsh and frequent evaluative comparisons enables individuals to know and accept themselves.[4] White stresses support for the child's feelings of efficacy and notes the importance of spontaneous activity, from which these feelings are derived. Though he does not deny the general importance of social approval, he proposes that "there are innate sources of satisfaction that

---

1. L. Kubie, in R. Porter, *The Role of Learning in Psychotherapy* (Boston: Little, Brown, 1968), p. 225.

2. *Ibid.*, p. 225.

3. C. G. Jung, *The Development of Personality* (New York: Pantheon Books, 1954), p. 56.

4. Stanley Coopersmith, *The Antecedents of Self-Esteem* (San Francisco, 1967), p. 35.

accompany mastery of the environment and they are independent of extrinsic social rewards."[5] According to Coopersmith, self-esteem is enhanced through democratic practices. He describes these practices as "freedom within established limits, encouraging the right to participate in ongoing dialogue within those limits and without penalty."[6] Limits, he says, should be well defined and enforced, but not harsh or unduly restrictive.[7] If limits are reasonable, children will internalize a set of definite values and attainable standards. "Without limits to gauge attainment, and (in the case of children) without the resource to form standards of their own, it is difficult, if not impossible, to gauge personal competence and success."[8] Support and limits such as those described above are found in the self-science curriculum.

Many studies from child-development research suggest that a child's self-concept is not innate; nor is it totally fixed by the magical age of five or six.[9] Consequently, the school holds tremendous potential for either enhancing or destroying a child's sense of worth. This grave responsibility has been too long ignored in education. If children hear from teachers and peers six hours each day that they are "stupid," "clumsy," "mean," "smart," "thoughtful," etc., their behavior will rise or fall according to these expectations.

Clearly, then, the indispensable basis of self-education is self-knowledge. Self-knowledge is gained partly from a critical survey and judgment of personal actions and partly from support and criticism of others. Appreciation of self and recognition of the importance of self-esteem are precisely what permit people to perceive the gifts of the heart. Lawrence Kubie summarizes this concept by saying,

> Without self-knowledge in depth we can have dreams but not art; we can have the neurotic raw material of literature but not mature literature. Without it we can have no adults but only aging children armed with words, paint, and atomic weapons; none of which they understand. It is

this which makes a mockery of the more pretentious claims of education, of religion, of the arts, and of science. Self-knowledge is the forgotten man [person] of our entire educational system and indeed of human culture in general. Without self-knowledge it is possible to be erudite but never wise. The challenge to all of us is to have the humility to face this failure and the determination to do something effective about it.

> This position should not be exaggerated. Self-knowledge is not all there is to wisdom. It is an essential ingredient which makes maturity possible. Yet, it is the one ingredient which is totally neglected . . .[10]

Self-science is an attempt to help educators meet one of their most formidable challenges—that of developing self-knowledge.

BIBLIOGRAPHY

Coopersmith, Stanley. *The Antecedents of Self-Esteem.* San Francisco: W. H. Freeman, 1967.

Jung, C. G. *The Development of Personality.* Translated by R. F. C. Hull, Bollingen Foundation. New York: Pantheon Books, 1954.

Kelly, G. H. *The Psychology of Personal Constructs. Vol. 1: A Theory of Personality.* New York: Norton, 1955.

Koch, Sigmond. *Psychology: A Study of Science. Study 11: Empirical Substructure and Relations with Other Sciences.* New York: McGraw-Hill, 1963.

LeFebre, L. *Psychotherapy Relocated.* Unpublished manuscript, 1975.

Lieberman, Morton A., Irvin E. Yalom, and Matthew B. Miles. *Encounter Groups: First Facts.* New York: Basic Book, 1973.

Maslow, Abraham H. *Motivation and Personality.* New York: Harper & Row, 1970.

Porter, Ruth. *The Role of Learning in Psychotherapy.* Boston: Little, Brown, 1968.

10. L. Kubie, op. cit., p. 226.

5. *Ibid.*, p. 41.

6. *Ibid.*, p. 205.

7. *Ibid.*, p. 208.

8. *Ibid.*, p. 208.

9. Sherif, in S. Koch, *Psychology: A Study of Science, Study II: Empirical Substructure and Relations with Other Sciences* (New York: McGraw-Hill, 1963), p. 60.

The Trumpet Process

Without self-knowledge it is possible to be erudite but never wise. The challenge of all of us is to have the humility to face this failure and the determination to do something about it.

—KUBIE

There isn't anything radical about the self-science concept. In practice, it merely extends traditional classroom norms. The extended norms are in no way meant to supplant the traditional; they are meant to supplement what already works.

Traditional Classroom Norms	Self-Science Extended Norms
1. Learning about the world is the legitimate subject matter for the school.	+ Learning about one's self (thoughts, feelings, and behaviors) is legitimate in school.
2. Remembering, planning and interpreting are important.	+ Experiencing the present moment, the here-and-now of students and teacher, is important.
3. Learning words and concepts for, and learning how to negotiate, the world of things and ideas is important.	+ Learning words and concepts for, and learning how to negotiate, one's emotions is important.
4. Critical judgment and evaluation (and earned respect for performance) are central in the learning process.	+ Nonjudgmental acceptance and respect is central to the process of individual personal growth.
5. Talking, thinking, and reading about experiences and ideas are central in the learning process.	+ Experiencing one's self and one's surroundings is central to personally important learning.
6. Well-thought-out expression about subject matter is valued in the learning process.	+ Appropriate, nonmanipulative disclosure of thoughts and feelings about self and others is valued and facilitates personal growth in self and others.

In the course of our investigations of humanistic education, we became aware of two recognizable problems besieging other affective curricula:

- Authors of other programs typically put together a series of fun-and-game activities with little logical ordering or psychological foundation.
- Authors of other programs helped students proceed through a series of exercises designed to help clarify values but without helping students learn process skills for appropriate behavior changes. Those who clarify their values reap little benefit if they haven't also learned how to take action.

Fortunately, our review of available materials in affective education led us to the University of Massachusetts where Gerald Weinstein and a group of colleagues (sponsored through a grant from the Ford Foundation) were researching various elements of an affective curriculum that seemed to offer theoretical and practical support.

Researchers at the University of Massachusetts did indeed have a solid base of foundation material, but little had been done to translate their findings from the laboratory discussion stage to the teacher-using-in-the-classroom stage. With approval from Weinstein and his permission to use the Trumpet Process, the lack of

THE TRUMPET

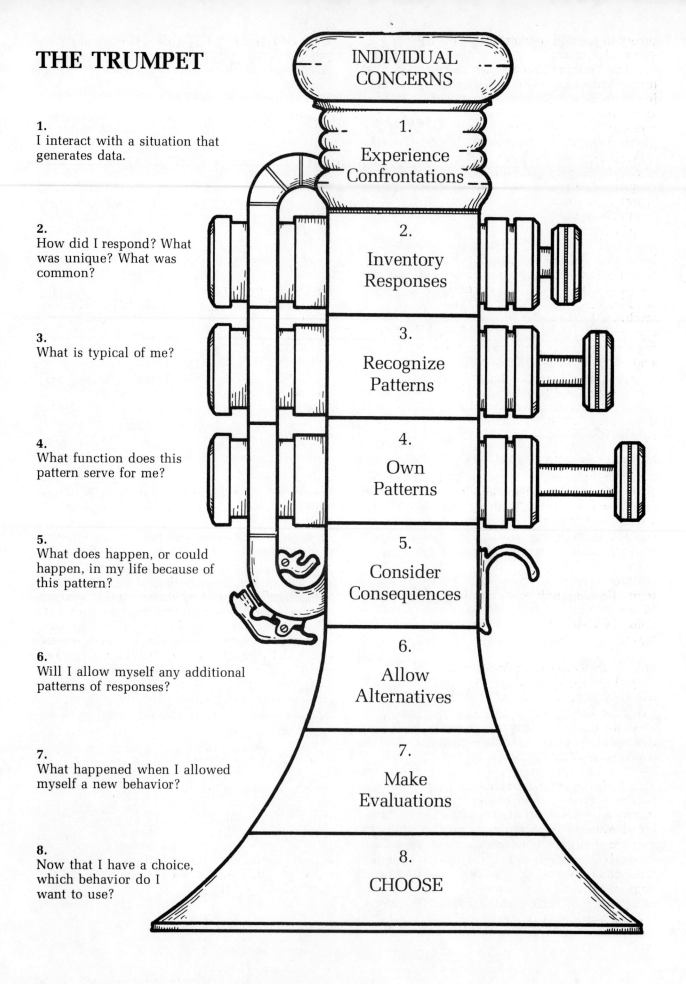

1.
I interact with a situation that generates data.

2.
How did I respond? What was unique? What was common?

3.
What is typical of me?

4.
What function does this pattern serve for me?

5.
What does happen, or could happen, in my life because of this pattern?

6.
Will I allow myself any additional patterns of responses?

7.
What happened when I allowed myself a new behavior?

8.
Now that I have a choice, which behavior do I want to use?

INDIVIDUAL CONCERNS

1. Experience Confrontations

2. Inventory Responses

3. Recognize Patterns

4. Own Patterns

5. Consider Consequences

6. Allow Alternatives

7. Make Evaluations

8. CHOOSE

theory to practice became ours. This book is a result of that effort.

The Trumpet Process (see tearsheet, p. 173) brings something to self-science that is seldom found in other affective curricula; it provides guidelines for action. As the scientific method is a process tool for making discoveries about the physical world, the Trumpet is a process tool for making discoveries about and acting on issues having to do with emotion and inner space. The purpose of self-science is to teach the cognitive Trumpet Process. This process is best learned through experiencing the curriculum's affective exercises.

Goals for the self-science curriculum have been outlined above. The first five goals help students work toward a group cohesiveness as well as orient them to certain skills they will need later on. The final six goals are built around teaching the Trumpet Process. The trumpet, in fact, provides the cognitive guidelines for making sense of the experiences in the lessons. Each step of the Trumpet Process will be presented in detail. The self-science teacher must have the process stored—and ready for use—at all times. The Trumpet Process offers the focal point for questions the teacher may ask, questions that help students internalize their experiences.

BEFORE BEGINNING THE PROCESS

A trusting atmosphere in which students feel safe to identify their concerns about themselves and others is essential. Children sometimes need alternative affective experiences in order to realize their concerns, particularly when they are working in a group. Many of the early games and exercises in the curriculum are designed to help children become aware of and share their problems. Games such as "Fear in the Hat" and "Three Wishes" help to evoke concerns and to unite the members of the class through common topics.

Step 1. Experience Confrontations

As just stated, student participation in the various exercises and games of the curriculum (affective experiences) has a unifying effect and provides the class with common reference points for discussion. Common affective experiences facilitate sharing of concerns.

Step 2. Inventory Responses

Students examine and explore what happened during an experience. (Other affective curricula fall short here as students are offered experiences and are then left to figure the answers out for themselves—if they can.) This step may be the most complex part of the Trumpet Process. It requires the ability to ask questions in three main areas: thought, feeling, and action. When inventorying responses to exercises, remember the questions, What did you think? How did you

feel? and What did you do? These questions provide simple guidelines for inquiry. Suggested discussion questions follow each exercise.

Step 3. Recognize Patterns

As the inventory process becomes more elaborate, patterns of unique student behavior begin to emerge. These patterns are evident in action, thought, and feeling. All people exhibit behavior patterns; that is, typical responses to typical problems or concerns; but most individuals need help in identifying and understanding their patterns. Learning about one's patterns is sometimes difficult. Most children need to be made aware of a given pattern on at least three separate occasions before they recognize its existence.

Step 4. Own Patterns

This step helps children examine the functioning of their own patterns, understand how a particular pattern serves them, and accept that it is theirs (own it). There is a serving aspect to all patterns of thought, feeling, and action no matter how negative the pattern may appear to one's self and others. A socially positive pattern, such as volunteering to clean the chalkboard, is easy for the child to grasp, because the child is quickly aware of rewards. Many children, however, find it difficult to discover the benefits that may accrue from a socially negative pattern, such as bullying other children. You may need to help them understand that even socially negative patterns serve the possessors in some way.

Step 5. Consider Consequences

At this point, the child is helped to examine the price one pays for a particular pattern. Phrased differently, the child is helped to understand what benefits come at what costs and to analyze how the rewards and punishments balance out. As all patterns have positive aspects, they, too, have negative aspects. Most people have at least one socially positive pattern behavior; they generally think only of the "good" things derived from these patterns. Something is given up for these patterns, a price is paid. Even the child who cleans the chalkboard has some costs involved.

Step 6. Allow Alternatives

The child is helped to search for alternative modes of responding (behavior). Students are often asked: "What else might you do?" They are not asked to evaluate their ideas but rather to think of as many ideas as possible, no matter how far-out, impractical, or useless some of them may appear. Using their imaginations in this way helps children realize there is more than one approach to any situation.

Step 7. Make Evaluations

Once alternatives have been generated, the children must begin to evaluate them first by discarding the most obviously inappropriate notions. After the alternatives have been narrowed down to one or two possibilities, a commitment to one is required of each student. After trying the chosen alternative, each child reports the results to the group using the Trumpet Process in order to evaluate the experience.

Step 8. Choose

Most important in this final step is the element of conscious choice. Children must be aware of making decisions and must take responsibility for them. The issue is not whether people choose one alternative over another, or that they supplant one pattern with another. The purpose, rather, in expanding the range of possibilities is to enhance students' ability to choose an appropriate pattern according to specific circumstances. Repetition of past response patterns may be appropriate in some circumstances but not in others.

Before launching a self-science program, teachers themselves have to face some difficult decisions.

The Lessons

If ever I am a teacher it will be to learn more than to teach.

—DELUZY

You would not be reading this book if you were not already convinced of the value of humanistic education. However, before you consider initiating a self-science program—whether as a teacher, an administrator, or a parent—we believe you should explore and clarify your own responses to these major questions:

- Are the goals of self-science philosophically consistent with my personal values?
- Are the goals of self-science philosophically consistent with the values of the school where I teach?
- Do I have the leadership qualifications to teach self-science?

Becoming aware of and recognizing patterns of responses to various situations is one of the prerequisites to having some control over reactions and increasing self-directedness. All adults can remember situations in which they did something and then said to themselves, "Why did I do that?" These situations may arise because we do not know enough about our patterns of behavior. Often children are completely oblivious to their own patterns of behavior. For instance, when two children have a fight and are asked what happened, each respond by saying something about the other child. Seldom are they aware of their own behavior.

Helping students become aware of their behavior patterns involves focusing on the here and now. Such questions as

- What are you doing right now?
- What did you just do?
- Do you usually do that when someone else does that to you?

help students recognize their patterns.

When beginning to work more directly with patterns of behavior, the teacher will usually find it easiest and most constructive to focus on patterns in the class. For example, in self-science classes made up of primary-level students, there is often a marked tendency for boys to sit on one side of the circle and girls on the other. The teacher might ask, "Has anyone ever noticed that we have a pattern in our seating arrangement?" At least some of the students will usually make the observation. You can then discuss the nature of patterns, the fact that we all have them, and the fact that some patterns serve us well and some do not.

As students become more aware of patterns, they become more willing to examine the functions and consequences of their own. Initially, children seem to need considerable help to understand how a pattern serves them. Useful questions for discussion are

- How many different patterns do you have?
- How many of us have similar patterns?
- What do we like about our patterns?
- What don't we like about our patterns?
- Can patterns be changed or expanded?

Fantasizing about various kinds of situations and possible patterns of responses helps students examine their own patterns. Role playing can also aid them in examining their own behavior.

Every pattern has its pluses and minuses. If the teacher can model a pattern and illustrate how it serves, students can usually understand the idea more readily and become more willing to share their own patterns. Nearly all of the games and activities can be utilized this way once the students' confidence has been gained and they are sufficiently willing to examine their own patterns of behavior.

There are ten "flow lessons" (explained later in this section) in the program sequence. These should be introduced in order, although you may want to spend more time on some lessons than on others. The sequence is carefully structured in accordance with the spiral theory of learning; i.e., that as a program advances, students work in greater depth and complexity, calling on approaches they have experienced earlier. Even though special group needs may call for the occasional detour, it is important that you return to the sequence as quickly as practical. And remember: the program may be repeated profitably with the same students in another year. Each time the learning is reinforced and deepened.

Each lesson in self-science follows a similar format and, where appropriate, includes these features:

1. Materials needed—Materials needed are indicated under the lesson number heading. Materials required have been kept to a minimum, generally limited to such items as pencils, paper, index cards, phonograph, etc.
2. Beginning—Suggestions for getting the lesson started, recommended discussion topics, and guides to working with previously assigned materials are noted.
3. Affective Experience—The core of each lesson is a directed experience which provides firsthand material for cognitive inquiry. The experiences include games, simulations, experiments, and other group activities. They make use of such inquiry techniques as

brainstorming, fantasizing, and role playing (see Appendix C, p. 152). Many other affective programs stop at this point; self-science uses these experiences to further the cognitive expectations stated. Each experience is followed immediately by discussion questions whose purpose is to help students learn and use such inquiry methods as identifying, observing, classifying, and noting similarities and differences.
4. Cognitive Inquiry—This portion of each lesson is devoted to comprehending and extending the reactions that developed during the experiences, usually by means of a group discussion guided by the teacher. Students develop relevant vocabulary and a grasp of central concepts during these inquiries.
5. Assignment—Follow-up assignments pertinent to the areas under investigation are suggested with nearly every lesson. The assignments integrate skills in reading, writing, creative expression (art, poetry), journal keeping, and so forth.
6. Teacher Comments—Space is provided for you to jot down any notes that may seem relevant to you.
7. Instructions for Games and Activities— Separate instruction pages accompany the lessons in which games are used.
8. Notes from Nueva—These sections follow many of the lesson plans. In them we share some of the vivid experiences encountered during several years of teaching self-science at the Nueva Learning Center. The extracts from journals and diaries may help you to anticipate or better understand similar experiences with your own group.

THE FLOW LESSONS

Ten unstructured lessons are suggested at various points in the self-science sequence. Their purpose is to provide opportunity for discussion of group-initiated topics. In themselves they constitute experiences in reaching some of the expectations of self-science, e.g., taking responsibility for one's own learning, participating openly, and dealing with sensitive subject areas. Appendix D (p. 161) contains suggestions for handling flow lessons, along with extracts from experiences at Nueva on various popular topics. Once familiar with the curriculum, you will likely increase your use of flow lessons.

TECHNIQUES FOR TEACHING SELF-SCIENCE

Anyone likely to be reading this book is probably fairly experienced at teaching or parenting or leading—certainly at using many of the tools required for teaching self-science: identifying, observing, classifying, finding patterns, integrating information, and analyzing critically.

Perhaps the main difference between teaching a traditional subject and teaching self-science is your role in the classroom. The traditional classroom teaching role often approaches that of a manager; i.e., the teacher is primarily concerned with controlling and directing students. In self-science, you must certainly maintain order and set limits, but think of yourself as a "facilitator," a person who leads and pulls and tugs and demonstrates how to negotiate and keep the process going.

Traditional curricula center around what you teach and how you teach it. In self-science, the focus is almost reversed. How you teach is in itself a demonstration of using the scientific method to study self. You might say that *how* you teach is *what* you are teaching in self-science. In such a curriculum, who you are and what you personally demonstrate is a great part of what you are teaching. The well-known Rosenthal effect* ("You get what you expect") certainly operates here.

None of this discussion is intended to dismay you. On the contrary, teaching a self-science class can be an exciting journey in your own development. Start by extending your own self-image and seeing yourself as a role model and group leader; these are parts of your teaching repertoire.

---

*Robert Rosenthal and Lenore F. Jacobson, "Teacher Expectations for the Disadvantaged," *The Scientific American*, no. 4 (April 1968).

BEING A ROLE MODEL

Willy-nilly, teachers are role models in any classroom. Children take cues and internalize judgments and values from the personal style of the teacher. In self-science, try to be as much aware of your role as possible.

Providing a role model is not a magical, mystical thing. It simply means being yourself, while perhaps changing the emphasis on certain skills you already have. Your hardest job may be to examine the conditioning behind your own (possible) tendencies to take control, wield authority, and moralize. While you will never let go completely (this is a classroom group, not an encounter group), your efforts should be toward working for greater initiative from the group and less direction from you as time goes on.

Those whose values are consistent with those of self-science should read on. Those who have doubts are referred to Appendix A for a few simple values-clarification exercises which are designed to help them know whether to continue.

Section 2
The Self-Science
Curriculum

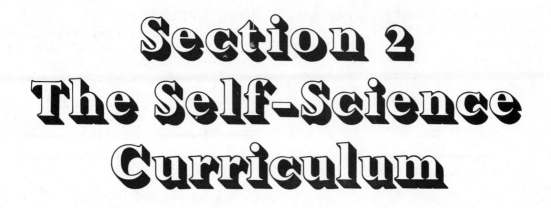

. . . knowledge per se does not necessarily lead to desirable behavior. Knowledge can generate feelings, but it is feeling that generates action. For example, we may know all about injustice to minorities in our society, but until we feel strongly about it we will take little action. A link to the affective or emotional world of the learner is therefore necessary. Unless knowledge is related to an affective state in the learner, the likelihood that it will influence behavior is limited.

—GERALD WEINSTEIN AND MARIO E. FANTINI,
*TOWARD HUMANISTIC EDUCATION:
A CURRICULUM OF AFFECT*

Getting Started

Currently there is considerable clamor to move "back to the basics." There is no question that today's children need the survival skills of the three Rs. To humanize or not to humanize, however, is hardly the question. A sensible balance between the two poles—cognitive and affective —is called for.

In some quarters there is greater opposition to affective education than in others. Educators who perceive that they will meet with little resistance are encouraged to proceed to the next section of the handbook, where information about lesson plans and teaching techniques are discussed. For those who anticipate some opposition, we recommend they read and study Appendix B. There they will find several suggestions for working with colleagues and parents. Make no mistake, careful planning and positive communication with all concerned are prerequisites for a successful program.

How the Program is Organized

It may be wise at this point to turn quickly to the lessons and preview the format. Each lesson follows a similar format. Note that, for easy reference, all instructions for games or activities mentioned in the lessons follow the lesson on separate pages. Even though the "Notes from Nueva" sections follow some lessons, you may wish to read the comments they contain prior to teaching the lesson. "Notes" are as close as we can come to sharing our personal experiences with self-science. All teaching and management techniques referred to throughout the book (brainstorming, role playing, etc.), are fully explained in Appendixes C and D.

We have found the following practices to be effective in self-science:

- Express your own feelings openly, letting your likes and dislikes show.
- Label behavior clearly. Express your feelings and values, but focus on naming clearly *what* action a child or the group has taken for good or ill. The emphasis on labeling the action but not the child is of crucial importance.
- Give feedback and reassurance. Trust is built when children feel there are no hidden surprises. The more you can let them in on what you are doing or attempting to do, the safer the group will feel.

- Experiment with several approaches, finding the discipline and group-management techniques that work best for you.
- Demonstrate good communication techniques: listen attentively, ask questions, promote dialogues (as opposed to monologues or lectures), and praise others as they demonstrate good communications skills.
- Participate in games and activities, taking part as a member of the group.
- Demonstrate openness and flexibility. Make it a point, for example, to choose from both sexes for partners in activities. (We have observed that boys and girls may find it hard to relate in open, friendly ways. Boys tend to stick with boys; girls with girls. Challenge this pattern.)
- Give praise, using reinforcement strategies and "appreciates" techniques (discussed in the sections which follow).

Appendix C contains advice and suggestions on several techniques that have been highly successful for the authors, including specifics on topics such as how to be a group leader, what to do about group dynamics and discipline, what affective experiential techniques are available, and how to use cognitive inquiry techniques. Clearly, however, each teacher brings a personal style to the process; use what feels comfortable for you.

Techniques for
Classroom Management—Logistics

SCHEDULING SELF-SCIENCE

The curriculum presented here has been designed to meet a variety of scheduling considerations. The sixty-four lessons break into two parts which may be taught consecutively as a year's course meeting twice a week or which may be divided into two mini-courses (Section 3 has thirty-eight lessons; Section 4, twenty-six lessons) meeting once each week.

GROUPING STUDENTS

Since social and emotional development are roughly related to chronological age, it is best to form students into groups about the same age. During the flow lessons, for example, older students may raise topics concerning drugs, sex, drinking, etc., which are not appropriate for younger students.

You should also try to include an equal number of boys and girls in the class. Class members are more likely to feel comfortable exploring their relationships to members of the opposite sex (an important part of self-science learning) if they receive support from members of their own sex.

SIZE

The optimum size for a class depends on the age of the students. With younger children, a group of eight to ten members is best. At that age, each child needs a chance to participate in every activity; attention spans are shorter, and children become restless if they are not actively involved. For older students, the best group size is between ten and fifteen students. With fewer students the group becomes exclusive and doesn't provide enough variety of opinion and attitude. If the group is too large, it is difficult to establish the intimacy and group solidarity necessary for teaching the tools and skills of the curriculum.

MEETING PLACE AND TIME

Each lesson is planned to last approximately forty-five minutes. When lessons call for the groups working outdoors, try to schedule the class meeting for the end of the school day so time can be extended if necessary.

The meeting place itself should be private. A sense of privacy and security allows students to open up and trust the class. Children have strong feelings about being overheard or interrupted, and the class will progress much more smoothly if the aforementioned conditions can be met. Do not, for example, attempt to hold a self-science class within an open classroom. Bear in mind the fact, for example, that some of the activities require shouting. While our school society generally does not encourage loud behavior, it is worth the effort to find a room that will permit this valuable self-science experience.

We have found that a classroom equipped with mirrors is a particularly stimulating environment. If that is not available, any private place with a comfortable atmosphere will do. You will need space for everyone to sit in a circle, preferably on bean bags or cushions, but if necessary, at desks arranged in a circle.

These are suggestions for basic classroom management; most teachers, however, will establish the setup most comfortable to them. We have found several other techniques that might be useful. For ideas on topics such as lesson preparation, important decisions, questions commonly raised, record keeping, student journals, and additional information about flow lessons, refer to Appendix D.

Alternatives for Classroom Teachers

While the logistics discussed in the preceding paragraphs may describe the ideal situation, many classroom teachers will need to use their imaginations in order to create circumstances suited to the curriculum. Most of the exercises can be performed by entire classes. The discussions, however, would generally be more superficial than they would be if held by a more intimate group of eight to twelve. If you are working with a large class, you may find that asking students to keep journals is a more effective means of fostering personal growth. It is important that teachers keep their expectations realistic.

Team teaching has become increasingly popular in the last several years. This technique frequently allows for flexible scheduling: one teacher's working with a larger group on math will allow another teacher to work with a smaller group on self-science. In many schools, large playground areas are vacant during parts of the day. These areas can provide a meeting place. In many schools, there are conference rooms, supply rooms, even basements. Any of these can be used as a meeting place.

Evaluating the Results of Self-Science

Several evaluation options and suggestions for when and how to use them will be provided in the course of this volume. The best measures, however, are to be discovered in reports made by teachers, students, and parents during the time a self-science course is in progress as well as after it has been completed.

Our experiences at Nueva have revealed considerable transference from self-science experiences to outside situations; that is, self-science can result in improved classroom behavior by individuals and groups of children, more purposeful study and learning behavior, better communication skills, and greater academic achievement. Anecdotal reports, which cannot be statistically charted (nor perhaps should they be), have nevertheless been of great use to us during the developmental years of the program. You may wish to keep your own anecdotal records.

If the goals of self-science, however, are to make each student aware of, responsible for, and involved in his or her own life and learning, then the best way to measure success is to discuss it with the child. We strongly recommend, therefore, that individual conferences be held toward the end of the program. (Additional elaboration on evaluation alternatives can be found in Appendix D, p. 154, under the heading "Some Common Questions."

Section 3
Getting Comfortable
with Yourself
and the Group

It is a part of our American heritage to resist being managed, and it should not surprise us if such techniques call forth in students ingenious and creative devices for sabotaging the system.

—ARTHUR W. COMBS, *HUMANISTIC EDUCATION SOURCEBOOK*

The curriculum is structured in accordance with the realities of group process. The first phase of the course is a group-growing-together time, a time for learning concepts and vocabulary, and for having basic experiences which are for the most part external and which take place in a climate of safety.

The thirty-eight lessons cover nineteen weeks if you are using the two-lesson-a-week plan. This brings you to approximately the end of February, if you start in September, or to the end of the school year, if you start after the winter vacation. Either of these is a convenient stopping place before the class moves on to the second phase of the curriculum (see Section 4).

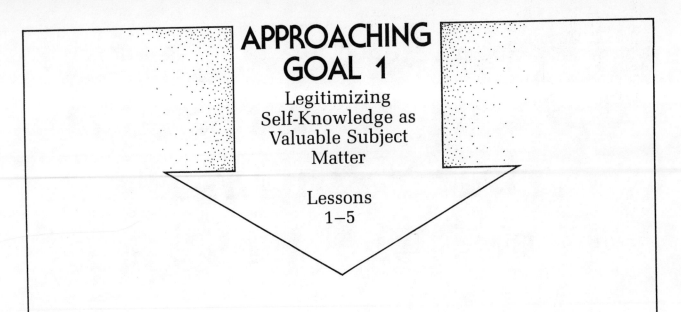

APPROACHING GOAL 1

Legitimizing Self-Knowledge as Valuable Subject Matter

Lessons 1–5

Most children have not thought that learning about themselves is a part of school. Nor have they thought about how you learn about yourself or about what there is to learn. Lessons one through five are concerned with establishing excitement and curiosity about using scientific methods to study one's self. Themes for future meetings will be discussed during these lessons.

GROUP BEHAVIOR

At this point in the program, the group is just coming together, with some anxieties, some curiosity—perhaps even some skepticism. Only later will individuals merge into a group characterized by trust and solidarity. In this first stage, you will be helping the group discover the purpose for their meeting. You will be providing experiences meant to demonstrate that self-science is a place where "we study ourselves like scientists do" and "where we learn about ourselves."

EVIDENCES OF STUDENT GROWTH

Growth toward the goal will be demonstrated by the students in a variety of ways:

AFFECTIVE EXPECTATIONS

- Choosing to take self-science.
- Participating in the activities and discussions.
- Talking about one's self.
- Verbalizing what is being learned about self and how this knowledge is useful.

COGNITIVE EXPECTATIONS

- Understanding the scientific process.
- Understanding concepts of investigating, manipulating, organizing, quantifying, generalizing, inventorying.
- Understanding how scientists observe. There are many ways of looking at things.
- Understanding different ways of learning.

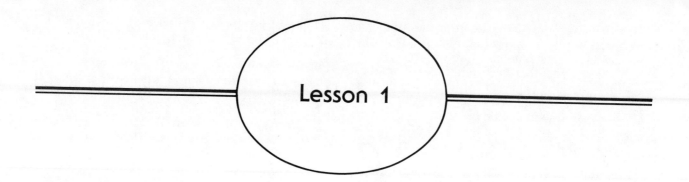

Lesson 1

MATERIALS

food (juice or cookies)

BEGINNING

Welcome the children. Introduce yourself. Break the ice by offering juice or cookies, explaining, "we're going to be working together as a group. We ought to get acquainted." Chat for a few minutes.

AFFECTIVE EXPERIENCE

- Introduce the "Bumpety-Bump Game," saying, "We play a lot of games in self-science. Let's start with a getting-acquainted game."
- Explain the rules. Play two or three times with first names.
- Play again with animal names, then with feeling words. (How the group handles feeling words is a good barometer of the group process at this point.)
- After each game, use the discussion questions to focus on what students are learning about themselves and each other.

This game will be used often throughout the program. Don't try to apply the discussion questions in depth at this time.

COGNITIVE INQUIRY

Have the students sit quietly in a circle and proceed with the first group discussion.

1. Ask, "What did we just do?" Elicit that we played some games. Talk about how we felt during the games.
2. Ask, "What did we do just *now*?" (referring to question 1). Elicit that we *observed* our behavior during a game. We *identified* some of the things we did and felt. We *verbalized* (talked about) some of the things we did and felt. Ask someone to write these words on the chalkboard as you discuss them.
3. Explain seriously that we're doing what scientists do. Scientists observe and identify and verbalize, among other things. Scientists use their eyes and ears and other senses to examine what it is they're studying.

4. Ask students to call out names of various sciences, having someone write the list on the chalkboard (e.g., biology, zoology, anthropology, astronomy, psychology, archeology, sociology, botany). Discuss what each "ology" is the study of.
5. Ask, "What did we just do?" (referring to question 4). Elicit that we talked about different sciences. We got our list together by means of another scientific tool called *brainstorming*. Brainstorming will be very useful in our self-science course.
6. Brainstorm. "What do you think self-science is?" Have someone list responses on the chalkboard (e.g., games, learning about ourselves, learning about feelings and behavior, getting to know ourselves).
7. Explain seriously that learning about yourself is a lifelong process. What we can learn in a group like this is something about the process. We can acquire tools for the process, such as brainstorming and observing and identifying and verbalizing and more. We can even learn about how we learn. Everyone has a special way of learning, for instance, and a different method of studying. We'll be talking more about what self-science is during our next meeting.
8. Explain logistics (such as when class meetings will be held) and ground rules. Classes are voluntary (if your structure permits) for the first four meetings. Anyone who wants to drop out, may. After that, contracts will be signed, and anyone signing a contract to participate in self-science will be expected to live up to the contract. "That's part of what we learn here, to make a decision and stick to it." During the classes, anyone who wants may "pass," i.e., decline to participate, without feeling uncomfortable.

There will be no grades (this is optional). If the students seem surprised, ask them how you, the teacher, can possibly make a judgment about how the group is learning and using the tools of self-science. Perhaps each person is the best judge for him or herself. If students seem interested, suggest that you discuss grading the first flow lesson.

Explain the flow lessons. For additional information on flow lessons, see Appendix D,

p. 161. Every so often, the group will have a chance to plan the meeting, and to talk about ideas of interest, such as grading.

Tell students that there will be assignments which they are expected to do. If they decide not to do an assignment, they are expected to write a short explanation of why they decided not to do it (e.g., didn't feel like it; had a dental appointment; felt uncomfortable—whatever they were thinking or feeling). This note will be kept private unless the student decides to share it with the group.

9. Thank the group for coming.

This first group discussion may run long. Skip questions 4 and 5 if time seems short.

ASSIGNMENT

Ask students to make a self-inventory and to include their birthday. An inventory is an itemized list. They must brainstorm anything they wish to list about themselves (physical description, likes, dislikes). The list may be as long or as short as they want.

Teacher Comments _____

_____
_____
_____
_____
_____
_____
_____
_____
_____
_____
_____

Bumpety-Bump Game

This is a good introductory, warm-up, or change-of-pace activity. It is useful in eliciting "here-and-now" feelings.

PROCEDURE

Have the group stand (or sit) in a circle. Each participant must ask and then remember the names of the people on either side (teachers play, too). Someone is asked to volunteer to be "It." It stands in the center of the circle, points to someone, and says out loud, "Bumpety-bump—one, two, three."

The person pointed to must say the name of one of the people next to him/her before It finishes counting. If the person wins, It points to somebody else. If the person cannot remember the names or say them quickly enough, then s/he becomes It.

VARIATIONS

1. Call out first and last names.
2. Call out first name of both people on either side.

3. Call out an animal you think is most like you today.
4. Pick a word that describes the way you are feeling right now.
5. Pick a word that describes the way you most like to feel.
6. Pick a word that describes the way you least like to feel.
7. Name something you want very much.
8. Name one good thing about yourself.

DISCUSSION QUESTIONS

1. "What did you observe during the game?" (During the first few days, you may have to probe for answers, either asking for volunteers or going around the circle—e.g., "Is there any pattern in the way the 'It' people made their choices? Do boys always choose boys? Do girls always choose girls? Do some people not try because they want to be It?") On future plays, you may want to let some children "monitor" the game by observing rather than playing, and then giving the group feedback afterwards.

2. "How does it feel when someone remembers your name?"
3. "How does it feel when someone forgets your name?"
4. "Does anyone in our group ever feel that way?" (Children learn a great deal about themselves and others by becoming aware of the similarities and differences in their responses. This question can be asked over and over, in almost every game and subsequent discussion.)
5. "What makes you want to be a _____ (name of animal)? What would you do if you were that animal right now? How do you imagine this animal right now? How do you imagine this animal feels about him or herself? Do you ever feel this way? When?"
6. "You chose _____ for your feeling word. Do you often feel that way? What made you feel that way today?"

Improvise questions along these lines depending upon the content of the game. Early in the program, remind everyone that they have the right to pass if they don't wish to respond.

Notes from Nueva

Co-leaders of the meeting, we introduced ourselves and initiated "Bumpety-Bump" with names. Everyone was excited and cooperative. We also played the game using animal names and feeling words.

	ANIMAL	HOW DO YOU FEEL RIGHT NOW?
Karl	Horse	Tired
Norma	Rabbit	Mad
Arthur	Lion	Sad
Drew	Tiger	Tired
Mimi	Cheetah	I don't know—horrible
Joyce	Jaguar	Happy

The games rose and fell in terms of attentiveness and noise. Patterns emerged: Karl always turned the game back so that he seldom had to be It, until we finally encouraged him to stand up and take a turn. ("I have a way of always keeping my place.") He seems to have trouble listening. This may be part of the reason for his defensiveness. Mimi acted up throughout the class. She didn't really want to be It, and her feeling word was "horrible." She disrupted the game by taking pillows and by kicking other people's pillows.

We introduced the idea of self-science, asking what each person thought might be learned from the group. Alice wrote this information on the blackboard:
nothing
everything I can learn
experiences
about me

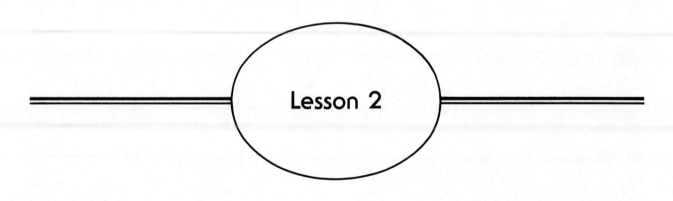

Lesson 2

BEGINNING

Share inventories brought in as lesson one assignment. Point out *kinds* of things being inventoried (probably predominantly physical or behavioral). Elicit a response of how little we really know about ourselves and each other.

AFFECTIVE EXPERIENCE

- Play "Bumpety-Bump" variation, asking players to "name one good thing about yourself" (see preceding lesson). Repeat the game, this time with some children monitoring.
- Proceed toward making children aware of how this game told them something more about themselves. Ask, "What did we just do?" (Play a game.) "What did the game reveal? Did

monitors see anything differently than the players?"
- Play "Elephant and Giraffe." Introduce a fantasy (specifically, the "No Teachers" fantasy), beginning with a relaxation technique.
- Ask discussion questions concerning behavior during the games.

COGNITIVE INQUIRY

Ask the students:

1. "What is fantasy?"
2. "What is monitoring?"
3. "What is feedback?"

Establish these techniques as ways of seeing ourselves. Develop the analogy of not being able to see yourself when you swing a baseball bat—but others can see you. Discuss self-knowledge by asking:

4. "Did you ever hear of self-knowledge?"
5. "Why isn't self-knowledge taught? Is it important? Why?"
6. "Are you an environment? How?"
7. "Where does the world around you begin?"
8. "What would you study if you could only study self? How?"
9. "How come we never have?"
10. "Can you see yourself learn?" (Promise you will say and do something about that later.)
11. "What is confidentiality?" (Add ground rule of not talking about anyone in the group outside, although you may talk about self.)

Teacher Comments _____

_____

_____

_____

_____

_____

_____

_____

_____

_____

_____

_____

_____

Elephant and Giraffe Game

This game is used as an introductory warm-up exercise to get people moving, thinking, and cooperating. The person who is It stands in the center of the circle, points to any person in the circle, and says either, "Elephant—one, two, three, four, five, six," or "Giraffe—one, two . . ." If you are pointed to and called "elephant," you bend from the waist and make a trunk with your arms. The people on either side of you put their hands to your head to make ears. If you are pointed to and called "giraffe," you put your arms together above your head and the people on either side of you place their hands on your waist to form legs. Whoever fails to do his/her part before the end of the count becomes It. This is a fun, fast-paced game that can go on as long as the participants are interested in playing.

Introducing Fantasy

The purpose of this activity is to help children to relax, to give free rein to the imagination, and to develop visual imagery.

"NO TEACHERS" FANTASY

Ask the children to relax as much as possible and imagine that they are students in a classroom—their own classroom or some other classroom. "On the first day you arrive and your classroom is absolutely empty. The walls are bare; the floor is bare. There is neither furniture nor equipment. Once everyone is inside the room, the teacher announces that for the next two weeks, all equipment, books, and teachers will be taken from the classroom. Your attendance is required and you must decide what you will do. What would you study? Would it be worth studying? How would you go about it? How would you know if you learned anything? How useful would such learning be? What tools or skills would you need to study that you don't have now? Who knows such tools or skills? Where did they learn them? What would scare you about such a learning time and subject? What would excite you? What would other people say?"

Children often have difficulty responding instantly, so you may lead some brainstorming on what they could learn. They usually begin listing activities concerned with external things, such as counting the number of squares on the floors, windows, and walls; progress to ideas involving ranking themselves according to height, hair color, eye color; eventually realize they could teach each other things that they know about; and finally begin to speak of their feelings, thoughts, and behaviors.

Notes from Nueva

We began the class with a modified fantasy about what school would be like without furniture, teachers, or books. There was excitement and enthusiasm. A number of children had a very difficult time closing their eyes, but when asked what they could study they suggested

Walls	*Carpet*	*Clothes*
Floor	*Eyes*	*How to kill each other*
Hair	*Lights*	*and ourselves*

No one mentioned feelings. We talked about whether learning about ourselves would be interesting and worthwhile, and whether it was something we did everyday. There were positive responses from some and negative responses from the older boys (typical of this age).

We summarized by saying that self-science was a place where we could learn more about ourselves and others. We would do this through activities and games. There was considerable interest on the part of the older boys, who had been negative throughout the introduction.

Hal asked everyone what they'd do if they didn't have to go to school:

JERRY:	*Be sad.*
GEORGE:	*I like school. I wouldn't have anyone to play with at home.*
ARTHUR:	*Not a lot to do. This is a fun school. We have good activities.*
NEAL:	*It would be boring. No one to play with.*
PETER:	*In a way, relieved, and in a way, sad. There wouldn't be anything to do. Just go downtown and look around. I wouldn't get an education.*
DARBY:	*During Christmas vacation, I really got bored. I was really happy to have the first day off, but then I got bored.*
SUE:	*I'd feel bored.*
HELGA:	*If I had a choice, I'd go to school for three weeks and then have one week off.*
SALLY:	*Bored.*

CONCLUSIONS

There was a definite pattern of "feeling bored if we couldn't go to school" and a pattern of liking school.

The older boys "cut down" the program and expressed discontent. There was little in their response about feelings, thoughts, or other people. There is a need to legitimatize study of self and a need to explore and gain a better understanding of the dimensions of self and the possibilities for learning.

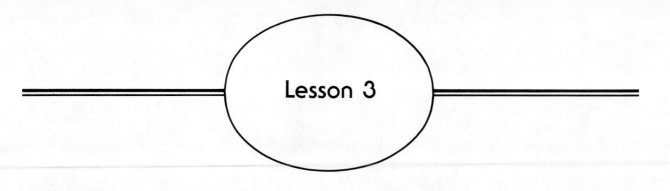

Lesson 3

BEGINNING

Review confidentiality (see pages 145, 147). Compare similarities in the group.

AFFECTIVE EXPERIENCE

- Just for fun, brainstorm games children already know and like. Play any one, first altogether, then with monitors.
- Discuss what we learned from this game. Ask questions pertinent to this game (see the discussion questions for the Bumpety-Bump game in Lesson 1). Ask "What did monitors see?"

COGNITIVE INQUIRY

1. Ask "What are games that are 'just for fun'? Do you like tag, hide and seek, hopscotch?"
2. "What do you learn about people who are strangers when you play a game?"
3. Focus on the value of games for learning. Ask "What can we learn from games? From football? From chess? From long distance running? Is this really learning?"

4. "What is a game in which you have to test your limits? What are the limits you test? Do you ever push your limits in your school work? In your relations with fellow students? Do you ever play games with yourself in which you test your limits, set goals, and try to reach them? What do you learn in this limit-testing? Is it important? Can someone else teach it to you?"
5. "Explain the difference between *What* you learn and *How* you learn it."

ASSIGNMENT

"Make a list of things you think you have learned in self-science so far—things you have learned about yourself or about someone else. How did you learn these things?"

Teacher Comments _____

_____

_____

_____

_____

_____

_____

_____

_____

_____

_____

Lesson 4

MATERIALS
paper, pencils

BEGINNING
Share the assignments students bring in. Introduce the concept of *experimenting* as a way of learning.

AFFECTIVE EXPERIENCE
- Distribute paper and pencil. Introduce this experiment: "If you were going to spend the rest of your life in this class, you would probably do some things differently and you might treat people differently. Write down two of these differences. Now, do one of these different things for the next ten minutes. How did your experiment with yourself turn out? What did you learn about yourself? Was that important learning? How did you do it?"
- Do another experiment. Ask students to make a list of:
  a. "three subjects you would find easy to talk about in this group;
  b. three subjects you would find hard to talk about;
  c. three subjects you would never want to talk about."

- Instruct students, "Do not write your name on your paper—make this list anonymous. Volunteer to turn in your anonymous list, for discussion."
- Discuss similarities of lists; discuss awareness of subjects hard to talk about as a learning experience; discuss what makes these subjects hard to talk about.
- Play "Explode" (see Appendix C) or "Elephant and Giraffe" (see page 22) for a change of pace. "Explode" at this point will probably be mild.

COGNITIVE INQUIRY
1. Ask students, "What did we just do? What have we learned about experimenting as a way of learning?"
2. "Did talking about the list of things you would never want to talk about change anybody's feelings about that?"
3. Discuss "exploding."
4. Tell the students that the next meeting will be a flow lesson and explain "flow lesson." (See Appendix D, p. 161)
5. Ask, "are there any subjects that came up in the experiment today that the group would like to explore?"
6. Briefly explain the term *consensus*. See if you can get a consensus.

[*No Assignment (before Lesson 5, a flow lesson)*]

Teacher Comments _____

_____

_____

_____

_____

_____

_____

_____

_____

_____

Notes from Nueva

We reviewed "exploding" and discussed the limited ways and places we have to "explode."

Kelly told about the bomb that was placed at her front door to kill whomever opened the door. She said that it was done because her father is important. She said she is afraid of front doors. She went on for some time in great detail, but the group was very willing to listen.

Tim said he is afraid of TV antennas and footsteps on the roof. He explained to Hal that when he was six and living in the Chicago ghetto, there was a terrible riot on the night Martin Luther King was killed. There was a lot of shooting, with fires and sirens, etc., down the street. Tim was on the second floor, looking at TV with six adults and eight children. They heard someone on the roof and the person broke the TV antenna. At that time, a brick flew through the window, and Tim knew they had to try to get to the hospital a half-block away.

As they went out onto the street, a bomb exploded in the downstairs of their building, starting a fire. They went to the hospital amidst the gunfire and sirens and were in the emergency room with many wounded people when a man came in with a shotgun and started shooting. Tim fell on the floor and someone threw a tiny baby on him. He put the baby under him and crawled out a side door with the baby. Tim was able to talk very openly about how scared he was. He cried and had nightmares afterwards.

There was a lot of discussion by the rest of the group on how they would feel if that happened to them—what they would do, etc. They decided that one very common way of "exploding" for many people is violence; examples: war, riots, murders, beating-up people, hitting little kids. All of these ways hurt other people. We asked what different ways they could think of to explode without involving other people. They mentioned a room where they could hit pillows, throw bean bags, smash dishes (this was very intriguing), hit a punching bag, and play the game "Explode." They all decided to ask for a punching bag for Christmas.

We agreed to play "Explode." During the game, Kelly deliberately tripped Bruce, who fell and hurt himself. We stopped the game and everyone sat down. Bruce was trying not to cry.

Tim and Drew both told Kelly she should not have done that. She said that she didn't care because Bruce had knocked her down when they were playing football in P.E. There was much discussion about the difference between getting knocked down in a football game and during "Explode." Kelly was unwilling to give an inch. Bruce was very angry and hurt. He had a difficult time controlling his tears. I thought he was going to hit Kelly when it first happened.

Finally, I asked Bruce how he thought Kelly was feeling. He said, "Angry and hurt, because I knocked her down during football—even though it was an accident." I asked him what he thought would make her feel better. He replied, "If I said I'm sorry." When I asked him if he could do that, he said, "Yes. I'm sorry I knocked you down. I didn't do it deliberately."

I then asked Kelly how she thought Bruce felt. "Angry and hurt."

"Why?"

"Because I tripped him and he got hurt." I asked what could she do to make Bruce feel better, and she said, "Say I'm sorry. But I'm not." At this point she was put down by everyone in the group. I asked her if she was sorry Bruce had really hurt his knee. "Yes."

"Could you tell him you're sorry about that?"

"I guess so. I'm sorry you got hurt, but I'm not sorry I did it." We were already ten minutes late so everyone had to leave at this point. We talked with Bruce for a few minutes and he was able to reduce some of his anger.

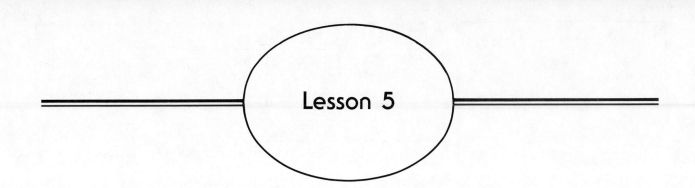

Lesson 5

MATERIALS
student contracts

FLOW LESSON
(See Appendix D, p. 161.) Use material generated by the group in Lesson 4, or select some from flow lesson materials.

ASSIGNMENT
Give out student contracts to be decided upon and brought back next time. Here is a sample student contract.

SELF-SCIENCE CONTRACT

I _____ agree to participate
          STUDENT'S NAME
in self-sciencing from now until the end of
the year (or end of semester).

_____
STUDENT'S SIGNATURE

_____
TEACHER'S SIGNATURE

(See Tearsheet, page 171)

Teacher Comments _____

_____

_____

_____

_____

_____

_____

_____

_____

_____

_____

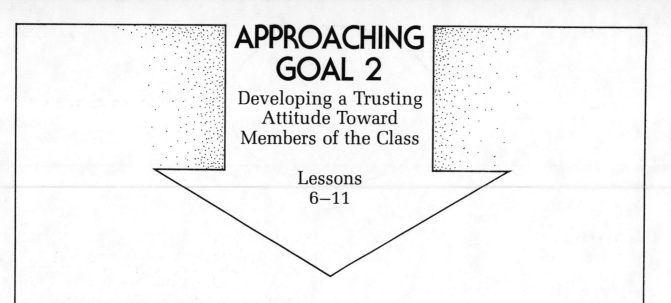

APPROACHING GOAL 2

Developing a Trusting Attitude Toward Members of the Class

Lessons 6–11

Nonjudgmental acceptance and respect is central to the process of personal growth. Indeed, it is central to simply hearing and seeing accurately, and thus learning. To put it another way, lack of trust generates defense mechanisms which get in the way of learning on any level.

Lessons 6 to 11 establish a basic trust among members of the group, as a foundation for the explorations to come. Cognitive awareness of how and why and when we trust or do not trust help to focus on this subject. Lesson 7 should be given outdoors, if this can be arranged. Lesson 9 is suggested as a flow lesson.

GROUP BEHAVIOR

These exercises in trust may generate the first testing behavior from some of the students. You may see some defiance, refusal to participate, or attempts to change the subject. Should this occur, it is important to maintain a firm but accepting attitude and to understand the difficulty of learning to trust others. Remember that learning to trust often creates anxiety and that we all have our own ways of dealing with this anxiety. Expect some giggling and embarrassment during the Killer Statements exercises. Your acceptance will, of course, help the group feel more comfortable.

The level of trust, acceptance, and respect that a group develops usually determines the degree to which members of the group are willing to explore "self" as a subject. Take your cues from the group as you move from Goal 2 to 3.

EVIDENCES OF STUDENT GROWTH

Growth toward the goal will be demonstrated by the students.

AFFECTIVE EXPECTATIONS

- Increasing willingness to utilize all members of the class as partners in exercises.
- Increasing willingness to disclose personal feelings and concerns.
- Accepting and respecting the confidentiality of the class.

COGNITIVE EXPECTATIONS

- Realizing the importance of trust, keeping confidences, accepting, respecting.
- Using reading, writing, observing, classifying, and judgmental skills in understanding *trust*.
- Learning ways of making decisions.
- Learning to classify by listening.

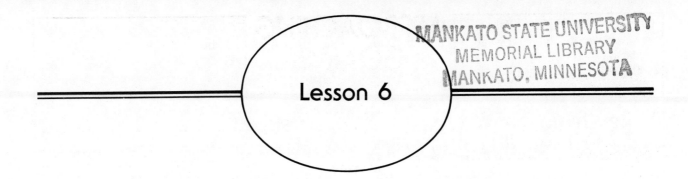

MATERIALS
journals

BEGINNIN_
Collect contracts. Discuss them. Use discussion questions to explore the subjects of trust and confidentiality. Discuss what aspects of self-science are appropriate to tell parents, other friends. Discuss what is *not* appropriate. Reassure students that this is a place where we can talk about things we cannot talk about anywhere else.

AFFECTIVE EXPERIENCE
- Play the Nickname Game (following).
- Play the Telephone Gossip Chain (following).

COGNITIVE INQUIRY
1. Ask the discussion questions (following).
2. Ask the discussion questions about trust.
3. Introduce journals. Have students write answers to their questions before discussion.
4. Discuss how journals will be used (as scientists keep logs—to identify, observe, find patterns, etc.).

ASSIGNMENT
Ask students to survey the friends and acquaintances they trust (least/most). (Show students a continuum of 1 to 5, 1 being the least, 5 being the most. Have them plot their findings on a continuum.)

Tell students that this assignment is due in a week and that the next meeting will be outdoors.

The Nickname Game

Ask everyone to think of a nickname they have that they really do not like or that embarrasses them. Have everyone share their names and how they got them, and explain why they do not like them. (Teacher shares first.)

Point out to the group that these names are confidential and may not be discussed outside the group. Also discuss the idea that there will be other feelings and thoughts we may want to share later on, such as things we are afraid of, and we will probably only do this if we feel sure others will keep this information confidential. (Note: We have never had a problem with this, but if a student should break this trust, it would be very important to deal with it as soon as possible, in the group. If there were a student who habitually broke the confidentiality of the group, it might be necessary to remove that person from the group and work with the person individually.)

DISCUSSION QUESTIONS
1. Ask the class, "Is it easy/hard for you to trust people?"
2. "What did you like about the game?"
3. "What was scary about the game?"
4. "Whom do you trust at school? At home? What makes you trust them?"
5. "What makes you feel as if you cannot trust some people? What do they do?"

Telephone Gossip Chain

This exercise is used to examine patterns of listening.

PROCEDURE
Direct everyone to sit in a circle. Start a message around the circle by whispering to a student a sentence about yourself that the class doesn't know. The first student whispers the message to a second, and so on—with each person passing to the next whatever they hear. The last person in the chain tells the class what they heard. Ask questions while students are in the circle.

ADDITIONAL DISCUSSION QUESTIONS

1. Ask "Was the final message the one that was started?"
2. "How did it change?"
3. "How well did you listen?"
4. "Is this a pattern of yours?"

Notes from Nueva

We reviewed what we could learn in self-sciencing and whether it was important. We also discussed the conditions necessary to make the group work. Some of the reasons and conditions suggested by members of the group are:

REASONS

So we can know ourselves and other people.
So we can learn to know ourselves.
So we can get to know people in the group well.
So we can gain self-confidence.
So we can learn to show feelings.
So we can come to understand our behavior.

CONDITIONS

We have to have trust.
We have to have confidentiality.
Gossiping about people is unacceptable.

At first the responses were vague, and eventually Bruce and Drew were able to explain about learning about ourselves. The group was quiet and attentive, although Mimi moved about. Hal sat her down on his cushion.

In closing we asked the children to say how they felt right at the moment. Some felt tired (Karl). Norma was mad because Mimi was kicking and making noise. Mimi really heard her and acknowledged how Norma felt. Arthur also felt sad because everyone was noisy. The children were attentive to one another's feelings.

Impressions: It was an insightful and elating session. My personal anxiety is gone. The group is good. Mimi and Karl will be a real challenge. Their disruptive influence is strong; however, it is just as strongly balanced by the influence of the more serious, attentive ones; i.e., Norma, Bruce, Arthur and Drew.

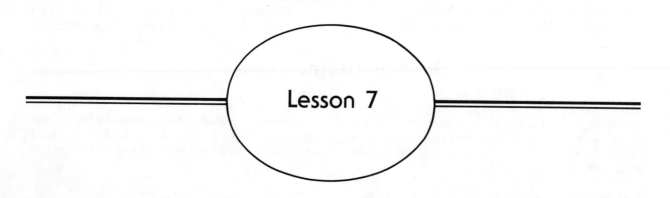

Lesson 7

FLOW LESSON

This lesson should be held outdoors, if possible.
Play the "Trust" games.

Trust Walk*

This exercise provides an opportunity for students to enhance trust in themselves and others, and it increases sensory awareness.

PROCEDURE

Ask students to choose a partner, someone they would like to know better. Then blindfold one of each pair or ask the "blind" partners to close their eyes. Students lead their "blind" partners on a "Trust Walk," the instructions being: "You have ten minutes to lead your partner around the class (classroom, school, gym, grounds). You are your partner's eyes. Establish a means of nonverbal communication. Stay with your partner and make the walk as interesting as possible. At the

---

*Reproduced by special permission from NTL Institute.

end of ten minutes, switch roles and continue for the next ten minutes. Then return to the whole group."

ACTIVITIES

Suggest that the partners discuss this experience, using the following processing questions as a "Trust Walk" guide. Reactions to the entire experience, noting high points, can be made in journals.

DISCUSSION QUESTIONS

1. Ask the group, "How did you feel leading?"
2. "How did you feel following?"
3. "Which was easier?"
4. "Which was more fulfilling?"
5. "Were you scared?"
6. "When did you feel most secure?"
7. "How did it feel to have someone dependent on you? To depend on someone?"
8. "What did it feel like to be deprived of your sense of sight?"

ASSIGNMENT

Make a list of names in your journal of the people you feel you can trust.

Teacher Comments _____

_____
_____
_____
_____
_____
_____
_____
_____
_____
_____

Notes from Nueva _____

I explained to the group what a Trust Walk is. Everyone picked a partner and had ten minutes for leading and ten minutes for following. I was impressed with how the leaders cared for their partners, introduced a great variety of touch experiences, as well as smell and taste (rocks, rough wall, glass, leaves, flowers, rope, grass, oranges, jasmine, dirt).

There was a definite mood of relaxation, easiness and peace during the discussion. We talked about: How students felt leading/ following. They noticed a time change; the walk seemed longer when they were being led. Most of them thought it more fun to be led, easier to be the leader, and felt scared when not in physical contact with their leader. No one expressed fear, although there was some uneasiness. Hal pointed out to Neal that he kept asking when it was time to stop and, at the end of the walk, took his mask

off quickly. We talked at length about being deprived of sight as well as other senses.

We ended the group meeting by complimenting them on their skills as leaders and on their ability to trust themselves and each other. We suggested that we later talk more about trust and what it means. We also commented on how much we can communicate non-verbally through touch. It was a very good day. I think we were all "high."

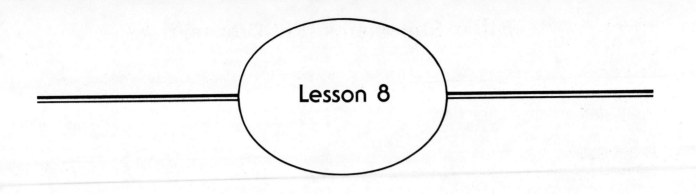

Lesson 8

BEGINNING

Explore how people felt during the Trust Walk. Talk about the trust survey of friends, which was the last assignment. Relate trust to acceptance and respect. What are some of the things that keep people from accepting and respecting each other? Elicit the group's ideas about put-downs.

AFFECTIVE EXPERIENCE

• Play "Killer Statements" (following).

COGNITIVE INQUIRY

1. Ask the group, "What are 'killer statements,' or 'put-downs'?"
2. "How often do you hear them in this class? In school?"
3. "How does it make you feel when someone directs a killer statement at you?"
4. "How does it make you feel when you direct a killer statement at someone?"
5. "Why do you think people make killer statements?"
6. "Let's brainstorm and list all the killer statements we can think of."
7. Ask them, "make a list of all the words and phrases that you and others use to 'put-down' others or to negatively judge them. Next to it make a list of all the words and phrases you use in praise or respect." For example:

Negative	Positive
dummy	tough
creep	sharp

8. "How long is each list? Which group is more in use? Is there anything good about using the negative words and phrases? Which ones particularly get to you?"
9. "What would be the three worst things that anyone could say to you in here (say them to yourself in your head)?"
10. "What are the chances of getting through the day without anyone saying them? The year?"
11. "When people make killer statements in here, what is the effect on the class?"
12. "If no one in this class made any killer statements or put-downs for the rest of this week, what would happen? What would you personally get out of such a truce? What would you or the class lose?"
13. "What would happen if *everyone* stopped making killer statements? What would be good about it? What would be bad?"

ASSIGNMENT

Ask students, "Listen for all the killer statements you hear around school and at home. Make a list in your journal. Include the killer statements you catch yourself saying."

Teacher Comments _____

_____

_____

_____

_____

_____

_____

_____

_____

_____

Killer Statements (Put-Downs)

This exercise is designed to help students become aware of hostile feelings—to learn that they are acceptable, normal emotions, and to discharge them without harming others.

PROCEDURE

Say to the students, "Everybody stand up. When I say, 'go,' all of you say or shout the killer statements you have held in until now. Use all the killer gestures, sounds, and words you want. You can talk to the air, to your neighbors, the whole group, your chair, or whatever feels comfortable."

ACTIVITIES

Journal entries
Small group sharing (two's)
Group discussion

DISCUSSION QUESTIONS

1. "What were your feelings as you were making the killer statements and gestures?"
2. "What or how did you feel after you made them?"
3. "Where in your body were those feelings?"
4. "Do you have any other comments about that exercise?"
5. "Did you like doing it?"
6. "How did you feel about waiting that long to make the killer statements and gestures? Was that feeling in your body somewhere?"

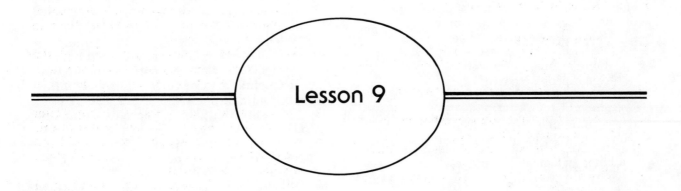

Lesson 9

FLOW LESSON

(See Appendix D, p. 161.) Because of the work on killer statements, the group may be ready to discuss angry feelings, or to explore why people make killer statements, or to pick a topic from the suggested list and process it.

Teacher Comments

_____

_____
_____
_____
_____
_____
_____
_____
_____
_____
_____

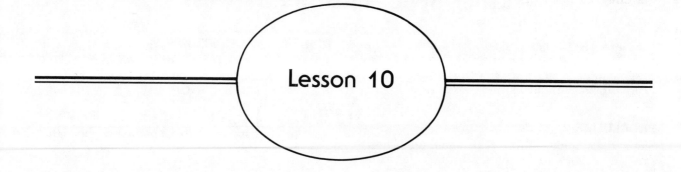

Lesson 10

BEGINNING

Discuss what "consensus" means. Decisions made by consensus meet everyone's needs. Discuss the concept of majority versus minority votes. Ask students to make a list of what is positive and what is negative about these two ways of making a decision.

AFFECTIVE EXPERIENCE

- Play "The Consensus Game" (following).
- Discuss observations; for example:
    "Some people were stubborn."
    "Some people changed easily."
    "Some people demanded."
    "Some people coaxed."
- Ask, "How do we all feel making a decision by consensus?" ("Fun ... good ... everybody agrees so no one feels bad.")
- "How might we feel with majority and minority?" ("Left out ... angry.")
- "Is consensus always practical?"

COGNITIVE INQUIRY

1. Ask the group to relate consensus to acceptance and respect.
2. Ask them to define "pattern" during the following discussions: "How are you evaluated here at school? Brainstorm a list of all the ways students evaluate teachers and other students. Pick the five that are the most important to you. Share them with the rest of the class by writing anonymous slips of paper or writing them on the board. What patterns are there in the way people are judged?"
3. "Who judges you in here? Who are the most important judges of you? What do they judge you on? How did you come to be judged on these standards?"

4. "Are you your own worst critic? Are there things others (parents, friends, teachers) are very critical of in you that you do not really care about? Do you put yourself down for things that others seem to ignore?"
5. "How do you know if you are accepted in here? Who decides? How do you know if you are rejected in here? Who decides?"
6. "Is the environment in the class basically accepting, positive, and respectful? Is your inner environment basically accepting, positive, and respectful of you?"
7. "Where do you feel most accepted and respected in your life? How does this make you feel? How do you perform there? How successful are you? How is this class different from that place?"
8. "What are the paths to acceptance in this class?"
9. "Are you 'playing for keeps' in here, or do you feel free to try out new ways of acting that may look foolish or dumb?"
10. "What effect does that have on you? Where do you feel okay about looking foolish once in a while? What is the difference between here and there? What can we do about it?"
11. "What are some of the ways people show acceptance and respect without words? Lack of acceptance and disrespect? Do you always know what you are communicating in this way? How can you learn what you are communicating without words?"
12. "What happens to people (children) who are not accepted by their parents? Teachers? How do you know? What can people do if they do not feel accepted or respected? What stops you from doing those things in here?"

ASSIGNMENT

Ask students, "Tell three people what you respect them for today. Tell yourself three things you respect yourself for today."

"When you feel like being sarcastic or putting someone down, don't! See if you can discover why you need to put that person down. Share what that need is, with the person or the class."

The Consensus Game

Have the group sit in a circle. Say that we are going to paint this room (chair or table) a different color. We are all going to agree on the same color or combination of colors. We will go around the circle and each person will name a color. *Nothing* more may be said by anyone except the leader, who may, if we reach an impasse between two colors, ask for a show of hands to indicate if the color is absolutely unacceptable to anyone. If it is, that color is no longer available.

Repeat with color two. The whole process may begin again at this point. The leader should observe as much nonverbal communication as possible. (Note who is aggressive, who goes along with the group or their best friend, who is frustrated, who are the leaders, who are the followers, and who pleads, orders, begs, or gets mad.) Once you have reached a consensus, ask for feedback:

1. How does it feel to make a decision by consensus?
2. Would it always be practical?
3. What nonverbal communication was going on?
4. What was your pattern? Is that usually your pattern?

Use this game often to make decisions within the group, e.g., should we have a visitor?

Notes from Nueva

We played the "Consensus Game" to decide if Shirley could join the group. Doug and Howard were negative, but the other children talked to them and they finally agreed. There were comments:

"How would you feel if you were Shirley?"
"Maybe you'd like her better if you got to know her."
"If she irritates you, you can talk about it here."
"I think they should have a better reason or Shirley can come."
"Your reasons sound personal."
"I think she should be in, if she wants to be."

We went out and brought Shirley in and Jay said, "Welcome to the group." We asked the class to tell her about our confidentiality agreement, the right to "pass" if you didn't want to say anything.

Shirley was reassured that she did not have to answer, but I wondered how she felt while she was waiting outside. I asked her, and her first response was, "Bored." Then she added, "I felt like I would not get in, because I do not have any friends in the group." Then she said she had some friends, but it was the boys who did not like her. I asked everyone to project themselves, to become Shirley and feel how she felt waiting to find out if she could be in our group. They had a lot to share:

"I would feel scared. I would feel like maybe no one would like me. I would feel uncomfortable. I would feel worried. I would feel like I waited and waited and waited."

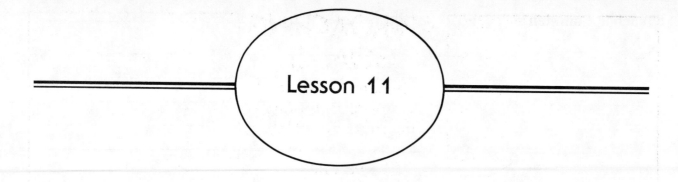

Lesson 11

AFFECTIVE EXPERIENCE

- Play "Bumpety-Bump" variation, with "Feelings."

Note: You will not be processing this in depth. It is a gauge as to how open the group is now, prior to moving to the Goal on Feelings.

COGNITIVE INQUIRY

This is a review of Goal 1 (legitimizing self-knowledge as valuable subject matter) and Goal 2 (developing a trusting attitude toward members of one's class). Start by discussing trust, acceptance, and respect. Ask the following questions:

1. "What are some of the ways people show acceptance and respect without words? Lack of acceptance and respect without words? Do you always know when you are communicating in this way? How can you learn what you are communicating without words?"
2. "Is there anything in your class other than the people that can cause someone to feel unaccepted or respected? What about the grading system? Competitive work schemes? Single standards for success, such as athletics for boys and appearance for girls?"
3. "Find a partner whom you most trust in the class and plan with his or her help to increase your own total acceptance and respect by doing something specific. First, the whole class can make a list of sample 'by-doing' experiments that might yield increased respect and awareness."
4. "Practice listening to the other students and just hearing and accepting them and their messages. Put off your ideas until another time; just focus on another person. Just hearing and accepting without 'yes, but,' 'that's dumb,' or stealing the focus with your concerns. This is the most acceptance-building thing one can do. The teacher must be the model."
5. "Brainstorm a list of things we can do to increase respect, e.g., when someone says something to you or acts (looks) in a way that causes you to feel put down or to doubt your worth in some way, tell the person how you are feeling right then."
6. "Brainstorm a list of things we can *stop* doing that gets in the way of creating respect; e.g., words and phrases to avoid saying, because they hurt other people.
7. "Review all the processes we have used so far to learn about ourselves; e.g., consensus, exploding, experimenting, fantasy, playing games, asking questions, talking, nonverbal cues, etc."

ASSIGNMENT
None

Teacher Comments _____

_____

_____

_____

_____

_____

_____

_____

_____

_____

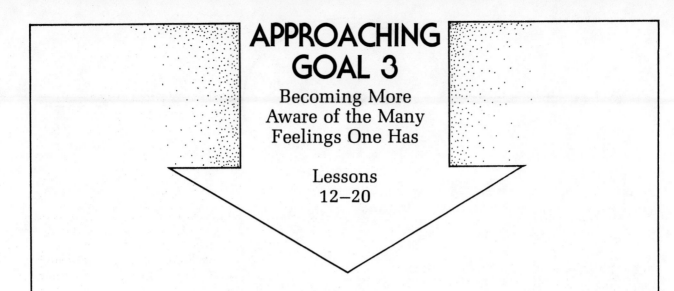

APPROACHING GOAL 3

Becoming More
Aware of the Many
Feelings One Has

Lessons
12–20

Experiencing one's self and one's surroundings is central to learning. Awareness of feelings, one's own and others', deepens learning about personal relationships, communication, language arts (tone, mood, character, inference, predictions in reading).

Children are often aware of their strong feelings, but have difficulty discriminating among more subtle emotional states. They need a vocabulary for feelings and an understanding of the various modes of "feeling" expression to be "in control" of this important aspect of their learning and growth. People neither think without feeling nor feel without thinking. Connections on this point need to be made. Lessons 12 through 20 deal with feelings on many levels; Lessons 14 and 20 are flow lessons.

GROUP BEHAVIOR

The group should begin to bond together a little more now. Exercises in the next lessons enhance the awareness of feelings. This period of time can be a very pleasant, growing time for the group.

EVIDENCE OF STUDENT GROWTH

Growth toward the goal will be demonstrated by the following.

AFFECTIVE EXPECTATIONS

- Increasing ability to inventory one's thoughts and feelings.
- Increasing awareness of the relationship between one's emotions and physical states.
- Increasing willingness to listen to others.
- Increasing acceptance and support of the thoughts and feelings of others in the class.
- Increasing awareness of the similarities and differences between one's own unique response to an experience and the responses of others.

COGNITIVE EXPECTATIONS

- Developing vocabulary for expressing and describing feelings.
- Understanding concepts of the process of feelings; labelling feelings.
- Understanding the relevance of feelings to self, home, and school (e.g., language arts—reading, films, TV stories).
- Understanding various modes of perceiving feelings.
- Acknowledging the responsibility for one's own feelings.

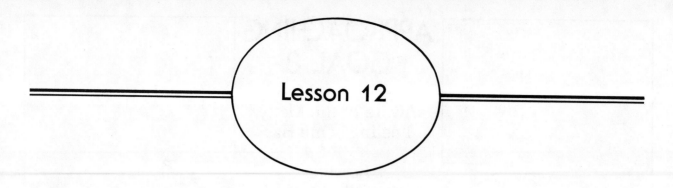

Lesson 12

MATERIALS
3 x 5 index cards (approximately 100)

PREPARATION
Before the class begins, draw a "feeling continuum" on the chalkboard.

Example:
Angry Upset Sad/Calm Indifferent Bored Happy Excited

BEGINNING
When the students come in, ask them, "How do you feel? How are you feeling today?" Give feedback that the usual response everybody makes is, "Fine." E.g., "How are you?"

"Fine."
"What's new?"
"Nothing."

Ask students to indicate how they feel right now by putting initials under the feeling words on the chalkboard. (Add any word that better describes the feeling.)

AFFECTIVE EXPERIENCE
• Use present feeling states to introduce *The Martian Fantasy* (following).
• Ask discussion questions that focus on feelings.

COGNITIVE INQUIRY
1. Ask, "What did we just do?" (Become aware of feelings.)
2. "Are feelings easy or hard to talk about? What makes it hard to talk about them?"
3. "How do you know when you're feeling a feeling? Can you stop yourself, or feel something more?"

(Encourage awareness of feelings and ways of identifying feelings. Continue through the Goal lessons—by tuning in to yourself through introspection and/or fantasy; by nonverbal cues; by behavior, action.)

ACTIVITIES
Brainstorm feelings—all the words the class can think of. Ask for volunteers to write the words on the board. Ask for other volunteers to write feelings words on 3 x 5 cards, one word to a card. Explain that for the next few lessons we will be collecting feelings words and making game cards.

Help the brainstorming by suggesting categories of feelings; i.e., good feelings, bad feelings, loving feelings, and neutral feelings. Teachers should add some complex words (i.e., embarrassed, content, indifferent).

List of Feelings Words

active	good	put-down
angry	great	puzzled
bad	hateful	rage
boiling	happy	rich
bold	helpful	sad
brave	helpless	safe
bruised	hot	scared
careful	hurt	shocked
chicken	hysterical	shy
clumsy	important	sick
cold	impressed	silly
comfortable	in-between happy and sad	sleepy
content	indifference	sly
cowardly	invisible	smart
crazy	itchy	sorry
cuckoo	joy	strong
curious	joyful	stupid
dejected	kind	surprised
depressed	lazy	terrible
down-in-the-dumps	like an idiot	thankful
embarrassed	love	thin
energy	mad	tired
enjoy	mean	unhappy
excited	miserable	unimportant
fat	nauseated	unprotected
fine	needed	upset
flattered	nice	warm
free	nuts	weak
frightened	overjoyed	wealthy
furry	physically-fit	weird
glad	poor	well
glum	proud	

Note: Do not expect a long list at first. The list will grow with awareness and time.

ASSIGNMENT

Ask the group, "Start collecting magazine or newspaper pictures that show some kind of feeling. Objects can generate feelings, such as a lonely city, a scary night. Any picture that has some feeling for *you*. Label the feeling. This assignment is due in two weeks." (Lesson 15)

"Start listening for feeling words at school and at home. Come in with at least one new feeling word next time."

Teacher Comments

_____

_____

_____

_____

_____

_____

_____

_____

_____

The Martian Fantasy

We use the usual fantasy induction methods (see Appendix C, p. 152); i.e., deep breathing and relaxation techniques. Ask the children, "Imagine that you are here at school and you see a flying saucer. It comes closer and closer and finally lands in the parking lot. There are blinking lights and strange sounds. A door opens and a strange creature emerges. It approaches the school and finds a place to enter. It has come to observe how we talk to each other. (Long pause.)

"What kinds of words would it hear? What kinds of positive things would it hear us saying

to each other? For example, I like you; that is a nice drawing; I appreciate you for helping me with my math; you are a good friend. What kinds of negative things (killer statements or put-down) would it hear us saying? For example, You are stupid; I don't like you; You're not my friend; I'm going to hit you. How do we say what we say? What kinds of words do we use?"

This game can be used with any aspect of communication. It's a good way to introduce "killer statements" or to stimulate a continued discussion on killer statements.

Notes from Nueva

We asked the children to list all the words they knew for feelings after telling them "The Martian Fantasy." How many words would the Martian hear?

Happy	*Marry*	*Disliked*
Sad	*Unhappy*	*Cool*
Confused	*Scared*	*Hot*
Mad	*Sticky*	*Great*
Angry	*Soft*	*Dull*
Joy	*Hard*	*Sleepy*
		Gay

Then we asked them how they could tell the Martian (who didn't know our language) what these words meant. They acted out some of the words while the rest of the group tried to guess the meanings.

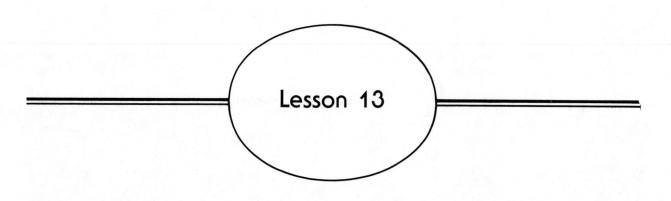

Lesson 13

MATERIALS
chalk; 3 x 5 index cards; straight pins.

BEGINNING
Collect feelings words by having a volunteer write them on the chalkboard. Ask another volunteer to add to the card list. Shuffle the cards and deal out one to each person.

AFFECTIVE EXPERIENCE
• Use the cards to introduce the "Milling Around" game (following). Each child should try to act out the word on his/her card. A student may put back any s/he might find difficult to work with.

COGNITIVE INQUIRY
Process what feelings were easy to act out. Which were hard? What is a feeling, anyway? (Give scientific stimulus-nerve response explanation.)

1. Ask, "What could we learn from knowing about feelings? (Understanding other people better, ourselves better, descriptions in books and poetry, society, etc.)"
2. "Can expressing feelings get you in trouble? When have you gotten in trouble expressing feelings? Are you having any feelings right now that would be risky to express? What are the feelings that have gotten people in trouble for expressing? (anger, frustration, love, affection, hate, hope?)"

3. "When you don't express a feeling, what happens to it? Does it just go away? What do you lose by not expressing a feeling? Do you remember a time when you didn't express a feeling and lost something by it?"
4. "What feelings are in this room right now? What difference does it make? What good does it do for a teacher to know how a student is feeling? A parent? A friend?"

Continue discussion of ways we can learn more about feelings.

ASSIGNMENT
Ask the children to collect magazine pictures showing feelings.

Teacher Comments _____

_____
_____
_____
_____
_____
_____
_____
_____
_____
_____

Milling Around Game

This is an exercise in low-level risk taking, which will generate data about patterns of interaction with others.

PROCEDURE
Collect feelings words by having a volunteer write them on the chalkboard. Ask another volunteer to add to the card list. Shuffle the cards and deal out one to each person. Direct students to pin on their feelings cards and stand in the class space in the center of the room and become aware of themselves in terms of the space and people around them. Direct students to start milling (walking slowly) around the room. After approximately two minutes, stop the milling and ask them to think about the following questions. "Stop and think for a second about the way you walked. Did you walk towards the center of the group, or stay on the periphery? Did you walk fast or slow? Did you feel as if you were following someone? Did you feel as if you were being followed? Did you change direction—pace at all? Did you look at people while you were walking? Did you make contact with others in any way?

How did you feel about the people you 'met' when you were milling? Did you feel the feelings word on your card? Anybody else's card?"

After giving people a few moments for processing their own responses, ask them to start milling again. Stop the milling after approximately one or two minutes, and ask the following "thought" questions: "Were there any changes in the way you walked during the second half of the exercise? Did you change the way in which you made contact or did not make contact with the people you 'met' while milling? Was there anything that you wanted to do that you did not permit yourself to do in this exercise?"

ACTIVITIES
Make and discuss journal entries.
Lead group discussion of reactions to exercise.

VARIATIONS

Have students wear blindfolds and mill. Then have them mill with eyes open. Focus on differences between the two experiences, the ways in which contact was made (or not made) blindfolded or with eyes open.

DISCUSSION QUESTIONS

"What sentences were you saying to yourself?"
"I discovered that I . . ."

Notes from Nueva

We introduced the Milling Around Game and the children were very involved for about ten minutes with milling around as an angry child, a critical parent, an unhappy little child, a pouting child, a crying child, a joyful child. We had a good chance to introduce new vocabulary and observe how freely each child was able to express feelings in nonverbal ways. We spent time discussing which feelings were the easiest, and which the hardest, to express.

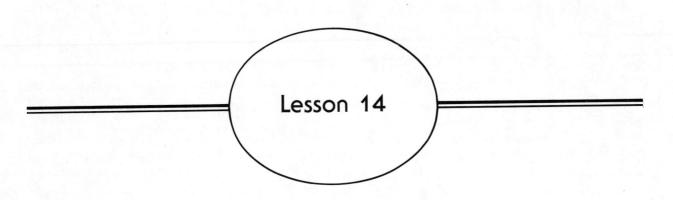

Lesson 14

FLOW LESSON

(See Appendix D, p. 161.)

ASSIGNMENT

Remind students to bring in magazine pictures for the next meeting.

Teacher Comments

_____

_____

_____

_____

_____

_____

_____

_____

_____

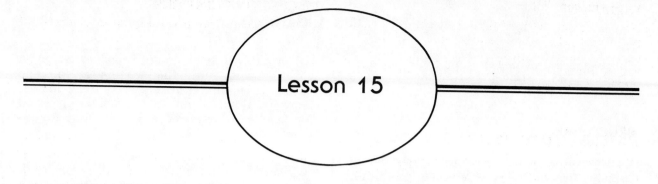

Lesson 15

MATERIALS

scissors, glue, large piece of oak tag for mounting "feelings" collage

BEGINNING

Ask everyone to share the magazine pictures they have brought in. Elicit how body expression, "body talk," can reveal so much.

AFFECTIVE EXPERIENCE

- Spend the lesson starting a "feelings" collage (following) which will stay in the classroom.
- Discuss and use discussion questions as the collage is being made.

COGNITIVE INQUIRY

Ask questions to elicit awareness of body talk as one means of learning about feelings. Pictures are one way of "seeing" feelings, receiving messages.

Encourage children to discuss sending and receiving as part of communication. Discuss *what* is sent (the message) and *how* it is sent (the feelings underlying the message).

1. "Do we all know what nonverbal is? When and how do we know when someone is using nonverbal communication?"
2. "How much of our communication is nonverbal?" (About 85 percent)
3. "Can we say one thing and express an opposing feeling nonverbally? Where? When? How?"

Such discussion will help students focus on what others are communicating to them and what they are communicating to others. This will allow them to be more effective in their communications and expand their repertoire of communication skills.

ASSIGNMENT

Bring in your favorite record, preferably a song with lyrics.

Teacher Comments _____

_____
_____
_____
_____
_____
_____
_____
_____
_____
_____

Feelings Collage

This exercise provides an opportunity for introspection and self-awareness as well as self-disclosure.

PROCEDURE

Provide many magazines, interesting pictures, scissors, glue, paste, and large paper for the students to work with. Have them go through magazines and create a personal collage. The pictures that the children choose may be a representation of their feelings. For example, a picture of a beat-up car represents the feeling of being hurt or picked on.

Working in small groups is preferable, but let children work individually if they wish. Each child then explains to the class what his/her representation is about; members of the class and the teacher are allowed to ask clarifying questions.

ACTIVITY

"Feelings" words can be listed on the board as positive or negative according to the quality of the original feeling described.

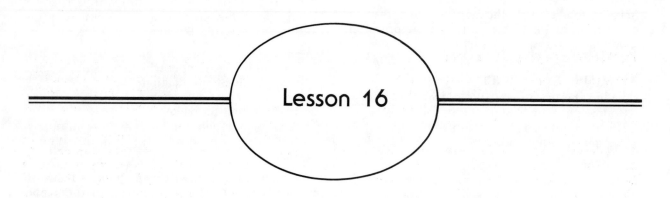

Lesson 16

MATERIALS

phonograph, 3 x 5 index cards

BEGINNING

Review last meeting, elicit information regarding "body language" they have observed since the last meeting.

AFFECTIVE EXPERIENCE

- Have students take turns playing the records they have brought in. Ask each student to tell why he or she chose that song, what feeling it evokes in them. Elicit similarities and differences in feelings.
- Play some of the records and encourage children to move to the music as they listen.

COGNITIVE INQUIRY

1. "Did you learn more words for feelings? (List and put on cards as before.) How do you usually learn more words for feelings? Is this useful learning? How?"
2. "Do you often discover how you are feeling by other people's expressions of their feelings?"
3. "Have you learned anything about your feelings today? This week? Is this real learning? Where else do you learn such things? (Offer books, films, TV, social interactions as other sources of learning about feelings.) What if feelings were outlawed? Would we be better off without them? In what ways?"

Close by pointing out that we have been naming words for feelings, *seeing*, feelings in pictures, *hearing* feelings in music. Continue thread with, "Is listening important? Why?"

You may wish to close this lesson with a game; e.g., "Explode," "Milling Around."

ASSIGNMENT

Ask the group to keep listening to people's feelings at school and home and to bring in another new word for the list.

Teacher Comments

_____

_____

_____

_____

_____

_____

_____

_____

_____

_____

_____

Notes from Nueva

The group agreed to meet during their lunch period Thursday because a field trip was planned. They had missed the previous two weeks because of half-day sessions and they were very upset.

Everyone ate lunch while we talked. We discussed our session with Lou Savery the week before and it was interesting to see how much the children remembered. We talked at length about altered states of consciousness and the fact that there are many inner spaces to explore and many "elevators" (Lou's term) to get us there. The students remembered: drugs, yoga, meditation, hypnosis, and music. We reviewed Peter's unpleasant memory state, which he shared today. Today, Peter happened to hear the same music being played that a friend and he had played one night at his friend's house, when he felt really weird things were happening. When he could not change his state and no longer wanted to be there, he opened his eyes. We again pointed out that with music as an "elevator," he had choices, but if he had taken a drug, for example, he would have had to wait until the drug wore off.

Jim began to tell about his dreams, particularly the ones that seemed to come true a week or two later. There were many agreements and lots of dream-sharing about scary things—dying, funny dreams, dreams of being attacked and jumped on, dreams of wishing to be somewhere else. We also discussed length of dreams and Hal told about a class he took where he studied dreams. Everyone thought it would be fun to keep a dream journal in order to remember dreams for sharing and discussing. I suggested that dreams were like messages and if we could understand the code we could understand ourselves better. Dana observed that while we were all sharing dreams, she realized how similar people really are. Not just that they have similar dreams, but that they are similar in many other ways, too.

Today was a great day. There was a close group feeling. Everyone but Sue was actively interested and we really were anxious to meet again. It was good feedback to hear them all complain about missing self-sciencing, really liking it, and being willing to meet during lunch so they wouldn't have to miss a session.

Lesson 17

MATERIALS
3 x 5 index cards

BEGINNING
Ask students to add new feeling words to cards.

Introduce idea of "inventory." Spend a few minutes inventorying the cards collected so far into categories of: Pleasure/Love; Pain/Hate words.

When the cards have been finished, ask students what feelings they have at this very moment. Also express your feelings.

AFFECTIVE EXPERIENCE
- Play *Tape Recorder Game* (following), sending messages about present feelings. Questions focus on receiving; i.e., listening.
- Play variations of acting out feeling cards, or *Bumpety-Bump* with feelings.

COGNITIVE INQUIRY
(Having developed awareness of feelings and ways they can be expressed, the focus now moves to accepting responsibility for one's own feelings.) Ask the following questions.

1. "Did you ever have a feeling you wished you knew what to do with? Do you have such feelings often? Do others have them too? How do you know if others are having the same difficulties with feelings that you are?"
2. "Do feelings ever make people sick? How? Do people really get headaches and ulcers from feelings?"
3. "Some say that each person has a 'gunny sack' into which all the sad, angry, frustrated feelings are put. We all have them everyday but we don't express them. Then when someone who won't hurt back does something the least bit annoying, we dump the 'gunny sack' all over our friends. Have you ever dumped your saved-up bad feelings on an undeserving friend? Has this ever happened to you? What did you do? How did you feel?"

4. "Do you have any 'unfinished' situations you are carrying around with you today? A quarrel with your parent this morning that you are still angry or sad about? An incident with a classmate that didn't turn out fairly or left you frustrated? Have you been planning for any situation that you have strong feelings about? What is the effect of these leftover feelings on what you've been doing today? If the effect isn't good, how can you free yourself from these leftover feelings? How long can a leftover feeling influence you? Do you sometimes still feel sad over a lost friend from a year ago? Can you recall a success or a happy feeling from it?"

Introduce concepts: perceptions, judgments, and values.

ASSIGNMENT
Tell the class, "Make a drawing of any thing that you think most expresses your feeling about yourself and your present mood; e.g., choose an animal, tree, flower, food, etc."

_____
_____
_____
_____
_____
_____
_____
_____
_____
_____

Tape Recorder Game

One child gives a short message (the subject can be open-ended or directed; i.e., "something I feel proud about," "what I like most/least," "something important to me"). Then this same child picks a member of the group to be the tape recorder. They must repeat back word-for-word the message. You can increase the difficulty by making the message longer, adding facial expressions, tone of voice, body movements, rate of speech, etc.

This is a good game to help children develop good listening skills.

Notes from Nueva _____

Hal was sick.

We found our space again in the Ballet Room. I think the mirrors in there are magic, making all of us more aware of our expressions, our movements, and of each other.

I asked Bob to be the scribe for the group, which he did with seriousness and pleasure. We all thought of words to describe our feelings after an initial romp around the room to relieve body tensions. We stamped, skipped, and hopped, the only verbalization being laughter. Talked a bit about expressing feelings through movement. The words for feelings came freely: uptight, happy, hungry, excited, angry, tired, confused, shy, thirsty, sad, relaxed, sick, weird.

We acted out nonverbally: How do you feel today? (Tape Recorder) Bob volunteered first; stomped around, snorted, threw himself on the floor and pounded with his fists, all in high good humor. Dana is thoughtful, moving around and tipping her ponytailed head like a miniature Oriental princess. Alice skips, she feels happy. Several show how tired they are. One is bored. We extend the actions into words and discuss how the movements convey feelings. "How would you call such a feeling?" Interpretations vary. Lila acted shy, which no one understood (some saw it as fear); so, we all tried being shy in her manner. Beth tried to be shy or tired but could not, which led to the closing discussion about how difficult it really is to understand someone else's feelings.

Lesson 18

MATERIALS
chalk

BEGINNING
Draw a feeling continuum on the chalkboard as in Lesson 12. This time don't put on labels.

Ask students to label and indicate their feelings at the present moment.

Discuss any past or present causes for the individual feelings (e.g., "happy because I'm going on a trip this weekend"; "sad because my goldfish died"; "hassled because I had a fight with my father this morning").

AFFECTIVE EXPERIENCE
- From any of the feeling situations raised, ask the group to choose some they would like to *role-play.*
- Teach the group how to role play and act out several of the situations. (See discussion on *role-playing* in Appendix C, p. 152.)

COGNITIVE INQUIRY
Discuss the role-plays.

1. Ask "Does this happen often? How does it start?"

Trace the situation through the feeling response. Introduce the idea of a *pattern,* a characteristic way of responding.

2. Ask the group, "Who/what causes your feelings? Many wise men have suggested that when we recognize and assume responsibility for our own feelings we are in control and do not blame others."

3. "Is it important for us to hear about someone's feeling even though that is not our feeling? What would make this important? Are we *taking responsibility for our feelings* when we identify them for the class? How? Is this useful to us?"

Tell the class that sometimes expressing feelings can be an attempt to cause someone to do or say something that the expressor wants. If you think someone is expressing feelings to influence you in a certain way, ask them directly if it is true. For example, "Are you saying you are feeling lonely so I'll invite you to come to the party we're planning?" Expressing feelings is often helpful, but you shouldn't expect people to guess what you want from your expression. Experiment with saying what you need directly to the person who can meet that need, *in addition* to naming your feelings.

ASSIGNMENT
Tell the class, "Watch for any situation that gives you a strong feeling. Write down a description of the situation and what feeling you had."

Teacher Comments

_____

_____

_____

_____

_____

_____

_____

_____

_____

_____

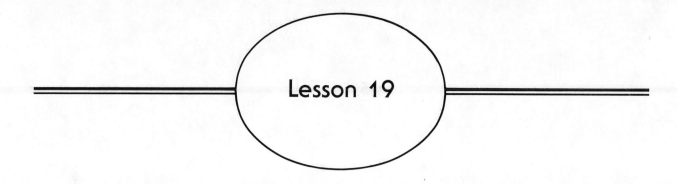

Lesson 19

BEGINNING

Share and discuss feeling situations the students encounter. Reinforce idea of *pattern* begun in Lesson 18.

AFFECTIVE EXPERIENCE

- Play "Bumpety-Bump" variation with feelings, choosing and acting out the feelings which surfaced in the homework assignment. Switch to present feelings. Note whether feelings changed.

COGNITIVE INQUIRY

1. "Try this experiment: Name your present feeling and then say to yourself, '*I'm making myself* feel _____ (angry, sad, alone) right now.' See how often you can believe this sentence. When it really seems as if someone is causing a feeling in you, say to yourself, 'I'm allowing _____ (Bill, Sue, etc.) to act as a catalyst and I am making myself feel _____ (happy, mad, lonely, etc.).' "

2. "What did you learn from this experiment? What was the most difficult part about it for you? What did you say to yourself to avoid the experiment?"

Introduce the Trumpet Process as a way of looking at ourselves. Show how we can use the Trumpet Process to see what we've been learning about feelings. Go through the first three steps— experiencing confrontations; inventorying responses; recognizing patterns (see page 9).

ASSIGNMENT

Ask the class, "Look for strong feeling situations and name them to yourself. Identify two such incidents and write them in your journal."

Tell the group, "Our next meeting will be a flow lesson."

Teacher Comments

_____

_____

_____

_____

_____

_____

_____

_____

_____

_____

Lesson 20

FLOW LESSON
(See Appendix D, p. 161.)

Teacher Comments _____

_____

_____

_____

_____

_____

_____

_____

_____

_____

_____

_____

_____

APPROACHING GOAL 4

Developing Communication Skills for Affective States

Lessons 21–27

In Goal 3, students concentrated on simply becoming aware of and labelling feeling states. Now they move into two new areas: an awareness of their present feeling state; i.e., recognizing their own feelings clearly at any given moment; and learning how to communicate their feelings as well as learning how to receive feeling communication from others. This involves observing the discrepancies between a sender's words, tone of voice, and body language. Also, cognitive inquiry continues, using experiences on which to build abstractions by cataloging the subject matter in terms of the Trumpet Process, Steps 1, 2, and 3. Lessons 21 to 27 concentrate on communications skills. Lessons 24 and 27 are suggested as flow lessons.

GROUP BEHAVIOR

(See Appendix C, p. 149.) During the lessons, you may want to adjust focus depending on the progress of the group. If the group has opened up expressed feeling states in Goal 3, progress in sequence through the lessons, emphasizing Cognitive Inquiry and the verbalization of communication skills. If the group seemed slow, or if the group had difficulties on the earlier lessons, focus more on the affective parts of the lessons. Allow for more experiences in surfacing feelings.

GROUP EXERCISE

These exercises help students focus on self. Children are asked to locate their zone of awareness; that is, everyone cycles on a continuum of awareness within the relatively distinct zones—inner, middle, outer. The inner zone consists of physical situations and feelings of the body itself.

The middle zone consists of memories, fantasies, planning, thinking, etc. or what is commonly called mental activity. The outer zone consists of the sensations which come from outside one's skin.

Have the students try to pay attention to the continuum of awareness. Some people are able to pay attention to two zones at the same time. Usually it's easy to name the focus of one's attention. The importance of what may seem commonplace, self-evident observation comes from answers to the questions: "What are your habitual patterns in terms of the continuum of awareness? How do the patterns serve you?" The questions aren't pursued systematically to a conclusion at this point, the practice is helpful for later learning.

EVIDENCE OF STUDENT GROWTH

Growth toward the goal will be demonstrated by the students as follows.

AFFECTIVE EXPECTATIONS

- Accepting new procedures for learning, e.g., fantasizing, role-playing, nonverbal communication.
- Improving listening skills and self-expression.
- Developing additional vocabulary.
- Relaxing and creating visual imagery.

COGNITIVE EXPECTATIONS

- Developing interpretation and inference skills.
- Distinguishing between fact and judgment.
- Learning the concept of negotiation in terms of negotiating problem situation.
- Understanding what communication is—sending and receiving.

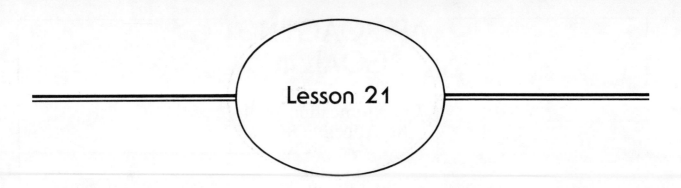

Lesson 21

BEGINNING

Ask students to sit in a circle. Begin a discussion of the "here-and-now." Rap about knowing when one is in touch with the "here-and-now."

AFFECTIVE EXPERIENCE

• Play the "Hot Potato Feeling" game (following).

COGNITIVE INQUIRY

Ask the discussion questions included with the "Hot Potato" game. Categorize the feelings; i.e., inner zone, middle zone, outer zone.

1. "Was there a preponderance of one zone over another?"
2. "Is this common for you?"
3. "What zone of feelings might you share with your friends? Strangers?"

ASSIGNMENT

Tell students, "In your journal, categorize three strong feelings you have from now until next meeting. See if you can identify which zone the feelings come from."

The Hot Potato Feeling Game

This exercise gives learners practice in inventorying their feelings.

PROCEDURE

Have students pair off and play "Hot Potato" with some object they can toss back and forth. When students get the "Hot Potato" they have to say what they are feeling right now, then toss the potato to their partner. This action continues for several minutes—even if students find it hard.

ACTIVITY

Aloud, or in journals, respond to the following questions.

DISCUSSION QUESTIONS

1. Ask, "Is this game hard or easy? What do you think makes it hard or easy?"
2. "How does it feel to have to say what you are feeling? How do you feel when you can't say anything?"
3. "Is there anything you would like to have said and censored? What?"

Teacher Comments _____

_____

_____

_____

_____

_____

_____

_____

_____

_____

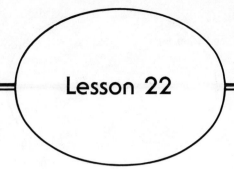

Lesson 22

MATERIALS

newsprint and magic markers, or a chalkboard

BEGINNING

Sitting in a circle, discuss strong feelings categorized on homework assignment.

Review "here-and-now" concepts.

Discuss vocabulary: metaphors, zones, habitual patterns, learning, brainstorming, etc.

Introduce the games.

AFFECTIVE EXPERIENCE

• Play the "Brainstorm-Feeling-Metaphors" and "Role-Playing-Feeling Metaphors" games.

COGNITIVE INQUIRY

Ask the following questions.

1. "What are habitual patterns? How do habitual patterns serve you? In what zone of awareness do you spend the most time? What zone is best for studying? Playing Monopoly? Baseball? Sleeping? Communicating with friends?"

2. "What can't you do if you're not aware of the outer zone? What is it like to be deaf? Blind? Without a sense of touch? Are you sometimes 'out of touch' with the outer zone? How do you really know when someone sees or hears you?"

ASSIGNMENT

Tell the group, "In your journal, identify three feelings, and indicate where in your body you felt them."

Teacher Comments _____

_____

_____

_____

_____

_____

_____

_____

_____

_____

Brainstorm-Feeling-Metaphors Game

This game is valuable for increasing affective vocabulary and improving inventorying skills—particularly feelings and sensations.

PROCEDURE

Divide the class into triads. Then explain that brainstorming is taking one special idea and thinking of everything you can about it, verbalizing and compiling a list of your thoughts. The quantity of ideas is what's important, not the quality. Thoughts about the brainstorming topic are not to be censored or judged. Each idea is acceptable, hitchhiking is both permissible and encouraged. You may want to give them a few examples such as "happy face, silly putty, shy shoes, angry plant, etc."

ACTIVITY

Work either in small groups or in a large group. In brainstorming, the whole group input is often invaluable.

VARIATION

After a list of feeling metaphors has been generated, the children may want to role-play them (like charades) as a guessing game.

DISCUSSION QUESTIONS

1. "How many of you had a word which was self-censored?"
2. "What prompted you to keep it to yourself?"
3. "Did you feel anxious about the reactions of others to your thoughts?"
4. "Did you feel you would seem silly?"
5. "Did you say to yourself, 'Anyone would have thought that?'"
6. "Did you do this often? Is it a pattern? If it is a pattern, how does it function for you?"

Role-Playing-Feeling-Metaphors Game

This exercise will help students both with self-disclosure and in their search for patterns.

PROCEDURE

Tell the children, "You're going to act out some of the feeling metaphors you brainstormed. Do this without using any words. Look at the lists on the newsprint (or chalkboard) and choose one you'd like to act out. Put the title on the board and then role-play your feeling."

ACTIVITY

Have the children in the audience describe what they saw, and how they imagine the role-playing student felt. Have a discussion either after each role-play or after all the role-plays, using the Trumpet Process questions to guide the discussion.

Children who are reluctant to role-play their feeling metaphor are to be allowed to tell their partner, support group, or class about it.

After all the role-plays, ask questions for students to respond to in their journals, and then share their answers.

VARIATION

This exercise may be role-played with a partner in support groups. After each role-play, ask the person questions to help analyze the feelings.

After all students complete their role-plays, ask questions for the students to respond to in their journals. Then the students can share, either again with partners, or support groups, or the whole class.

Students can also role-play feeling metaphors without first writing them on the board. Other students can try to identify the feelings from the nonverbal cues.

DISCUSSION QUESTIONS

For the role-player, ask: "How did your body feel as an (eggbeater)? Where in your body did you feel this? Did you notice your body? (Example: clenched fists, crouched position, etc.) What did you do with different parts of your body? How did they feel?"

For the audience, ask: "What did _____ do that made you feel s/he was feeling _____ (confused or mixed up, etc.)? How do you think s/he felt? How accurate were your observations of the feelings?"

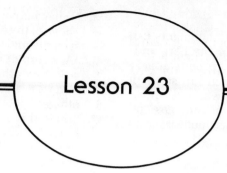

Lesson 23

MATERIALS
newsprint for each student; magic markers for all.

BEGINNING
Share one feeling and its body placement (see Lesson 22).

Review vocabulary words, and add new ones: perceptions, concepts, awareness, preference, satisfaction, senses, etc.

AFFECTIVE EXPERIENCE
- Play the "Here-and-Now" statements and the "Here-and-Now" Wheel game.

COGNITIVE INQUIRY
Ask the following questions.

1. "How aware are you of your middle zone of thoughts, memories, and fantasies?"
2. "Are there some thoughts that you have over and over?"
3. "Do you spend a lot of time planning?"
4. "How often are you aware of your feelings? Your inner zone?"
5. "Strong feelings usually force themselves to our attention, but do you ever deliberately check out your body, your inner zone, to see what is happening with your feelings? Check now!"

ASSIGNMENT
No assignment. Lesson 24 is a Flow Lesson.

Teacher Comments _____

_____

_____

_____

_____

_____

_____

_____

_____

_____

_____

_____

Here-And-Now Statements Game

This activity will increase awareness of perceptions and feelings as they are being experienced.

PROCEDURE
Have students sit in a circle. Explain the rule that for this exercise only things happening at the moment can be mentioned. Go around the circle having each complete the statement, "Right now I see . . ." Each has the option of passing. Repeat, using "Right now I hear . . . ," "Right now I am touching . . . ," "Right now I feel . . . ," "Right now I am aware . . ."

ACTIVITY

Group sharing of "I learned ..." statements can be useful in illustrating some of the here-and-now experiences that usually go consciously unnoticed. Brainstorm with the group some of the factors that affected their awareness positively or negatively. Discuss the advantages and disadvantages of heightening consciousness to so many stimuli.

DISCUSSION QUESTIONS

Ask the following questions.

1. "What did you become aware of that you normally wouldn't have noticed?"
2. "What usually gets in the way?"
3. "What helped your awareness here?"
4. "How many different senses can you attend to at one time?"
5. "Are certain combinations of senses easier for you than others?"
6. "Do you attend to certain senses more than others?"
7. "Does this match up with some of your patterns?"
8. "Are there alternatives that might be useful for you?"

ASSIGNMENT

None (next meeting is a Flow Lesson).

Teacher Comments _____

_____

_____

_____

_____

_____

_____

_____

_____

_____

_____

_____

Here-and-Now Wheel Game

This activity increases awareness of the variety of feelings students may be experiencing at any given moment, broadening the perception of those feelings.

PROCEDURE

Tell the class, "Draw a circle with four spokes so that the circle is divided into four quarters. Write four words, one in each quarter, which describe how you are feeling right now. Then take one of those words and expand it into two sentences."

ACTIVITY

Using paper and magic markers, have the children depict their feelings, emphasizing the one feeling they expanded. Tell them, "With this wheel in your journal, make another wheel that would have just the opposite feelings; then compare the two wheels in respect to your preferences, pleasantness, satisfaction, goals, etc."

With the class divided into triads, have them share what they wish from the here-and-now wheels.

Group members can volunteer to share with the whole class what they wish from their wheels.

DISCUSSION QUESTIONS

Ask the following questions.

1. "Are your present feelings typical of your day-to-day feelings?"
2. "Did you get in touch with any feelings that surprised you?"
3. "Are you satisfied with the way you are feeling? If not, what could you do to change your feelings in the direction you'd prefer? Do others feel as you do?"

Notes from Nueva

We were able to return to the "here-and-now" to talk. Heidi suggested we tell about our sicknesses and scary things. Taylor agreed, but he also wanted to talk about death. He is afraid of dying. Everyone agreed that it was a concern. Eric is going to be a doctor when he grows up and he will discover a pill that will help us live forever.

We asked if there were any other topics people would like to talk about. Eric wanted to talk about "asking stupid questions." We were able to help him clarify that he sometimes feels stupid when he asks questions. The other children told him he should not feel that way; that he had to ask questions to learn. We all agreed to think of a question we would feel stupid asking, and that we would talk about it next time.

Lesson 24

FLOW LESSON
(See Appendix D, p. 161.)

Teacher Comments

Lesson 25

BEGINNING

Discuss the Flow Lesson. Was anything learned?

Five minutes into the class, ask these questions:

"What have you been doing in the last five minutes?"

"What have you been feeling?"

"Have your feelings changed in that time?"

"What have you been thinking?"

"What were you saying to yourself in your head?"

"What did you learn about yourself just now?"

Discuss meaning of new vocabulary, e.g., attending, perception, nonverbal cues.

Play *Telephone Chain* (Lesson 6).

AFFECTIVE EXPERIENCE

• Play the "Nonverbal Gossip" and "Indian Chief" games.

COGNITIVE INQUIRY

Ask the following questions.

1. "What skills (identify) were useful while playing the games?"
2. "Write in your journal five communication skills. What do the terms mean?"
3. "Can you learn about yourself by studying yourself? How?"
4. "What tools do scientists use to study cells? Do people need tools to study themselves?"
5. "What if you were to do exactly the opposite of what you're doing right now? What would you be doing?"

ASSIGNMENT

Write down in your journal two changes you have deliberately made in your life and be prepared to share them with other members of the group.

Teacher Comments _____

_____

_____

_____

_____

_____

_____

_____

_____

Nonverbal Gossip Game

This exercise will offer experience in attending, perception, and nonverbal communication skills.

PROCEDURE

Students sit in a circle. One student volunteers to express a feeling nonverbally to the one next to him/her, who passes it on to the next, and so on until it goes all around the circle. Play several rounds, with different students initiating different feelings to be expressed.

ACTIVITY

The group may share their experiences in "I learned . . ." statements. Opportunities for feedback may be useful. Discussion of changes that developed as something proceeded around the circle are beneficial.

DISCUSSION QUESTIONS

Ask the following questions.

1. "What was easy to communicate without words? Hard?"
2. "What part of your body did you use most?"
3. "Did you learn any ways to improve your nonverbal communications or to make your meaning clearer?"
4. "Did you find yourself exaggerating your usual expressions or adding new ones?"

Indian Chief Game*

This exercise is designed to develop communication skills of attending and being aware of nonverbal behavior.

PROCEDURE

Have the students sit in a circle. The group picks one person to be the "Guesser," who then leaves the group. While the "Guesser" is gone, one person is asked to be an Indian Chief. The Chief makes different nonverbal signs, such as clapping hands, snapping fingers, or yawning, which everyone imitates. The "Guesser" returns and tries to guess the identity of the Chief. Several rounds can be played.

ACTIVITY

Have the group discuss the following questions.

1. "What did you do to enable you to guess the Chief?"
2. "How well did you imitate the Chief?"
3. "What things make it easy to imitate a person?"
4. "What makes it hard?"

*Adapted from Allen Evey, Professor, University of Massachusetts.

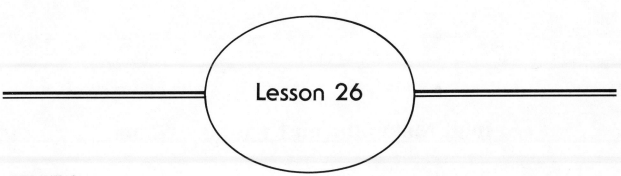

Lesson 26

BEGINNING

Tell the group to share experiences of deliberately made changes in life action.

Introduce the concept of communicating "here-and-now" feelings. Ask, "What kind of person would you be if you had no inner zone? How do you know what zone you are in?"

Say to the group, "When you feel you are in the inner zone of awareness for what you are trying to do, try naming that pattern to yourself, either inside or out loud. For example, if you're supposed to be studying your math, and you can't think because you are feeling sad about losing a friend, say just that to yourself, your classmate, or to the teacher. If you are supposed

to be listening to your friend talk, and you are thinking about what you are going to do tonight and not hearing the friend, tell the person (or at least tell yourself).

"When you are in an argument or feel one coming on, pay attention to what zone you're in. Win-lose arguments and fights usually happen to people who are in their middle zone. If, instead of staying in your awareness of your thoughts, plans, and expectations of others, you name the feelings you're having (inner zone), and what you are seeing and hearing in the other (outer zone), it will be difficult to keep the argument going. For example, when someone cuts in line in front of you, try saying, 'I feel frustrated, having waited my turn and seeing you cut in line. You look a little embarrassed at having done it.'"

"Who controls actions? Who manages the present situation better than you?"

Review vocabulary: expectations, change, deliberate, fantasy, experiments.

AFFECTIVE EXPERIENCE

• Play the "Animal Metaphor and Fantasy" Game.

COGNITIVE INQUIRY

Ask the students:

1. "Describe in your journal what happened, what you were feeling during the games."
2. "What changes have you made in your life on purpose?"

3. "What do you do differently than you did before because you decided to do it differently? Who helped you decide to do it differently? Who helped you make the decision to change? What are some of the things you would like to do differently in here? Who can help you?"
4. "When you want to do something differently, like talking to someone new, trying a different way of talking to teachers, or asking for what you want, what do you say to yourself in your head that stops you?"

ASSIGNMENT

No assignment; Flow Lesson to follow.

Teacher Comments _____

_____

_____

_____

_____

_____

_____

_____

_____

_____

_____

Animal Metaphor and Fantasy Game

PROCEDURE

(This exercise is relatively low in risk and is a good one for a transitional unit.) "Imagine a huge forest. In the middle of it is a large open field. The animal that is you and the animal that is the person you dislike the most are in the center of the field."

Continue the fantasy. (Give the students a minute or two at this point.) "Now briefly try to wipe the slate clean. That scene fades and suddenly the field appears in your mind again. This time as you approach the middle of the field you meet the animal that is the person you love most."

Continue fantasy. "When you're ready, return to this room and slowly open your eyes."

ACTIVITIES

Immediately after the exercise, students should be given the opportunity to make an entry in their journals, describing in some detail what happened during the fantasy. Students should then be encouraged to share reactions with other members of the group and to consider a few questions, such as the following.

1. "How did you feel during each of the encounters?"
2. "Is this the way you usually react to these people?"
3. "What did you learn about yourself from your reactions?"

4. "How were your thoughts and feelings in both the first fantasy of the exercise and the last fantasy similar to and different from those of others?"

Finally, students should be given the opportunity to make an additional entry in their journals, based on the questions and the group discussion.

Notes from Nueva

We asked the group to "Think of the person you like the most. Now think of an animal that's like that person."

ERIC: Cat. My friend, Frank. He is twelve. He reminds me of a cat because he is nice.

STUART: Deer. My girl friend. We play "Bambi" when we are together.

KATRINA: Dog. My friend. She loves dogs. Wonderful!

HEIDI: Horse. A horse is gay, nice. My friend, Kathy, who lives next door.

"Let's think about all the words we know that relate to the person we like the most."

Happy	Overjoyed	Gay
Great	Good	Silly

"Now let's make a list of words that might describe someone we do not like."

Sad	Angry	Mad	Cuckoo
Bad	Hurt	Yucky	Gooey

TAYLOR: Ox. My neighbor is like an ox. He bothers everybody. Always runs into me.

HEIDI: Lion. I do not like Scott. He is mean and sneaks up on me.

ERIC: Cheetah. A boy named Miller, who lives down the street. He is really mean, and he never plays with me, and he can run fast.

"Now let's think of an animal that is most like you."

KATRINA: Cat. Silly.

ERIC: Person. Energy, happy (sort of).

STUART: Squirrel. Sometimes I feel small because I feel like I have no friends.

TAYLOR: I could not listen to Stuart because I was so anxious for my turn. That is what happens when you do not listen. That is bad. I get sent to my room; get sent home. If you do not listen, then, when it is your turn, they will not listen to you.

Heidi suggested we all brag about how we do not listen. We did. The group agreed we have a pattern of not listening.

We dealt with projections and got the group to think about the fact that they are responsible for their own reactions and responses.

Lesson 27

FLOW LESSON
(See Appendix D, p. 161.)

Teacher Comments _____

_____

_____

_____

_____

_____

_____

_____

_____

_____

_____

_____

APPROACHING GOAL 5

Disclosing One's Thoughts and Feelings

Lessons 28–33

Lessons 28 to 33 further emphasize communication skills by helping the students feel comfortable about disclosing themselves; when it is appropriate, and when it is not, as well as how to encourage openness in others. Material dealt with so far is integrated and reviewed prior to completing Section 1 of self-science.

Lesson 31 is suggested as a Flow Lesson.

GROUP BEHAVIOR

Most self-disclosure at this point is external, i.e., outer zone. Usually children need considerable practice before they move into areas of personal concerns. Think of this Goal as seed-planting time. Results will come later in the course. You can contribute a great deal here by active role-modeling, i.e., demonstrating disclosure by discussion about yourself. Concentrate on the similarities within the group by reassuring and promoting a safe climate for disclosure, and permitting shy students to "pass" without fear of shame.

EVIDENCE OF STUDENT GROWTH

Growth toward the goal will be demonstrated by the students as follows.

AFFECTIVE EXPECTATIONS

• Showing an increasing ability to disclose thoughts and feelings.
• Showing an increasing ability to participate in self-disclosure exercises.
• Ask, "If others do not know what you feel, need or want, what do you lose by their not knowing? What do you avoid?"

COGNITIVE EXPECTATIONS

• Classifying behavior into categories.
• Seeing patterns.
• Understanding the connection between behavior and communication.
• Valuing open communication.
• Conducting and reporting on experiments.
• Improving listening and question-asking skills.

DISCUSSION QUESTIONS

Rap sessions on the importance of appropriate self-disclosure for its own sake and in support of the other class norms can be structured around the following kinds of questions and strategies.

1. "How smart is it to reveal or tell about yourself in here? Your real thoughts and feelings? Do you feel freer to disclose yourself somewhere else? What is different there? Do you learn anything by disclosing yourself?"
2. "People say if you keep your thoughts and feelings to yourself, you are better off. What do you think? When isn't that so?"
3. "Who can say what you are really thinking or feeling? Anyone? Many people?"
4. "When was a time you said more about yourself than you should have? When was a time you said less than you should have? What happened? What did you learn?"

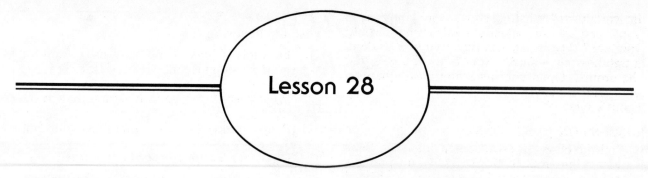

Lesson 28

BEGINNING

Ask students to sit in a circle. Discuss what has been learned so far in self-science. Discuss vocabulary: disclose, inner self, sender, receiver, pattern, consequences.

AFFECTIVE EXPERIENCE

- Play the "Volunteer Game" and the "Rehearsing Game."

COGNITIVE INQUIRY

Ask questions to the first game as follows.

1. "How much do you reveal about yourself when you volunteer?"
2. "Are you affected by how much others disclose about themselves?"

Discuss questions for the second game.

ACTIVITY

Have the class write journal entries in response to what was learned through the games and discussions.

ASSIGNMENT

Tell the children, "Note two patterns in your journals that you identify during the week."

Teacher Comments _____

_____

_____

_____

_____

_____

_____

_____

_____

_____

Volunteer Game

This exercise will help the students understand their feelings leading to the decision to volunteer or not to volunteer.

PROCEDURE

The class is asked for volunteers to present something to the group. After giving the class a few minutes to make their decision and acknowledge those who want to volunteer, the teacher

then can say, "I don't need the volunteers right now, but I would like you to focus on your decision to volunteer or not to volunteer."

ACTIVITY

Tell the class, "Close your eyes for a few minutes and see if you can play back that scene we just experienced. What were you feeling after I asked for volunteers? What questions were going on in your head? If you looked in a mirror, how would you look? What was your body saying? Was there a tightness anywhere?" After a few minutes, tell the group, "Open your eyes and write down in your journals anything you might have observed about yourself."

DISCUSSION QUESTIONS

1. Tell the class, "Here are some other questions you might like to think about and perhaps note in your journal." (These also can be put on newsprint or on the board.)
2. "Were you affected by others' responses? How?"
3. "Were you concerned about how you might appear to your classmates or the teacher?"
4. "Did this concern affect your decision?"
5. "Can you state briefly how you decided to volunteer or not to volunteer?" (The answer to the last question might be shared with the entire class by several who wish to share— Volunteers.)

PATTERNS

Ask the group, "I would like you to now take a look at your usual behavior, your pattern. How do you usually respond in a similar situation?" Students may find that their responses vary with situations. They may discover some interesting data by answering the question, "Under what circumstances do you make a similar response? a different response?" Their pattern of behavior, however, will be the response they most often make in a volunteer situation. It is that pattern they will take through the Trumpet.

FUNCTION

Ask the following.

1. "Let's take a look at the patterns of those of you that volunteered."
2. "What does volunteering get for you?"
3. "What does it give you? What are the advantages?"
4. "Does it enable you to do something you want to do?"
5. "How does this pattern make you feel?"

The same questions can be used for the students who don't usually volunteer. An additional question might be: "What does not volunteering protect you from or help you avoid?"

CONSEQUENCES

The following questions can be used to help students identify the consequences of either pattern. Ask the students, "What price do you pay for volunteering or not volunteering? How much does it cost? Are you losing out on anything? If so, what? If someone were thinking of adopting your pattern, what precautions might you give them?"

EVALUATION

Tell the children, "If you tried on an alternative behavior pattern, you might make a comparison with your first pattern. To help, you might complete the following statements: 'I learned . . . ,' 'I disliked/liked it because . . .'"

CHOOSE

After evaluating the alternative behavior and comparing it with the original pattern, the student can select either behavior or both as part of his/her repertoire.

Rehearsing Game

This exercise is designed for use with other disclosure exercises. It increases the awareness of the process of rehearsing inner self dialogues.

PROCEDURE

When there is a lull and while the students are being asked to share their unique and common responses to a given activity, ask the students if there are any who are rehearsing an answer. Ask those who are rehearsing to share their inner self dialogues.

ACTIVITY

Have the class make journal entries, using the following sentence stubs: "I discovered that I . . . ," "I learned that I . . ."

VARIATION

Ask a volunteer to role-play an inner dialogue, using a separate chair for each voice. Miming with words works well here.

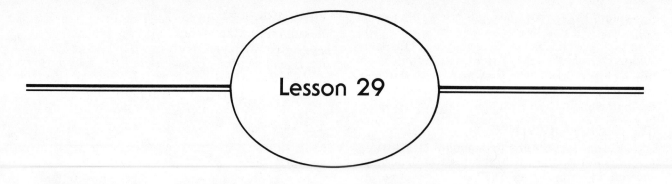

Lesson 29

BEGINNING

Ask students to share patterns identified in their journals. Review the concept of patterns.

AFFECTIVE EXPERIENCE

- Play the "One Minute Autobiography" Game.
- Play the "Empty Your Wallet, Pockets, or Purses" Game.

COGNITIVE INQUIRY

Ask questions related to the first affective experience. Ask questions related to the second affective experience, as follows.

1. "How much were you willing to reveal about yourself?"
2. "Are you embarrassed to talk about yourself? Why?"

Have the class add "I learned . . ." statements to their journals.

ACTIVITY

Have the class make journal entries, using "I learned . . ." statements. Then follow with small-group feedback.

DISCUSSION QUESTIONS

Ask the following questions.

1. "What thoughts did you censor (hold back) as you were saying your autobiography out loud?"
2. "Did you give a well-rounded picture of yourself or did you reveal only your good side?"

ASSIGNMENT

Ask the class to conduct two one-minute autobiography sessions with their friends and/or members of their families, and record notes about each in their journals.

Teacher Comments _____

_____

_____

_____

_____

_____

_____

_____

One-Minute Autobiography Game

This exercise will help students view their lives in a variety of ways they may not have considered before. It offers a chance to share views with others, to become more aware of their own pictures of self, and to share some of their patterns.

PROCEDURE

Divide the class into groups of five or six. Ask each child to think about his/her history from birth to the present. Tell the children that each will have one minute to relate personal autobiographies. Give children time to think. Then have them share their autobiographies orally in the small groups.

VARIATION

Since children like this exercise, you can repeat it periodically, having them do one-minute autobiographies around relevant themes such as: houses I have lived in; friends I have had; new toys I have gotten; etc. For the first run of this exercise the teacher should avoid modeling any particular style or theme of autobiography. This will make it possible for each child to express unique views. Sometimes children tend to copy each other's themes. For example, if one child describes personal experiences in terms of various medical operations, other children may follow, describing their lives with special emphasis on operations. Be alert to this possibility and note themes that emerge.

Empty Your Wallet, Pockets, or Purses Game

This exercise has many possibilities, depending on the students' interests and concerns. They may explore their own feelings about themselves and others, their values, and their willingness to share or disclose themselves.

PROCEDURE

Have groups of three to five students empty their pockets or wallets in front of them. Allow students to censor (eliminate items from) those things they want to put in front of them. Then each student can take a turn describing the contents of his/her wallet or purse.

VARIATION

The groups can also successfully be either dyad or larger support groups of eight or more, depending on the class.

DISCUSSION QUESTIONS

Ask the students the following questions.

1. "What are your feelings about the contents of your purse or wallet compared to the others?"
2. "What are you censoring or not showing? What are you protecting by not showing it?"
3. "What feelings are you having about individual items of yours—sadness, pride, etc? Are you surprised by what others show?"
4. "How are the contents of your wallet or purse the same as the others? How are they different?"
5. "Do you have vivid memories associated with some of the things? What feelings did you have then? What are your feelings about that memory right now?"

ACTIVITIES

After the discussion, the teacher can ask the students to "be a detective" about themselves. Have the students write a list of the habits, likes, dislikes, and probable hopes or fears of "the suspect whose wallet this is." Each entry should have the supporting evidence listed from those items in the wallet or purse. Then, the group can be interrogated to see if the habits, etc. are consistent with those recognized by acquaintances. This is very helpful for the pattern clarification section of the Trumpet.

Journal entries, letters to the teacher, or further group sharing can include what the student hopes to have (or expects to have) in the purse or wallet one year from now, five years from now. Explore how each student is judging or evaluating him/herself based on what is not now in the purse or wallet. Anxieties about sharing, fantasies about what others are thinking about one's self, and how that makes one feel may also be appropriate here.

ADDITIONAL DISCUSSION QUESTIONS

In addition to the above questions for side-coaching and suggestions for journal content, the teacher might ask the following.

1. "What did you say to yourself immediately after I gave instructions? How did your feelings change during the activity? What was happening when they changed?"
2. "Did you make any discoveries during this activity?"
3. "What things would have made you feel better if they had been in your wallet or purse?"
4. "What would there have been if you were the person you want to be (should be? will be?)?"

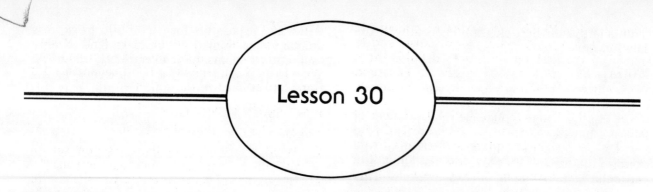

Lesson 30

BEGINNING

Share one-minute autobiographies, taken from journal entries, with the class. Discuss terms: disclosure, self-description, intimates, acquaintances, concentric.

AFFECTIVE EXPERIENCE

• Play the "Privacy Blocks" Game.
• Play the "One Special Thing about Someone Else" Game.

COGNITIVE INQUIRY

Ask questions to the first and second games, as follows.

1. "Was the Privacy Blocks diagram helpful?"
2. "Would you change it in any way?"
3. "Are there some areas easier to disclose than others?"
4. "How much is it smart to reveal?"
5. "Can people be trusted with your real thoughts and feelings?"
6. "Do you learn anything by disclosing information about yourself?"

ASSIGNMENT

Tell the students, "In your journal, draw in a series of concentric squares and mark them with: self, intimates, friends, acquaintances, everyone. Put two names of people within each of the concentric squares."

Privacy Blocks Game

This is an exercise to help students take a look at their patterns of disclosure. They will take a look at some of the criteria they use as individuals in deciding what things they talk about to whom.

PROCEDURE

Put the following diagram on the board and then give the explanation below.

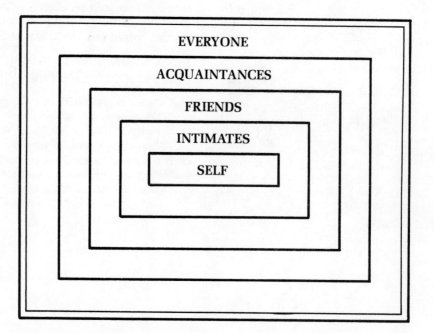

"The Privacy Block is a series of concentric squares dealing with what you disclose, and to whom. In the first square is self; it holds those things which you say to yourself. The next square, outside of that one, is for intimates, defined as one or two close friends, or members of the family. They are just the small number of people with whom you can share most of who you are. In the next square are friends, from school, from the community, and also including family members who are not as close as intimate ones. The next square is for acquaintances; classmates you really do not know very well, other students in the school that you meet, and neighbors a couple of doors down that you do not see very often. The final square includes absolutely anyone."

Ask the children to write a key word in one of the privacy blocks for each of the following instances. Who would you tell if you hit a dog with your car and did not stop—key word, DOG; if you cheated on a test—key word CHEAT; if you love someone—key word, LOVE; if you hate someone—key word, HATE; if you knew your best friend shoplifted—key word, BEST FRIEND; if you knew you only had six months to live— key words, SIX MONTHS.

ACTIVITY

Action can take place either in the form of journal entries or dyad or small group sharing. Whole group "I learned that I . . ." statements is a third way to finalize the action.

DISCUSSION QUESTIONS

Ask the class the following questions.

1. "What kinds of statements do you say to yourself that you can't share with anyone?"
2. "What kinds of statements can you share with your intimates, friends, and acquaintances?"
3. "What kinds of things can you share with acquaintances and not your intimates?"
4. "Do you find yourself keeping a lot of things to yourself?"
5. "Do you have confusion about what 'people' consider private to you?"
6. "How does it serve you to reveal certain things only to intimates, only to friends, only to acquaintances?"
7. "What are you protecting by keeping some things private?"

One Special Thing About Someone Else Game

In this exercise students try to share something important about themselves and perhaps will learn some things of which they are not aware.

PROCEDURE

Divide the class into dyads. Each pair is asked to carry on a normal conversation for five minutes in which the content is self-description. Each student is asked to share what s/he considers important about himself/herself. (Acknowledging the usual reluctance and concern about "bragging" helps dispel those obstacles.)

ACTIVITY

At the end of the five minutes, the class comes together as one group. Each student in turn tells who s/he talked with and shares one special thing about that person that seemed most important. Group sharing of feelings about talking to someone else about yourself can be preceded by some quiet reflections along that line in personal journals. Individuals can be asked to consider what they learned about the listening process while doing this exercise.

VARIATION

This format can be used with variations in the content of the conversations to encourage easier self-disclosure, to build trust and caring, and to contribute to group cohesiveness (e.g., "Spend two and a half minutes each sharing what you like best about your favorite movies or TV programs. Share with each other what you think we might do to make this class better.") The input to the total group involves what special thing this sharing conveyed about one's partner.

DISCUSSION QUESTIONS

Ask the following questions.

1. "Was it difficult to talk about yourself in this way? Was it enjoyable?"
2. "Did you like being told that it was okay to share this part of yourself?"
3. "Were there things that came to your mind that you decided not to share?"
4. "Do you know why? What was it like hearing your partner tell about you?"

Lesson 31

FLOW LESSON
(See Appendix D, p. 161.)

Teacher Comments _____

_____
_____
_____
_____
_____
_____
_____
_____
_____
_____
_____

Lesson 32

MATERIALS
crayons, butcher paper

BEGINNING
Review the concentric square concepts and the relationships between friends, intimates, etc.

AFFECTIVE EXPERIENCE
• Complete the "Me" Picture activity.

COGNITIVE INQUIRY
Ask the class the following questions.

1. "Do the pictures of others match your feelings about them?"
2. "Are some congruent and others not? Why do you think this is so?"
3. "Can you tell from the pictures the things others like most about themselves?"
4. "Can you tell from the pictures the things others have the greatest concern about?"

ASSIGNMENT

Tell the students, "In your journal draw a picture of your teacher and show the things the teacher is happiest about and the things the teacher has the most concern about."

Teacher Comments _____

_____

_____

_____

_____

_____

_____

_____

_____

_____

"Me" Picture

This exercise is to help students begin to: share facts about themselves, observe themselves, and share some of their concerns.

PROCEDURE

Instruct students to draw pictures of themselves as well as two things they think about a lot. While they are working, when you have finished your own picture, walk around and informally discuss pictures with the students. Listen to their conversations and observe. Have students share their pictures. Make it clear that this is voluntary. The sharer merely explains the picture to the group. Teacher asks questions such as, "Will you tell us about this part of your picture? What does this make you feel?"

VARIATION

Ask the students to write explanations of their pictures and attach them. Put the explanations and pictures up on the wall someplace in the room. Have them share their pictures in quartets for about twenty minutes.

DISCUSSION QUESTIONS

Have the class complete the following statements.

1. "The thing on my picture I think about most is . . ."

2. "There seems to be a pattern about my concerns which is . . ."

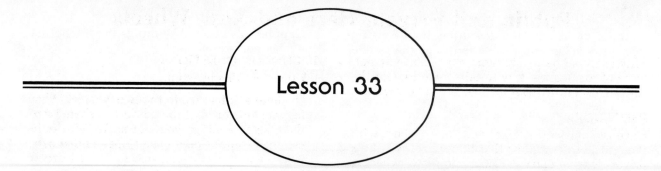

Lesson 33

BEGINNING

Have a few students share their drawings about "teacher." The teacher then shares feelings about the things the students expressed. (This is an important time for the teacher to illustrate openness—with sincerity.)

Explain the "Here-and-Now" wheel concept (see pages 55–56).

AFFECTIVE EXPERIENCE

• Complete the exercises on the "Public and Private Here-and-Now" wheels.

COGNITIVE INQUIRY

Ask questions associated with the private wheel. (Students need not share.) Ask questions associated with the public wheel. (Students share.) Ask the following additional questions.

1. "To whom can you say what you are really thinking or feeling? Anyone? Many people?"
2. "Are there times when people say more than they should about themselves? Have you?"
3. "Are there times when people say less than they should about themselves? Have you? What happened?"
4. "If others do not know what you feel, need or want, what do you lose by their not knowing? What do you avoid?"

ASSIGNMENT

Tell the children, "Look over your journal for the past three weeks and see if you can write two paragraphs about things learned during that time."

Teacher Comments

Public and Private Here-and-Now Wheels

This exercise helps students examine their patterns of disclosure. It will help them look at the ways and reasons why they censor their feelings.

PROCEDURE

Have the class do a "Here-and-Now" wheel with the added instructions that this wheel will be a private journal entry. A "Here-and-Now" wheel is a circle divided into quarters with a feeling that one has at the moment written on each spoke. One of the feelings is expanded. A sentence is written about it to get to the essence of that feeling. Now have the class do a Public "Here-and-Now" wheel.

ACTIVITY

Both wheels should be entered in the journals. Answers to discussion questions should be recorded. Discussion can take place in small groups or dyads. To finalize processing, open-ended sentences may be used in a large group setting.

DISCUSSION QUESTIONS

Ask the class this question:

1. "Is there a difference in the two wheels? What feelings do you find the hardest to share? Are there some feelings you can share with only certain people? Some useful open-ended sentences are: 'I discovered that I . . . ,' 'I learned that I . . . ,' 'I was surprised that I . . .'"

Winding Up Goals 1-5

The lessons so far were designed to help the student become comfortable in the group; to permit the group process to develop to a middle "safe" stage, and to provide affective experiences and cognitive inquiry. Learning has been primarily general and external—observing, identifying, classifying, developing a mental framework for the study of self.

The next five lessons provide the cognitive framework within which the rest of the course will proceed. Students are already familiar with the first three steps of the Trumpet. Now they will learn the entire Trumpet pattern as a forerunner for applying the pattern to deeper studies of self.

Students in self science may take a break after Lesson 38 (end of Section 1), or continue without stopping. In any event, a party or special outing is suggested as a final event to create a sense of accomplishment and closure.

ANTICIPATED OUTCOMES

Students at this point will learn an eight-step cognitive "road map" for charting affective experiences. An understanding of the Trumpet model is essential. The teacher may need to try a variety of approaches to help the student learn this new tool.

MATERIALS

For each of the following lessons the teacher is encouraged to have available (on display) the Trumpet diagram (p. 8). Students can quickly identify with the parts of the Trumpet that match the process they are learning. After practice with the visual model, it can be removed; students should be able to work without it.

Lesson 34

MATERIALS

Cookie Monster Scenario, Part 1

BEGINNING

Put the Trumpet diagram up on one of the walls or draw the trumpet on the chalkboard.

Discuss the need for problem-solving skills. (Use information before the Cookie Monster.)

AFFECTIVE EXPERIENCE

- Role-play Part 1 of the Cookie Monster. (A scenario follows.)

COGNITIVE INQUIRY

Ask these questions for Part 1 of the Cookie Monster.

1. "What is a confrontation?" (Confrontation is anything that you are involved in, within yourself and with other people. Deciding what to wear to school, telling your parents about what happened in school, playing with your friends, fighting, telling jokes, *anything* can be a confrontation. We feel things. We think things. We do things. Confrontations can tell us about ourselves. They give us data, information about ourselves.)

2. Explain: "We can use anything we do, any confrontations, for studying ourselves. In this class, I am sometimes going to arrange special exercises or games for us to do. We will use what happens during these times to gather data for our own self-study."

3. "What is inventorying responses?" (Response means very simply reactions of self during a confrontation.) Self can be observed on these different levels:

    feelings or bodily sensations
    thoughts
    actions or behaviors.

    When inventorying responses we explore the WHAT? HOW? WHEN? WHERE? rather than the WHY?

4. "At what level was the Cookie Monster inventorying his responses? Jane? Mark?"

BECOMING A SELF-SCIENTIST

5. "What would you need to know in order to do one of these things?
    a. A double backflip off the high diving board;
    b. The 50-yard dash in 6.5 seconds;
    c. A double-play in baseball;
    d. A perfect spiral pass in football;
    e. Write a best-selling novel;
    f. Compose a piano concerto."

At this point, allow discussion about what we need to know in order to do anything well. Give special emphasis to:

Skills	Learn to hold, catch, throw, etc.
Language	Description for explaining.
Processes	Techniques; e.g., analysis, identification, classifying, etc.

"Learning how to be a self-scientist is similar to learning how to play ball, solve math problems, etc. You need to have certain skills to use a precise language (vocabulary), to understand certain processes. You've already developed some *skills*, such as attending (paying attention, listening) to one another, keeping each other's trust, and so forth. You've also begun to learn a new *language* for talking about your thoughts, feelings, actions. You have many of these new language words in your journal. Now, we will learn a *process* for studying ourselves. This process is called The Trumpet.

"The Trumpet is an eight-step process, a road map, which can help us become self-scientists. It can help us better understand ourselves, how we relate to others, how we can be in control of our lives.

"At this time we are our own textbooks. We are our own educators. We are the content, the material, the process of self-science because the subject of this course is each of us as people. As we begin at the narrow end of the Trumpet and proceed through the wide end, we will grow as people. For the next few lessons we will study each step of the Trumpet more carefully. The first two steps in the process are what we call 'Confrontation' and 'Inventorying Responses.' The chart (the Trumpet) shows what I'm talking about."

"To get at these first two ideas (process steps), we'll role-play a part of a story about the Cookie Monster. As we listen, pay particular attention to the confrontation parts and to the times when individuals inventory their responses. If the terms 'confrontation' and 'inventorying responses' aren't familiar to you, do not worry. We will define them after we have had a chance to talk about the Cookie Monster and his escapades."

ASSIGNMENT

Put the words "confrontation" and "inventory" in your journal; copy from the dictionary interpretations of these terms.

THE TRUMPET (STEPS 1 AND 2)

Step 1. Interact with a situation that generates data.

Step 2. How did I respond? What was unique? What was common?

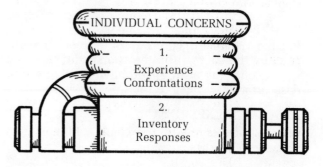

Cookie Monster Meets the Trumpet—Part 1

SCENE: Instruction to the class: "Imagine that we are going to have a party in this room. What do you think the room would look like? Do you think there would be crepe paper streamers? Colored balloons? Down at one end of the room imagine a table of refreshments, punch, cookies, and ice cream." (Ask for more elaboration from students.)

PROCEDURE

Cookie Monster role-play Steps 1 (confrontation) and 2 (response). Assign people to play the different roles. This might be done a few days in advance so people can study their scenario lines.

TEACHER: "The room is ready for a party, but no one has come in yet. Softly the door opens and a head peers inside. It is the Cookie Monster! He looks carefully around, sees that no one is there and tiptoes to the refreshment table. As fast as he can, he grabs all the cookies and gobbles them down. Just as he's finished, Mark, Jane, and two other kids come in. They are disappointed because there are no cookies left for them. I am going to go over and talk to the Cookie Monster and Mark and Jane about what just happened and have them try to remember what they did during this confrontation. A confrontation is just something that happens— something specific that happens. I am

going to see what each of their reactions were to the situation. While I am talking with them, I will try to have them describe some of their thoughts and feelings."

TEACHER: "First, Cookie Monster, you tell us a little about what happened. Tell us what you did from the time you came into the room until now." (recap)

C.M.: "Well, I got to the party first and saw two plates of cookies. I love cookies so I ate *all* the cookies off both plates." (identification of situation)

TEACHER: "What were you thinking about as you looked around the room?"

C.M.: "I was thinking about how hungry I was in my tummy. I saw the cookies and I wanted all of them. I started toward the table." (connection between thought and action)

TEACHER: "Okay, can you tell what kinds of things you were *saying to yourself* as you went to the table?" (internal sentences)

C.M.: "I said, 'Oh, look at that plate. Look at all those cookies. I love cookies the best.'"

TEACHER: "You did not think of anything else at all?"

C.M.: "No, just cookies. Just me and the cookies."

TEACHER: "What kind of feelings were you having?" (identification of feeling)

C.M.: "I was hungry."

TEACHER:	"Where did you feel hungry? Can you show us?"
C.M.:	"Right here. My tummy was hurting a little because I was so hungry."
TEACHER:	"Was any other part of you hurting, or was your tummy the thing you felt the most?" (clarifying question)
C.M.:	"Just my tummy. I felt my tummy the most."
TEACHER:	"What did you do?"
C.M.:	"Well, I went to the table and I looked over by the punch, and there were two plates of cookies and my tummy was real hungry and it was hurting a little. So I said, 'Make my tummy feel better,' and I took all the cookies and ate them."
TEACHER:	"Did you think at all about the other kids? Did you have any second thoughts?"
C.M.:	"I don't think I thought about the other kids."
TEACHER:	"No? Just the cookies?"
C.M.:	"Just the cookies."
TEACHER:	"Did you think about getting caught?"
C.M.:	"No. I don't get caught. I eat so fast."
TEACHER:	"How do you think the other kids, who came in later, felt?"
C.M.:	"They know I like cookies the best. Maybe they didn't feel anything."
TEACHER:	"How do you *think* they felt about what you did?"
C.M.:	"I don't know. I thought maybe they would be mad at me, but I wanted the cookies so badly I ate them anyway."
TEACHER:	"Let's try and find out what some other people saw. Jane, you were the one that came into the room next?"
JANE:	"The Cookie Monster is mean!"
TEACHER:	"Oh? Tell me what just happened to you. What did you notice first?"
JANE:	"No cookies."
TEACHER:	"Is that the only thing you saw?"
JANE:	"I was hungry too."
TEACHER:	"And did you see anybody else in the room when you came in?"
JANE:	"No, there was just this big monster."
TEACHER:	"What was he doing?"
JANE:	"Eating."
TEACHER:	"And when you saw that, how did you feel?"
NOTE:	Jane is not responding to the questions asked. We assume many students will have a hard time at first and the facilitator or teacher must keep refocusing him/her.)

JANE:	"A little scared because I wanted to eat the cookies, too."
TEACHER:	"Just scared?"
JANE:	"A little scared so I didn't go up to the cookies." (feeling causing behavior)
TEACHER:	"Do you know what frightened you?"
JANE:	"How big this monster is."
TEACHER:	"Well, he might hurt you. Is that what frightened you?" (source of feeling)
JANE:	"He might eat me."
TEACHER:	"He might eat you?"
JANE:	"Yes, he might eat me!"
TEACHER:	"So then what did you do, Jane?"
JANE:	"I stood in the corner and watched."
TEACHER:	"Can you remember what you looked like when you were in the corner watching?" (clarifying question)
JANE:	"Yes."
TEACHER:	"What did you look like?"
JANE:	"Scared."
TEACHER:	"How do you look when you are scared?"
JANE:	"Like I look now."
TEACHER:	"Here's a mirror. Take a look at yourself." (confrontation)
JANE:	"Oooh!"
TEACHER:	"How does scared Jane look?"
JANE:	"I see my shoulders are rounded over and cover my body a little. My face, I feel my lips twitching a little." (response)
TEACHER:	"You're a little folded up?" (reflective listening)
JANE:	"Yes."
TEACHER:	"And so when you were in the corner, what kinds of things were you saying to yourself?" (internal sentences)
JANE:	"When is that Cookie Monster going to finish eating?"
TEACHER:	"So that what?"
JANE:	"So I can get my cookies."
TEACHER:	"So that was your big wish—that he would stop?" (reflective comment)
JANE:	"Yes."
TEACHER:	"How do you feel about the Cookie Monster now?"
JANE:	"I think the Cookie Monster is very mean."
TEACHER:	"And what would you do now? Would you try to be near him?"
JANE:	"No."
TEACHER:	"You want to stay away from him?"
JANE:	"Yes."
TEACHER:	"Mark, could you tell what happened to you?"
MARK:	"I came into the room and he had done it again. There were no cookies."
TEACHER:	"You saw him eating the cookies?" (reflective question)
MARK:	"Yes. Well, I heard him burp, brush off his mouth, and there were no more cookies, as usual."

TEACHER: "So what did you do?"

MARK: "I shrugged my shoulders and I said, 'He did it again' and I looked around to see if maybe there was some other cookies that I could find in the corner somewhere. Maybe the bag was still there and they were going to bring out some more."

TEACHER: "You remember any of the kinds of feelings that you had at the time?"

MARK: "I felt a little angry."

TEACHER: "At whom?"

MARK: "At the Cookie Monster and I felt a little angry at myself."

TEACHER: "Really? What were you angry at yourself about?"

MARK: "He always is there ahead of me."

TEACHER: "Yes?"

MARK: "And I always say to myself, 'He's smarter and faster.'" (internal sentence)

TEACHER: "So how did you blame yourself?" (naming the feeling)

MARK: "I know he's going to do it because he always does it and I saw him walking in here, but I let him go into the room first. When I got here the cookies were gone. I should have known."

TEACHER: "So you are angry for not knowing what to do or what you should have done?" (reflective listening)

MARK: "Yes."

TEACHER: "So what did you do next? Where did you go?"

MARK: "I looked in the corners to see if there were any bags. There were no bags there, and there were no more cookies. I don't know, I just sort of said, 'Yeah, that's it. No cookies again. He got them.' So I walked away and went over to some of the other children who had just come in. It's still on my mind though. It *really* annoys me." (naming feelings)

TEACHER: "These are examples of unique and common responses, done by inventorying of things you said to yourself, the kinds of feelings you had, and the kinds of things you did in the situation. At our next session we'll go to the next part of the trumpet which is the step called 'identifying patterns of behavior.' A pattern is the way you usually behave in a situation. We'll talk to the Monster again and also to Mark and Jane."

DISCUSSION QUESTIONS

Ask the class the following questions.

1. "Why were the others upset with the Cookie Monster? Would you have been upset?"
2. "Were they all upset about the same thing?"
3. "Have you ever acted the way the others did? When? Why?"
4. "Was the teacher able to help the Cookie Monster, Jane, and Mark identify their feelings? How?"
5. "What feelings did you have during the story?"
6. "Whom did you like best? Why?"
7. "Whom did you like least? Why?"

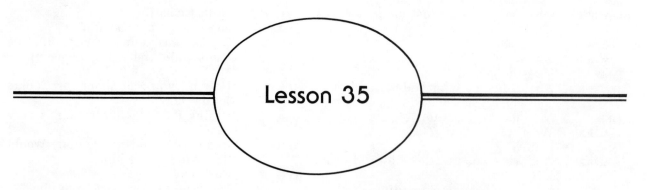

Lesson 35

MATERIALS
trumpet display, Cookie Monster scenario, Part 2

BEGINNING
Review concepts of "confrontation" and "inventorying responses." Discuss idea of "pattern." Where are patterns seen? What math patterns are you familiar with?

AFFECTIVE EXPERIENCE
Cookie Monster—Part 2

COGNITIVE INQUIRY
Ask questions for Part 2—Cookie Monster.

Discuss recognizing patterns. (Recognizing patterns is the third step in the Trumpet.) "What this means is discerning which patterns are typical of you. You can discover this in several ways. One way is to look at data you gather about yourself. Another way is to have other people show you what they see as typical responses of yours. Then you decide whether or not you agree with their observations."

Brainstorm situations in real life where students can identify patterns. *Discuss Owning Patterns.* (Owning patterns is the fourth step of the Trumpet. Owning a pattern means both recognizing that a certain behavior really is my pattern and understanding how that pattern helps me.)

When we discuss a pattern we do not like, we can waste considerable energy telling ourselves it is not our pattern; that we really are not like that most of the time. We can't work on changing ourselves until we acknowledge that some patterns we want to change are really a part of us. So owning a pattern is saying, "This is my pattern and this is what I gain by behaving in this manner."

Tell the class, "To discern what your pattern does for you or how it works for you, you'll ask yourself questions. Try considering your pattern as a servant you've hired to work for you. Give your servant a name. What did I hire this servant to do? How does my servant serve me? What does my servant help me to get? How is my servant comfortable for me? What does my servant protect me from? Or lets me avoid?" (This is a good place for the teacher to discuss personal pattern functions.)

Review the Trumpet steps covered so far.

THE TRUMPET—STEPS 3 AND 4

Step 1. I interact with a situation that generates data.

Step 2. How did I respond? What was unique? What was common?

Step 3. What is typical of me?

Step 4. What does this pattern do for me?

Set the stage for Part 2 of the Cookie Monster scenario.

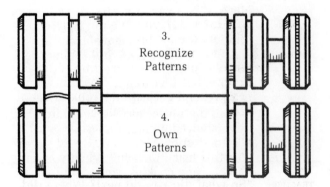

Cookie Monster Meets the Trumpet—Part 2

PROCEDURE

Step 3. Patterns

TEACHER: "Cookie Monster, when you come into a place is this something you usually do—immediately look for the cookies and eat them?"

C.M.: "I think I always do—always look for the cookies first."

TEACHER: "Always look for the cookies?"

C.M.: "Always."

TEACHER: "Do you ever do anything different?"

C.M.: "Don't think so."

TEACHER: "Most of the time, whenever you come into a situation with cookies, the first thing you do is grab them and eat them?"

C.M.: "Yep."

TEACHER: "No matter who is around?"

C.M.: "No matter who's around. I get there first."

TEACHER: "That is your pattern, then." (identifying a pattern, Step 3 of Trumpet)

C.M.: "What's a pattern?"

TEACHER: "Your pattern is the thing you do most of the time."

C.M.: "Yeah, I do that most of the time."

TEACHER: "One of your patterns is, you eat cookies whenever you get a chance, regardless of who is around."

C.M.: "Yep."

TEACHER: "All right. That is your pattern."

C.M.: "That's my pattern."

TEACHER: "Now, what is your pattern, Cookie Monster?"

C.M.: "My pattern is I get to the cookies first and eat all the cookies right away."

TEACHER: "No matter who else wants them?"

C.M.: "Every time. That's my pattern."

TEACHER: (to Jane) "Remember what you did? Is that something you are likely to do?"

JANE: "What do you mean—likely for me to do?"

TEACHER: "You came into the situation and could not get what you wanted. You got scared and then you went right into a corner."

JANE: "You mean is that what I do if I can't get something I want?"

TEACHER: "Yes."

JANE: "Oh, yes."

TEACHER: "Do you usually do that?"

JANE: "Just kind of move to the side."

TEACHER: "And then what?"

JANE: "I wait to see—yeah, I just wait."

TEACHER: "To see if things get any better?"

JANE: "Yes. I don't do anything."

TEACHER: "Is that your pattern?"

JANE: "Pattern?"

TEACHER: "The thing you do most of the time when something happens."

JANE: "Yes, yes, I do that."

TEACHER: "So could you tell me what your pattern is in a situation like that?"

JANE: "Yes. I think that if I can't get something I want, I just move away."

TEACHER: "And stay by yourself until things cool off a little?"

JANE: "Yes."

TEACHER: "Mark, you've heard the other two talk about their patterns. Did you think that you showed a pattern of your own?"

MARK: "I don't know."

TEACHER: "Is this usual for you? When you cannot get any cookies, you begin looking around for some more, and you also become angry at yourself for not knowing better?"

MARK: "Yes, I get angry at myself a lot of times when people get what I want, and I don't get any."

TEACHER: "Then you get angry at yourself?"

MARK: "Yes. Like I got angry because the Cookie Monster was quicker than me."

TEACHER: "You're a little bit angry at him, but you're also angry at yourself?"

MARK: "Yes, I get angry at myself."

TEACHER: "So when you are angry at yourself, what are you saying?"

MARK: "I'm saying I could have done better or I could have been smarter, or I could have been quicker."

TEACHER: "Is that something you say to yourself a lot?"

MARK: "Yes."

TEACHER: "That's your pattern. Could you say what your pattern is?"

MARK: "My pattern is that when somebody gets what I want or when I don't do what I would like to do, I blame myself and I say I could have been smarter, or I should have been faster or I'm not too good. That's my pattern."

Step 4. Function

TEACHER: "Each of you has identified a pattern. Now let's look at the way these patterns function for you—how they work for you. All right, Cookie Monster, can you tell me what your pattern is again?"

C.M.: "My pattern is when I come into a new place, I look for the cookies right away and then eat them up very fast."

TEACHER: "How does that work for you?"

C.M.: "Oh, it makes me feel very good because it fills up my tummy and makes me smile because the cookies taste so good. Makes me feel very good to be first and get all the cookies." (identifying how a pattern functions—Step 3 of the Trumpet)

TEACHER: "So that pattern really helps you?"

C.M.: "Oh, yeah. Because then I get all the cookies."

TEACHER: "Right. And what happens to your stomach when you eat all the cookies?"

C.M.: "Oh, my stomach feels good. It's all filled up."

TEACHER: "So the hurt moves away a little bit?"

C.M.: "Oh yeah, the hurt moves away then."

TEACHER: "So that pattern really helps you? It lets the hurt go away and gives you a nice sweet taste in your mouth."

C.M.: "Oh, yeah, it tastes so good."

TEACHER: "And even when you're not eating cookies, you can think about how good it was when you ate them."

C.M.: "I think about it for a long time afterwards. I think about cookies a lot."

TEACHER: "Jane, can you tell me what your pattern is again?"

JANE: "When I can't get what I want, I feel sad and I just leave."

TEACHER: "Tell me, when you leave, how does that help you—to kind of pull away and go to a quiet place for awhile?"

JANE: "I don't know."

TEACHER: "You don't know how it helps you? How would that be compared to something else? Like suppose you had jumped up to the Cookie Monster and said . . ."

JANE: "No! No! I would be too afraid."

TEACHER: "So going away helps you be less afraid?"

JANE: "Yes. I'm not so afraid when I'm far away."

TEACHER: "You are much less scared and don't have to get into things that are too scary?"

JANE: "I just wait until things get better."

TEACHER: "Mark, remember what your pattern was?"

MARK: "Yes, I blamed myself. I should be smarter, or faster, or better."

TEACHER: "All right. It is blaming yourself for not being good enough. What do you think is good about that?"

MARK: "Well, sometimes I get smarter the next time. I say, 'I'm not going to let that happen again to me. I'm going to be better next time,' and then sometimes I really am. And I think one of these days I'm going to get the cookies first."

TEACHER: "Right. So, if you keep correcting yourself and seeing where you are weak, you might know better the next time and you will be stronger."

MARK: "That's right!"

DISCUSSION QUESTIONS

Ask the following questions.

1. "What was the Cookie Monster's pattern? Jane's? Mark's?"
2. "How did the patterns serve the Cookie Monster? Jane? Mark?"
3. "What is a pattern?" (Something a person does most of the time.)
4. "Are patterns hard to own? Why?"
5. "Do patterns sometimes help? Do they ever get in the way?"

6. "Can patterns help and hurt at the same time?"
7. "What were the patterns of the three characters? Let's talk about the Cookie Monster pattern and how it works for him."

Functions	Consequences
Tastes good.	He has to face the kids.
Gets all the cookies.	Thief.
Felt good.	Fat.
	Lost friends.
	Rotten teeth.
	Tells lies.
	Mad when the cookies ran out.

8. "Pretend you are all Cookie Monsters. Would you like to have Cookie Monster friends?" ("Yes.")
9. "What could you do to get some friends?" (". . . don't know.")
10. "How could you act so the children would like to be your friends?"
11. "What are some alternative things the Cookie Monster could do?"
   ("Wait.
   Not eat all the cookies.
   Find something else to eat (chocolate, vanilla ice cream, graham crackers, banana splits, meat, vegetables, cake, cherries, fruit).
   Ask for a cookie.
   Give some to other children.")

ASSIGNMENT

Tell the children, "Before the next class period, write in your journals four patterns, of any kind, that you have noticed."

Teacher Comments _____

_____

_____

_____

_____

_____

_____

_____

_____

_____

_____

_____

_____

MATERIALS
trumpet display,
Cookie Monster scenario—Part 3

BEGINNING
Discuss patterns observed and noted in journals. Review concepts of "confrontations," "inventorying responses," "patterns," "owning patterns."

Introduce concepts of: "Consider consequences," "allow alternatives," (see information preceding Cookie Monster, Part 3).

Set stage for Cookie Monster, Part 3.

AFFECTIVE EXPERIENCE
• Cookie Monster—Part 3

COGNITIVE INQUIRY
Ask questions for Cookie Monster, Part 3.

1. "See if you can remember, with your eyes closed, the steps learned so far in the Trumpet. Can you remember them by heart?"

DISCUSSION QUESTIONS
Ask the following questions.

1. "What were the consequences of the Cookie Monster's patterns? Jane's? Mark's?"
2. "What other consequences might have been possible?"
3. "Can you identify a pattern and a consequence of your own?"
4. "Will you share it? When do you see your pattern? Do you think other people recognize your pattern?"
5. "What alternatives were considered by the Cookie Monster? Jane? Mark? What other alternatives could they have thought about?"

CONSEQUENCE
(Teacher explanation re: Trumpet) "The fifth step of the Trumpet is to consider the consequences of your pattern. During this step we'll explore what happens when you behave according to your pattern. This involves looking at how you see yourself and how other people see you. You have an idea of what you want to accomplish by using your pattern. How effective is that pattern in achieving your goal? You pay a price for your servant.

"Whenever we decide to behave according to a pattern, we gain something and we pay something. When a person goes to the grocery store, money is used to pay for food. When a person always buys hamburger and never buys any other kind of meat, one benefit gain is knowing what the hamburger will taste like. One disadvantage is missing out on the experience of tasting other kinds of meat.

"What price do you pay? What do you miss out on because of having one particular pattern and no other? What does happen, or could happen in your life because of your pattern? Exploring consequences is looking at the benefits and the disadvantages of one's patterns. Does your pattern serve you well enough in reaching your goal to be worth its disadvantages? Or are you paying too much for the product?"

ASSIGNMENT
Tell the children, "In your journal list two of your patterns and the consequences of each. Also list two alternatives that you might take if you wanted to." (Teacher: use Trumpet display in explanation for "consequences" and "allow alternatives.")

THE TRUMPET—STEPS 5 AND 6

Step 5. Consider consequences.

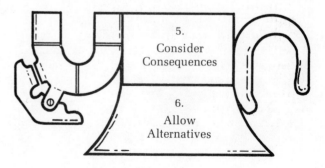

Cookie Monster Meets the Trumpet—Part 3

TEACHER: "All right, Cookie Monster, we are back to you again. Let's see now, we are coming to the consequences part of the trumpet."

C.M.: "What's consequences?"

TEACHER: "When you buy something, you pay for it. Did you ever buy cookies, by the way?"

C.M.: "No, I never bought any cookies."

TEACHER: "Remember you told me about what good happens—you feel so much better when you get all those cookies to eat and the pain in your stomach goes away and everything. Does anything bad happen when you do that?"

C.M.: "Sometimes I don't have many friends."

TEACHER: "That's a consequence. Sometimes that is what happens. There are two things that happened to you. You get to feel good. Your pain goes away. You get those nice sweet tastes in your mouth. That one is a function, a good thing that happens to you. But another thing that happens, too, is that sometimes you don't have as many friends as you would like to have, or your friends get angry and won't talk to you and that makes you feel bad. That is a consequence. So sometimes things we do make us feel good, but at the same time they make us feel bad. All right?"

C.M.: "Right."

TEACHER: "Jane, when you go away, one of the things that happens to you is that you feel less afraid. That is the way going away helps you. Is there anything about what you do that is not helpful?"

JANE: "I don't get my cookies."

TEACHER: "You don't get your cookies. So sometimes by going away you give up getting the things you want."

JANE: "No, sometimes people feel so sorry for me that they bring me cookies."

TEACHER: "That is the good part about their feeling sorry for you."

JANE: "Yes."

TEACHER: "Is there anything that makes you feel bad about their feeling sorry for you?"

JANE: "Yes, sometimes."

TEACHER: "What might bother you about that?"

JANE: "They might say, 'Look at her. She can't do anything for herself.' I don't like that. I want to do things for myself."

TEACHER: "So it makes you feel a little smaller?"

JANE: "Yes, I feel small already."

TEACHER: "So some of the good things that help are: sometimes you feel much less frightened and sometimes people feel sorry for you and you do get the things you want. But a lot of times you don't get what you want, and when people feel sorry for you, you feel smaller."

JANE: "Yes."

TEACHER: "Mark, let's talk about the consequences of your pattern. You said before that when you tell yourself that you're not as good as you could be, it helps you do better the next time."

MARK: "That's right. Next time I'm going to get those cookies."

TEACHER: "So that's a function. Is there any kind of consequence that's not so good when you say that to yourself? Is there anything bad about saying that?"

MARK: "I don't know. I know I'm going to get the cookies. I'm going to get the cookies eventually. I say that to myself, 'The next time, I'll be better.' So I'm not sure there's anything bad."

TEACHER: "You're not sure there is anything bad at all?" (clarifying question)

MARK: "No. Well, I get a little nervous."

TEACHER: "What do you mean, nervous?"

MARK: "Like am I going to be able to get them next time? Or is he always going to be better than me? And I feel bad that he's better than me. I'd like to be better than him."

TEACHER: "So, it would really be nice if you were as good as he. Then you would be able to get what you want. That would be really nice." (focusing on the positive)

MARK: "Yes."

Step 6. Will I allow myself any additional patterns of response?

TEACHER: "Cookie Monster?"

C.M.: "Yeah?"

TEACHER: "Let's try to imagine a situation or a thing happening in which the results would be mostly good, rather than some good and some bad. I wonder if there is a way you could have cookies and still have friends? Would you think about that a little bit? And maybe we could all help you imagine ways. We will make up ways in which you could have cookies and have friends."

C.M.: "I have an idea. Do you think somebody could teach me to bake cookies myself? And then I could give one to Jane and I could give one to Mark. And then they could be my friends and I could eat all the rest."

TEACHER: "Good! Then let us see how many different ideas we might have. Like one idea I have is maybe you could learn to like some other things, too, like apples, bananas, candy bars, ice cream."

C.M.: "I never tried those."

TEACHER: "Spinach?"

C.M.: "I don't know. I never tried it. Is it good, too?"

TEACHER: "Well, right now you only have one thing to pick, right? Cookies. They're the only thing."

C.M.: "But I love cookies."

TEACHER: "I know, but they are the only thing that makes you feel good. Do you know if there is anything else that can make you feel good, too?"

C.M.: "I don't know."

TEACHER: "Well, maybe you would want to try it and see if there is anything else that could give you the same good feelings as cookies do, because if you could find more than one thing that makes you feel good, you would not have to go after only one thing."

C.M.: "Maybe I could try something new."

MARK: "Cookie Monster, I have a lot of candy. Candy is very good and maybe you'd like to trade candy for cookies."

C.M.: "I don't know. Maybe I could try it. I never ate candy."

MARK: "It's very good."

C.M.: "Very good? Does it taste like cookies?"

MARK: "Yeah, very much like cookies. But it tastes different too."

C.M.: "It tastes different? Maybe I could try one."

MARK: "You give me cookies and I'll give you candy."

C.M.: "Maybe I could try that."

MARK: "I'll give you ice cream."

C.M.: "What's ice cream?"

MARK: "You don't know what ice cream is?"

C.M.: "I never tried it. I only eat cookies."

MARK: "Oh, it's so great. Ice cream and cookies are good together. Ice cream is cold and it's sort of sweet like cookies and it's sometimes crunchy like cookies."

C.M.: "Crunchy? I like crunchy."

TEACHER: "What you just talked about are different ways of experimenting with try-ons. So you, Cookie Monster, may try candy, may try ice cream. Just to see. It may be that you don't like anything as well as you like cookies. But how will you know if you never try anything else? All right, Jane, let's think about what the best results for you would be. What kind of situation could get you what you want and help you to be less scared? Does that sound like it would be the best idea?"

JANE: "You mean to be less scared and get what I want? Oh, yes."

TEACHER: "It would be the best idea?"

JANE: "Oh, yes."

TEACHER: "Do you have any ideas that you could experiment with to get what you want and yet be less scared? Or, can anybody else think of any ways?"

JANE: "Need courage."

TEACHER: "Like the lion in the 'Wizard of Oz'?"

JANE: "Yeah."

MARK: "You could try what I do. You could try to get there first next time, and get the cookies first."

TEACHER: "Or you could say to yourself that you're just not going to be afraid of that Cookie Monster."

JANE: "Oh, no, no, no. He's too big. But I could get a friend who's bigger."

TEACHER: "Hey, that is another one. Say that again. What could you do?"

JANE:	"Make friends with somebody else who's just as big as the Cookie Monster."
TEACHER:	"And what? He could protect you?"
JANE:	"Yes."
C.M.:	"Jane, if you'd be my friend, I'd give you one of my cookies."
JANE:	"Well, that's OK, too, Cookie Monster."
C.M.:	"And maybe I could even protect you."
TEACHER:	"You're looking at the Cookie Monster now. You said earlier you were too afraid to look at the Cookie Monster."
JANE:	"I feel a little different now."
TEACHER:	"You do?"
JANE:	"Yes."
TEACHER:	"What is helping you do that?"
JANE:	"Well, the Cookie Monster asked me to be his friend and he seemed to like that."
TEACHER:	"And that made you feel better?"
C.M.:	"It made me feel good."
TEACHER:	"So one experiment that you could try is talking to the thing you're afraid of."
JANE:	"Yes, that helped. Wow!"
C.M.:	"Okay, that makes me feel good."
JANE:	"Good."
MARK:	"You could come with me next time. We could both try to get there first together."
JANE:	"All right."
C.M.:	"But you better save me a cookie if you get there before me."
MARK:	"Oh, I'll share them. We won't eat them all. We just want a couple."
C.M.:	"Thank you, Mark."

TEACHER:	"Mark, what could you do to try on some new behavior?"
MARK:	"I could try saying to myself, 'you're not dumb just because you didn't get the cookies.' Also, maybe I could say, 'It wasn't all my fault that I didn't get the cookies.' Also, 'Well, it's not only me. Maybe I could be with somebody else next time. It's not only up to me.' " (examining alternatives)
TEACHER:	"Do any of you have any other ideas or experiments Mark could try?"
JANE:	"You could say to yourself, 'Cookies aren't that important. Why should I worry about them?' "
MARK:	"Yeah, I like other things."
TEACHER:	"But you like cookies a lot."
MARK:	"Yeah, I like cookies a lot. Yeah, I do."
JANE:	"Why couldn't you just talk to the Cookie Monster?"
TEACHER:	"Like Jane did?"
MARK:	"Yes."
JANE:	"And maybe the Cookie Monster will share more with you."
MARK:	"You know, I just never thought of talking to the Cookie Monster. I wasn't afraid of him. Maybe a little—a little afraid because I think he's better than me, faster and smarter."
C.M.:	"I'm very fast."
JANE:	"But the Cookie Monster is clumsy and you're not clumsy."
MARK:	"Yes, that's true. I might talk to the Cookie Monster."

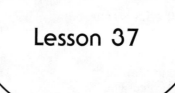

Lesson 37

MATERIALS
Trumpet display,
Cookie Monster Scenario—Part 4

BEGINNING
Discuss patterns and alternatives from the journals. Review concepts learned so far (up to Step 7). Introduce concepts of: "make evaluation" and "choose." (See information preceding Cookie Monster—Part 4)

Role-play Cookie Monster—Part 4.

AFFECTIVE EXPERIENCE
• Cookie Monster—Part 4

COGNITIVE INQUIRY
Ask questions for Cookie Monster—Part 4, as follows.

1. "How are action choices made? How do you make your choices?"
2. "How do you evaluate new choices?"
3. "Do new choices cause new confrontations?"
4. "How is the Trumpet process used when new situations occur?"

ASSIGNMENT
Tell the class, "In your journal, write up one complete Trumpet process for something that happened to you lately."

Teacher Comments _____

_____

_____

_____

_____

_____

_____

_____

_____

_____

_____

EVALUATION
(Teacher explanation re: trumpet) "The seventh step of the Trumpet is the evaluation of your various choices. Now you test your new pattern of behavior. You'll ask yourself questions such as: Which patterns get me what I want? Which patterns are worth the cost I pay? Which patterns cost more than I want to pay? Which do I prefer? Am I willing to work for changing to a new pattern? Which pattern do I prefer?"

Step 1. I interact with a situation that generates data.

Step 2. How did I respond? What was unique? What was common?

Step 3. What is typical of me?

Step 4. What function does this pattern serve for me?

Step 5. What does happen, or could happen, in my life because of this pattern?

Step 6. Will I allow myself any additional patterns of responses?

Step 7. What happened when I allowed myself a new behavior?

Step 8. Now that I have a choice, which behavior do I want?

THE TRUMPET

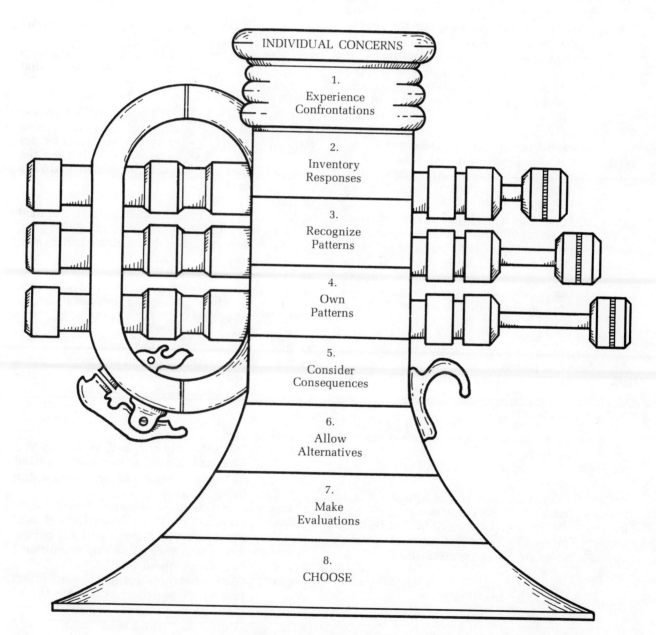

INDIVIDUAL CONCERNS

1. Experience Confrontations

2. Inventory Responses

3. Recognize Patterns

4. Own Patterns

5. Consider Consequences

6. Allow Alternatives

7. Make Evaluations

8. CHOOSE

Cookie Monster Meets the Trumpet—Part 4

Describe what has happened thus far in the Cookie Monster scenario. Continue scenario.

PROCEDURE

Steps 7 and 8. Evaluation and Choice

NARRATOR: "A week later the teacher visits the class again. The purpose now is to evaluate the experiments."

TEACHER: "Hey, Cookie Monster, did you try any experiments this week?"

C.M.: "Yeah, remember my pattern about getting all the cookies first?"

TEACHER: "Yes."

C.M.: "Well, I saw Jane, and Jane gave me some candy, and I gave her a lot of my cookies back. And I tried the candy and it was chocolate, like chocolate chip cookies, and it was crunchy. It was real good! I liked it. So now Jane and I are friends and now I like some kinds of candy. Now I have two things I like. I like cookies—still like cookies very much—very much. But now candy, candy is very interesting."

TEACHER: "In addition, you have a friend, too."

C.M.: "Oh, that's real good. And Jane's not so quiet, and I can talk to her. She's my friend, kind of."

TEACHER: "So what would you say about your experiment? Do you like what happened?"

C.M.: "Oh yeah. I feel really good now. Now I've got two things to eat. I've still got my cookies. Jane's my friend now. I've got somebody to talk to and she's not afraid of me."

TEACHER: "Thank you, Cookie Monster. Jane, did you try an experiment this week with your pattern?"

JANE: "Well, I continued talking to the Cookie Monster."

TEACHER: "And how did that make you feel?"

JANE: "I was scared. The Cookie Monster didn't know it though. So that made it easier."

TEACHER: "Did you feel less scared when it was easier?"

JANE: "Yes, I got less scared and it made it easier. The Cookie Monster . . ."

TEACHER: "What did you do that was different?"

JANE: "I approached the Cookie Monster—went to the Cookie Monster."

TEACHER: "You used to go away."

JANE: "Right. I used to hide. But I went right to the Cookie Monster."

TEACHER: "Right to the thing that you were afraid of?"

JANE: "That's right. It was different. I didn't hide."

TEACHER: "And do as many people feel sorry for you?"

JANE: "No."

TEACHER: "Do you have any feelings about that?"

JANE: "Yeah, I feel good."

TEACHER: "Do you think you might try that again sometime—to talk to the thing that you are afraid of?"

JANE: "I don't know. Yes, I guess so."

TEACHER: "Mark, what happened with your experiment?"

MARK: "Well, I said to myself, 'You're not dumb just cause you couldn't get the cookies.' 'Cause it happened again the next day."

TEACHER: "It did?"

MARK: "Yeah. The Cookie Monster the next day got there ahead of me, with Jane, and they got the cookies and candy, too."

TEACHER: "My goodness!"

MARK: "And I said to myself, 'You're not dumb. You're not dumb because this happened.'"

TEACHER: "What are you?"

MARK: "I said, 'Darn!' to myself."

TEACHER: "Can I try something and see if it fits?"

MARK: "Sure. I don't feel good about not getting the cookies. I'm disappointed, but not dumb. But I wish I had gotten them. That's the way the cookie crumbles."

TEACHER: "So you only felt half as bad as you used to feel before, because you used to feel bad before for not getting the things you wanted."

MARK: "I still felt a little dumb. I said that to myself, that I still felt a little dumb. But I didn't feel as bad as I did before. And I also didn't think as much that I have to get there first."

TEACHER: "And what does that do for you? When you don't feel that you have to get there first?"

MARK: "I don't feel so nervous inside."

TEACHER:	"You're more relaxed?"
MARK:	"Yes."
TEACHER:	"You like the feeling of being more relaxed?" (reflective listening)
MARK:	"Yes, I felt better. I wasn't even nervous that night when I went to sleep. I wasn't thinking about how I didn't get the cookies or how dumb I was and how the next day I had to get there first."
TEACHER:	"The most important thing now in completing the Trumpet experience is time. You need time to continue your experiments and see if this is a behavior you want to use more often."
C.M.:	"Then what?"
TEACHER:	"Then you make a choice. If you do like this new way of behaving, then you may want to keep it as another way of acting. If you decide you don't like it, then there's no reason to keep it. The best thing about the Trumpet is that you can make your own choice after trying on something new."

DISCUSSION QUESTIONS
Ask the following questions.

1. "How did the Cookie Monster test new ideas for behavior? How did his patterns get what was desired?"
2. "What evaluations were made by Jane? Mark?"
3. "Can people get friends sometimes by changing their patterns? Should you always change your pattern to get a new friend?"
4. "What new choices were made by Jane? Mark?"
5. "What other choices might have been made by the Cookie Monster? Jane? Mark?"

Lesson 38

MATERIALS
Trumpet display

BEGINNING
Review the preceding journal entry. Introduce and discuss the Trumpet, reviewing each of the steps.

AFFECTIVE EXPERIENCE AND COGNITIVE INQUIRY
The format for this lesson is purposely different from the others. In this lesson, a number of situations are established. These situations (confrontations) should be reviewed by the children using the Trumpet. Discussion questions are provided.

Situation
David is in the fourth grade, the unannounced leader of the boys. In many ways he has instigated ridicule and laughter among the boys toward the girls of the class. But the girls were aware of the situation and confronted David by telling him how his behavior makes them feel. David's response is, "Tough! It makes me feel good."

DISCUSSION QUESTIONS
(Confrontation and Response) Ask the following questions.

1. "How do you think David feels?"
2. "What sentences do you think he was saying to himself?"
3. "How do you think he is affected by the response of others?"
4. "How might his face and body look as he says the above quote?"

Patterns

Ask the class, "See if you can think of several patterns for David. What are they? How would you describe the typical David?"

Own Patterns

"Can you think of anything he gets out of being the way he is? Try to list five things he gets from his actions."

Consequence

Ask, "If you were David, would you be missing out on anything? When you ridicule someone, what price do you pay?"

Alternative

Ask, "What other alternatives could David choose?"

Situation

Sue has come late to spelling class five days in a row. The lingering in the halls is due to her involvement with Armando at the lockers. Finally the teacher asks her to stay after class to speak to her about her tardiness. From the back of the room George calls out, "You'd better get Armando in, too." Sue blushes.

DISCUSSION QUESTIONS

(Confrontation and Response) Tell the class, "Let's write some words on the board about how you think Sue feels, George feels, and the teacher feels. Who is most comfortable? Least comfortable?"

Patterns

Ask, "Is there any part of the story which surprised you? If you were Sue, how would you have responded?"

Own Patterns

"Obviously Sue is getting something out of being late. What might make it worth her being late for class? Can you relate this to your life?"

Consequence

"Think of a similar situation in your life and remind yourself what you have done, how you have acted. Are you willing to share your experiences with the rest of us?"

Situation

The football team has had a 4-0 season so far. The coach is putting more and more pressure on the team to practice, keep curfew and be on time. Finally one of them speaks up and complains about the price they have to pay to be on the team: "I'm quitting unless the pressure starts cooling off." The others chime in, "Right on!"

DISCUSSION QUESTIONS

(Confrontation and Response) Ask the class, "How do you think the team felt right after the one team member spoke up? What sentences would you be saying to yourself if you were them?"

Patterns

Tell the children, "Identify patterns that you see in the situation. Think of the time you spoke up and how you felt about it. What were they? Are there things you feel comfortable or uncomfortable about, things which you feel quite strongly about?"

Own Patterns

"What will the team gain by going along with the coach? What will the team gain by opposing the coach? What will the coach gain by pressuring the team or by not pressuring the team?"

Consequence

Ask the following questions. "What are the team members willing to take? Are they missing out on anything? What precautions must they consider?"

Alternatives

Ask, "What alternatives are open to members of the team?"

Evaluation

Ask, "What ending to the story would you choose?"

Situation

Louise is an honor student, has been since sixth grade. Now in the tenth grade she has lost interest in school, studies, and friends. Most of her evenings she spends in her room reading. On weekends she seldom joins the crowd for any fun. Last year her father and mother decided to get a divorce after years of family conflict. When called in by the counselor about her grades, the counselor inquired, "Can you tell me what's bothering you?" Louise responded, "What difference does it make?"

DISCUSSION QUESTIONS

(Confrontation and Response) Tell the class, "Imagine you are Louise. What is she feeling? Try to look like Louise looks. If you had to choose one word to describe her, what would it be?"

Patterns

Ask the following questions.

Name Louise's pattern.

"In what circumstances have you felt like Louise? Did you do anything the same or different from Louise? What does Louise get from her pattern? What need does she satisfy?"

Own Patterns

"How does Louise's indifference help her? Why would this attitude help her deal with her situation?"

Consequence

Ask the class, "What is Louise avoiding? Or protecting? Is she missing out on anything?"

Alternative

Ask, "If you were Louise, what other things could you say to the counselor? What are the first steps you would take, if you were Louise, to change?"

Evaluation

Ask, "If you were Louise, what would be the most scary part about making a change?"

Situation

Tim just moved to a new community. He knew none of his fellow students in the second grade. When his dad took him to school the first day, Tim started to cry.

DISCUSSION QUESTIONS

(Confrontation and Response) Ask the following questions.

"If you were Tim, describe the feelings you would have. Are you more concerned with yourself or how others view you? When have you responded in a similar fashion?"

Patterns

Ask the following questions.

"In what kind of setting do you respond as Tim did? Are these settings similar in any way?"

Own Patterns

"If this is your pattern, what do you get out of it? What do people do to or for you when you cry?"

Consequence

Ask the class, "What is the result of your behavior in a similar setting?"

Alternative

Have the children tell their stories with different endings. Ask, "What has to happen for these new endings to be real?"

Closure

This concludes the first five goals of the self-science curriculum.

Section 4
Moving Ahead

Approaching Goal 6: Enhancing self-esteem in terms of awareness and accepting one's strengths

Approaching Goal 7: Accepting responsibility for one's self

Approaching Goal 8: Becoming aware of one's major concerns

Approaching Goal 9: Recognizing one's present behavioral patterns; learning about one's own learning styles

Approaching Goal 10: Experimenting with alternative behavioral patterns

Winding Up Part 4: Reviewing the Trumpet
Evaluating self-science tools

Section 4, in traditional terms, gets down to business. Self-science business is like peeling an onion, Section 3 was necessary just to peel off the outer layers. Now proceed with the twenty-six lessons that get to the heart of the matter. Material in Goal 9 is particularly valuable. If you get no further than that with your group, you have the right to be very well pleased.

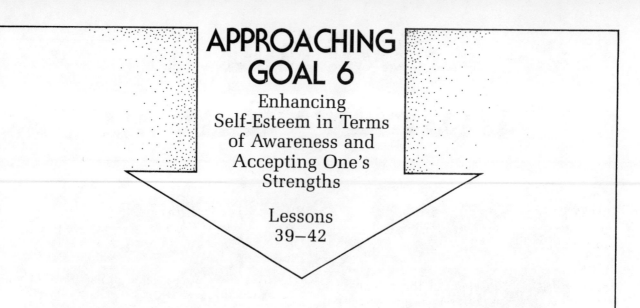

APPROACHING GOAL 6

Enhancing
Self-Esteem in Terms
of Awareness and
Accepting One's
Strengths

Lessons
39–42

Lessons 39 to 42 build the foundation for the harder work in self-exploration which follows. It is impossible to "dig" for weaknesses and self-improvement without a sense of where one's strengths are. We too often harp and nag and chide on weaknesses, ignoring the very real need to feel pride before permitting criticism (from self or others). Lesson 42 is suggested as a flow lesson.

GROUP BEHAVIOR

Some students, oddly, have a harder time than others in bragging or just talking about their strengths and accomplishments. Or, perhaps not oddly enough! Certain myths in our culture about "humility" cause confusion about personal worth; this must be dealt with. The experiences are short, but rich in the potential relief and release when pride is clarified and sanctioned.

EVIDENCE OF STUDENT GROWTH

Growth toward the goal will be demonstrated by the students as follows.

AFFECTIVE EXPECTATIONS

- Thinking and feeling more positively about self.
- Liking self.
- Laughing at self.
- Expressing pride in self.
- Describing personal strengths and weaknesses with greater accuracy.

COGNITIVE EXPECTATIONS

- Learning to make evaluations and judgments.
- Relating "moral" concepts to characters in fiction and myths.
- Reinforcing skills in classifying data.

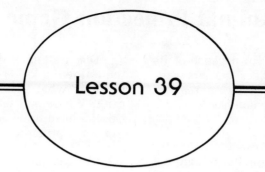

Lesson 39

MATERIALS

student contract forms, list of self-science goals, paper and pencils

BEGINNING

Review the first five goals of the self-science curriculum. Ask the children to give you feedback on what they learned about the goals. Was it worth learning? What could be done to make it better?

Talk briefly about Goals 6 through 10. Explain what will be covered in self-science during the remaining class meetings. Ask for questions. Since the children have signed a self-science contract before, have a brief conversation about the need for commitment to the group in order to effectively participate in self-science. Ask each child to sign a new personal contract.

AFFECTIVE EXPERIENCE

• Distribute paper and pencils and explain the *Animal Projection Game* (following).

COGNITIVE INQUIRY

Discuss what "projection" means. (See page 231.) Discuss the term "reown." Ask the following questions.

1. "Was there at least one projection that you reowned that seemed true about yourself?"
2. "How did you feel when you were reowning your projections?"
3. "What were you thinking? What were you doing?"

It is hard sometimes to be aware of all three states, or zones. The teacher can often make a note and give the student feedback when the child is unable to answer the question, i.e., "I imagined that you were feeling embarrassed," "shy," "surprised," etc.; "that you were thinking this was fun;" "was hard to do;" "wasn't true;" "was true;" etc. "I observed that you were tapping your foot," "looking away," "smiling," "frowning," etc.

ASSIGNMENT

Tell the class, "In your journal list three qualities you really like about your best friend. Reown them for yourself."

Teacher Comments _____

_____

_____

_____

_____

_____

_____

_____

_____

_____

Animal Projection Game

This game is particularly useful because of its flexibility. This exercise enhances learners' self-concepts and self-disclosures by increasing awareness of strengths and weaknesses.

PROCEDURE

When using the game for self-esteem, have students choose their favorite animal or the animal they would most like to be. Have the students write down the name of their animal and three positive qualities or characteristics of the animal. Students may then act out the qualities nonverbally or share them verbally with the group.

ALTERNATE PROCEDURE

Tell the class to choose the animal they like least, are afraid of, etc. Then have the students identify three positive and three negative qualities of the animal.

DISCUSSION ITEMS

Verbally share with the group the qualities chosen. Ask the students to "reown" the qualities for themselves. (See the description of "Reowning" following.)

NOTE TO THE TEACHER FOR LESSONS 40 AND 41

Enhancing a student's self-esteem isn't easy. Frequently a student's self-esteem is intimately related to academic performance. Needless to say, there isn't a one-to-one relationship between self-esteem and academic performance. This happens both because the term is vague and because of people's general difficulty in accurately assessing their own self-esteem.

Many students, when beginning a new class, want to impress the teacher with their self-confidence and abilities. Consequently, measuring self-esteem during the initial phases of a self-science class often yields an inflated measure. As the year progresses, however, students realize their self-science class is a safe place to admit weaknesses as well as to accentuate strengths. A more accurate measure of true self-esteem can be obtained midway through the year.

Discussions at this point can be focused on the following kinds of questions. Is it important to know what you can do well and what you can't? Where is it safe to talk about these things? Do you have to be good at everything? What are the ways others can make you feel good about yourself? What are the ways you can make yourself feel good about yourself? Is there a difference between accentuating your strengths and bragging? What is the difference?

Such discussions provide a basis for students to both assess their own capabilities and potentials, and to distinguish these qualities from their own worthwhileness. As students become more familiar with their many and varied strengths and weaknesses, they generally develop a more trusting attitude toward their own capabilities as well as toward other members of the class. They start to learn that even the "smartest" and most popular students have weaknesses, and that the "dullest" and most unpopular people have strengths. This attitude allows students to begin feeling better about themselves; they are able to begin developing foundations for accepting responsibility for personal thoughts, feelings, and actions.

Reowning

After a brief description and modeling by the teacher, students will quickly understand the concept of "reowning."

"Reowning" means repeating what has been said about someone or something else as though it were true of yourself. For example, if a student chooses an animal like a dog and states that a dog is kind, the "reowning" process would be to have the student say, "I am kind." Some projections are appropriate when "reowned" and some are not.

A brief illustration enables students to decide for themselves when a projection is appropriate to "reown." One word of caution: students shouldn't be forced when dealing with a highly negative projection. Under these circumstances, simply going through the process of reowning the projection is enough without saying to everyone, "Yes, this is true for me."

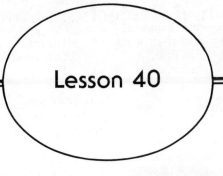

Lesson 40

MATERIALS

pencil and paper (for each student)

BEGINNING

(See authors' note, preceding, for Lessons 40 and 41.) Review yesterday's assignment. (Be careful not to take too much time on this as the lesson is packed.)

AFFECTIVE EXPERIENCE

- Introduce and play the *Bragging Game* (following).
- Introduce and play the *Pride Line Game* (following).

COGNITIVE INQUIRY

Ask the questions to the *Bragging Game*. Ask the questions to the *Pride Line Game*. Ask the following questions.

1. "Is it easier to talk about strengths than weaknesses?"
2. "Do most people focus on strengths or weaknesses?"
3. "How do people feel when they learn only negative comments?"

ASSIGNMENT

Tell the class, "Write in your journal five things you feel are positive about your teacher and five weaknesses."

Teacher Comments _____

_____

_____

_____

_____

_____

_____

_____

_____

_____

_____

Bragging Game*

This exercise is useful for enhancing learners' self-concepts, for helping them feel more comfortable about acknowledging their strengths and abilities, and for increasing rapport and self-disclosure.

PROCEDURE

Ask students to form groups of five or six. Instruct them that they have a total of fifteen to

twenty minutes in which to brag and boast about anything they can think of.

VARIATION

Each member of the group writes three things done well and later shares them. Proud quip: The class sits in a circle and everyone completes the sentence, "I'm proud of . . ."

---

*Emily Coleman, Graduate Student, University of Massachusetts.

DISCUSSION QUESTIONS

Ask the students to make journal entries regarding their feelings about bragging, and then ask the following questions.

1. "Did you enjoy it?"
2. "Were you uncomfortable?"
3. "How did you feel when others were bragging?"
4. "Did you feel competitive?"
5. "Did you want to make 'killer statements' to different people in the group? To whom? What brought on those feelings?"

Pride Line Game

This exercise is used to enhance positive self-concept, to clarify values in regard to action, to increase self-disclosure.

PROCEDURE

Ask the students to make a statement about a specific item, beginning with, "I'm proud that ..." For example, you might say, "I'd like you to mention something about your work in school that you're proud of. Please begin your response with, 'I'm proud that ...'" Students may say, "I pass," if they wish.

VARIATIONS

Below are some suggested items for use in the Pride Line.

Things you've done for your parents.
Things you've done for a friend.
Things you've done for yourself.
Things you've made.
How you spend your free time.
Habits you have.

Something you tried hard for.
How you've earned some money.
Something you've done to fight pollution.
Something you've done athletically.
The thing you're most proud of.
Something you've done in school.
Something you believe in.
A new skill you've acquired.
The nicest thing you did last week for someone.

ACTIVITY

Have the class make the appropriate journal entries.

DISCUSSION QUESTIONS

1. "How did you feel when you gave your 'Pride Line'?"
2. "Was there anything you wanted to say and censored? What?"

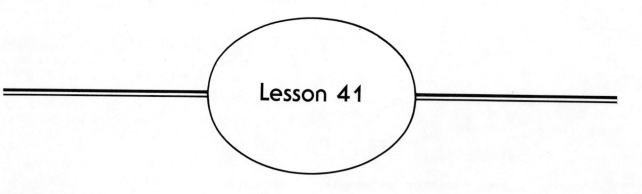

Lesson 41

MATERIALS

newsprint, felt pens

BEGINNING

Review assignment. Discuss concepts of: censorship, symbols, self-esteem, bragging, projections, owning, fantasy, self-disclosure.

AFFECTIVE EXPERIENCE

• Introduce *Strength Bombardment Game* (following).
• Introduce *Success Symbols Game* (following).

COGNITIVE INQUIRY

Ask questions for the *Strength Bombardment* experience. Ask questions for the *Success Symbols* experience. Ask the following questions.

1. "Are we more prone to criticize than to support people?"
2. "What price do we pay when we are critical?"
3. "What do we gain when we are positive? Lose?"

ASSIGNMENT

None. Flow Lesson to follow.

Teacher Comments

_____

_____

_____

_____

_____

_____

_____

_____

_____

_____

Strength Bombardment Game*

This exercise is valuable in helping students gain a clearer recognition and overview of their strengths, personality resources, capacities, and potentialities.

PROCEDURE

The first step is to spend about ten minutes brainstorming a list of personality strengths that are written on the chalkboard or on newsprint. To "prime the pump" the teacher may start by giving a couple of examples. Then have the class break into groups of five or six. Focusing on one person at a time, each group member is to "bombard" him/her with all the strengths they see in him/her. The person being bombarded should remain silent until the group has finished. One member of the group should act as recorder, listing the strengths and giving them to the person when the group has finished. (It may be necessary to caution the students that no "put-down" statements are allowed. This is a time to share only positives.)

VARIATIONS

If the teacher wishes to continue the exercise further, the group fantasy strategy can be used. After the list of strengths has been completed, the teacher asks, "How would you see (_____) functioning five years from
NAME OF STUDENT
now if s/he used all the strengths and potentialities?" The group then shares their fantasies and dreams about the chosen person.

The following optional question can be addressed to the student. "What is your own fantasy or dream for yourself?" An additional follow-up activity is to have the students ask their parents to list strengths and then to add these strengths to the list collected in class.

ACTIVITY

Have the class make journal entries; verbal sharing with group members whose input the student wishes to pursue further.

---

*Herbert A. Otto, *Group Methods to Actualize Human Potential.*

1. "How did you feel while this process was happening?"

2. "Were you surprised at any of the strengths you heard?"
3. "Do you consider any of the strengths you heard about yourself to be weaknesses?"

Success Symbols Game

This exercise is used to enhance the learner's positive self-concept and to increase rapport and self-disclosure.

PROCEDURE

Have the students imagine bringing to class one or more tangible objects that recall or symbolize some past successes or accomplishments they've had. During the class period have each student share one or more of the "success symbols" either with the rest of the class or with a small group. Instruct the students to share the feeling and meaning connected with the specific object as well as the success symbolized.

ACTIVITY

Ask students to make journal entries regarding their feelings before, during, and after the sharing of their success symbols.

DISCUSSION QUESTIONS

1. "What sentences were you saying to yourself when others were sharing?"
2. "'As I was sharing, I noticed . . . ,' 'What I liked best was . . .'"

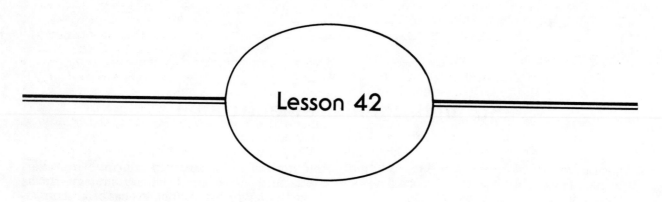

Lesson 42

FLOW LESSON
(See Appendix D, p. 161.)

Teacher Comments _____

_____

_____

_____

_____

_____

_____

_____

_____

_____

_____

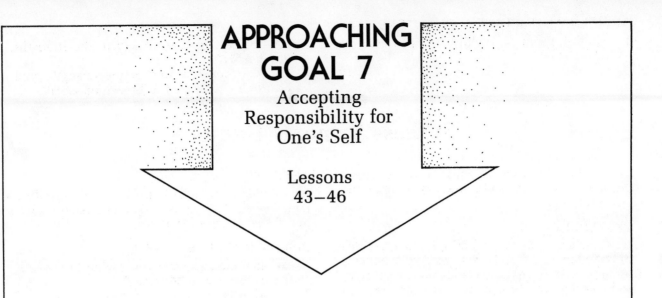

APPROACHING GOAL 7

Accepting
Responsibility for
One's Self

Lessons
43–46

Lessons 43 to 46 explore some of the dynamics behind taking responsibility, "owning" one's feelings, thoughts, and actions. Students survey their own study habits (applying the Trumpet concepts) to encourage experience and responsibility in evaluating important areas of student life.

GROUP BEHAVIOR

For this Goal, you'll be further "peeling the onion" in trying to promote awareness of how people project in order to avoid taking responsibility. Here you will have to move carefully, letting the awareness come out as students are able. Danger here is one of moralizing, i.e., "Stand on your own two feet"; "Who's to blame?"; "Did *you* do this?"

EVIDENCES OF STUDENT GROWTH

Growth toward the goal will be demonstrated by the students as follows.

AFFECTIVE EXPECTATIONS

- Gaining an increasing acceptance of feelings, moods, conduct, and the consequences of personal behavior.
- Gaining an increasing ability to follow through on a commitment.

COGNITIVE EXPECTATIONS

- Beginning to understand the concepts of projection and avoidance.
- Applying evaluation skills to personal study habits.

NOTE

(Background information for the teacher) Learning to accept responsibility for one's self is probably a life-long task. The difficulty becomes evident when we see the two-year-old child with cookie crumbs on his/her face deny having eaten a cookie, or the adolescent student who proclaims the stupidity of the teacher when the student has just failed an exam, or the husband who blames his wife's talking for the car accident, etc. We can all think of times when we have been either on the giving or the receiving end of similar situations.

A major impediment to accepting responsibility for self is the tendency to blame someone else for a given action. There are relatively few situations where this can't be avoided, by having each person accept responsibility for one's own behavior. To be sure, there are many situations and social issues over which we have little control. We do control our reactions and we can accept responsibility for our reactions. For example, in the situation with the husband, wife, and car incident, it wasn't the wife's talking that caused the accident but the husband's attending to the conversation rather than to driving. Being able to accept responsibility for self also allows others to accept responsibility for themselves, ultimately decreasing the need to establish fault.

Discussion about accepting responsibility can revolve around such questions as: "Is it hard to admit something when you are wrong? Do others seem to have control over you? Does anyone really make you do something? How do these situations make you feel?"

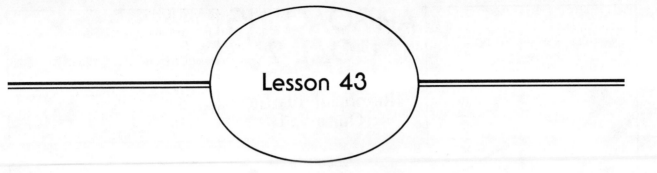

Lesson 43

MATERIALS

study skill sheets (one for each child)

BEGINNING

Introduce the ideas of accepting responsibility and why all of us must accept responsibility for our own actions. Review the "alternatives" and "choosing" steps in the Trumpet.

AFFECTIVE EXPERIENCE

• Play the *Robot Game* (following).

COGNITIVE INQUIRY

Ask the questions for the *Robot Game.*

Introduce the Study Skill Experiment. The Study Skills Experiment is an assignment for the students to keep a time-and-pattern diary of study habits over the next week. The purpose of the study is to demonstrate responsibility in a relevant form; i.e., each person is clearly responsible for his/her own studying. The Trumpet will be applied to this experience. (See information following the *Robot Game.*)

ASSIGNMENT

Tell the class they are to maintain a diary of study habits for a period of a week.

Teacher Comments _____

_____

_____

_____

_____

_____

_____

_____

_____

_____

_____

_____

Robot Game*

This exercise is useful for gathering data about how students feel about following orders. Structure and freedom can evolve from this exercise.

PROCEDURE

Students are requested to become robots with you as their master. They move in a stiff manner, follow your every command, doing only what they are programmed to do. Give them a series of repetitious, boring commands, such as requesting they take a step back and a step to the left when they bump into another person or object. Give some commands they can't possibly do; then chastise them for their inability to follow orders. Don't stop the exercise until some of the class is upset with following commands.

---

*Marianne Simon, graduate student, University of Massachusetts.

ACTIVITY

Have the class do a Here-and-Now Wheel, journal entries, or a group discussion of process questions.

VARIATION

Students can get into dyads. One becomes the robot, the other the master. Then switch.

DISCUSSION QUESTIONS

1. "What feelings are expressed in the Here-and-Now Wheel?"
2. "Do you ever feel like a robot? When?"
3. "Who are your masters?"
4. "What do you like, dislike about being a robot?"
5. "Do you feel trapped?"
6. "How much freedom did you feel you had to untrap yourself?"

Study Skill Experiment

Hand out a Study Skill Time Diary to each student (see following page). Put sample ideas on chalkboard. Discuss "power" and "powerlessness."

Each person with a sense of responsibility has power over his/her actions. By studying one's behavior, one is able to consider alternatives for improvement and making choices. (This is a good opportunity for the teacher to use personal examples, in keeping with the adult modeling role.)

PROCEDURE

Work through the first of the diary for that portion of the day up to the time self-science class meets.

DISCUSSION QUESTIONS

The personal time diary should be discussed each class meeting to help the students think through their personal records. Ask these questions.

1. "What situation arose which caused time to be wasted?"
2. "Was this in keeping with your usual pattern?"
3. "What did you gain from your pattern?"
4. "Did you miss out on anything?"
5. "What alternatives might you choose?"
6. "What would you gain?"
7. "What would you lose?"

Notes from Nueva

The class looked at last week's videotape on the birthday party. There was a lot of giggling and embarrassment. They all shared their feelings about seeing themselves and there was general agreement that they did not recognize their own voices.

Then we played the Robot Game.

First we played it as a whole group and then in dyads. This group really enjoyed the game and had a very good discussion. Peter feels like a robot at home because of the way his older brothers and sisters treat him. He was able to go into detail and really get in touch with his resentment, which is important as he's always trying to live up to his image of his family. George doesn't feel like a robot but thought about his brother, whom he treats as if he were one. He decided his brother must not like it very much, and he would try to treat him differently.

The group generally related robot feelings to home where they felt they were being bossed around.

Again, today, the boys were particularly "high" when the group began. The whole group was talking and didn't stop even though I said we wouldn't be able to play a game until they settled down. I waited about ten minutes, and then I had everyone "Freeze." I told them sitting in their bean bags was available while we talked for a minute about why they came to self-sciencing.

They responded:

". . . to learn about ourselves."
". . . to learn about others."
". . . to learn about our feelings."
"How do we do this?"
". . . playing games."
". . . talking."

I felt a great deal of frustration dealing with the group today. On one hand I'd like to just let them go until they take control, but I don't feel that it's fair to the other children who want to do other things.

Study Skill Time Diary

DAY _____ Monday _____

TIME USED		TIME WASTED	
Writing	9:00–9:25	9:25–9:30	(5)
Math	9:30–9:50	9:50–10:10	(20)
Art	10:10–10:40		
Recess	10:40–11:00		
Music	11:00–11:30		
Reading	11:40–12:00	11:30–11:40	(10)
	(etc.)		

© 1978 Goodyear Publishing Co. from Karen Stone and Hal Dillehunt, Self-Science: The Subject Is Me.

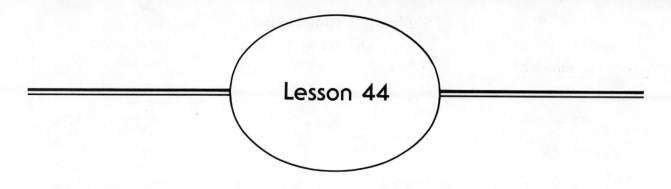

Lesson 44

MATERIALS

Trumpet display, power continuum (one for each student)

BEGINNING

Review the Study Skill Time Diary for the period charted. Discuss the "wasted time," using the "Trumpet." Introduce the concepts and vocabulary words of "approach" and "avoidance." ("Approach" is moving ahead or taking action; "avoidance" is keeping away from or ignoring, or disliking certain actions.)

AFFECTIVE EXPERIENCE

• Complete the *Power Continuum* exercise (following).

COGNITIVE INQUIRY

Ask the questions for the *Power Continuum*, as follows.

1. "How much power do you have over your own actions?"
2. "Do people always think before they talk? Act? Do you?"

ASSIGNMENT

Have the class continue with the Study Skill Diary.

Power Continuum

This exercise is designed to help kids inventory where they are in relation to fighting—"toughness."

PROCEDURE

Create character descriptions of "Meek" Mel, "Sort-of-Mean" Sally, "Tough" Ted. Pass out copies of the Power Continuum (see sample, following). Request students to mark on the continuum where they are now, and then mark in a different color where they would like to be. Volunteers can share their actual and desired continuum positions with the large group.

ACTIVITIES

Have children in the small groups discuss their continuum positions, using discussion questions as a guide. Have the children respond in their journals to the questions and complete the statements: "I learned that I . . . ," "I feel . . ."

DISCUSSION QUESTIONS

Discuss the following questions.

1. "What's really good about the position you marked?"
2. "Is there a difference between your actual position on the continuum and your desired position?"
3. "If there is a difference, what stops you from getting to your desired position?"
4. "Imagine a time when you have acted in your actual positions. How did you feel then?"
5. "Have you ever acted in your desired position? How did that feel?"

Power Continuum

Name _____ Date _____

Meek Mel

Won't even hurt
a fly; won't ever
fight or yell,
even when really
pushed around.

Sort-of-Mean Sally

Tough Ted

Beats everyone
up all the time
even if he likes
them.

I learned _____

_____

_____

I feel _____

_____

_____

Lesson 45

MATERIALS
Trumpet display

BEGINNING
Review the preceding journal entry. Review Trumpet steps. Review purposes of self-science.

AFFECTIVE EXPERIENCE
• Have each student use Study Skill sheets.

COGNITIVE INQUIRY
Ask the following questions.

1. "What does your diary suggest about your use of time? Do you notice any patterns? What kind? Is there anyone else who helps you waste time? Does it occur at any regular times?"
2. "Are you responsible for yourself?"
3. "Are you responsible for others?"
4. "Are you willing to process (out loud) your wasted time through the 'Trumpet'?"
5. "Are there any group patterns similar to individual patterns? How is this possible?"
6. "Are there any times during the day when more people seem to waste time than at others?"

ASSIGNMENT
Tell the class, "Keep your time diary for two additional days and see if you have the personal power to waste thirty minutes less time than for the same days the preceding week."

Teacher Comments

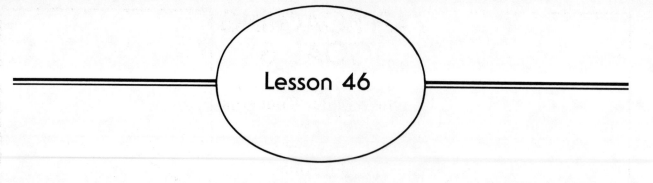

Lesson 46

MATERIALS

Trumpet display

BEGINNING

Combine regular and flow lesson. Review preceding journal entries. Review concept of "projections."

AFFECTIVE EXPERIENCE

• Play the projection game, *Give the Teacher a Voice* (following).

COGNITIVE INQUIRY

Ask the questions (in individual journals) for the *Give the Teacher a Voice* experience.

Have individuals act as teacher and have the children do their projections out loud and continue discussion questions.

Continue with flow lesson.

ASSIGNMENT

None

Teacher Comments

_____

_____

_____

_____

_____

_____

_____

_____

_____

_____

_____

_____

Give the Teacher a Voice Game

This exercise is designed to get at students' concerns through projection.

PROCEDURE

Have the children look at you. Say, "I am going to sit here. I want you to imagine what I might be saying if I were to talk. Give me a voice; make it sound the way you think it would."

ACTIVITY

Make journal entries on the following questions.

1. "How did it feel to be my voice?"
2. "Did you think of things for my voice that you did not say?"
3. "If so, what kept you from saying them?"

VARIATIONS

Have the children write their answers in their journals instead of giving them aloud.

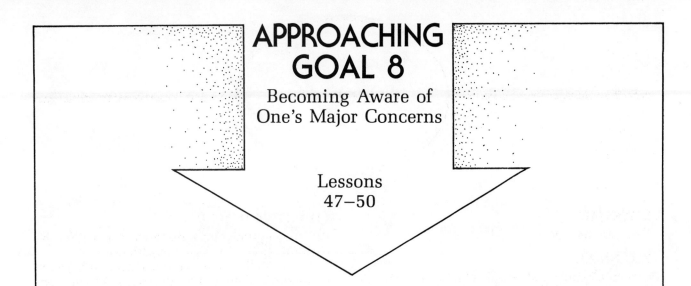

APPROACHING GOAL 8

Becoming Aware of One's Major Concerns

Lessons 47–50

Lessons 47 to 50 use all the cognitive steps of the Trumpet to understand personal concerns and the validity of the concerns is, in effect, final preparation for the "pay-off" of self-science—feeling free to examine and make changes in any one of a number of behavioral patterns.

GROUP BEHAVIOR

The work in this Goal is a "cleansing" action, in a sense. Students use the skills and concepts they learned all along to zero in on deep-seated concerns. The ability to do this creates an internal freeing-up, a release, a letting-go. (It takes much energy to keep fears and concerns inside.) Obviously, some students will participate more deeply than others. Again, the seed-planting concept functions. Accept the group on whatever level they can reach.

EVIDENCE OF STUDENT GROWTH

Growth toward the goal will be demonstrated by the students as follows.

AFFECTIVE EXPECTATIONS

• An increasing ability to state specific personal concerns and relate personally to the concerns of others.

COGNITIVE EXPECTATIONS

• Integrating and using the skills and concepts developed so far.

NOTE TO THE TEACHER

It may seem unusual to think a person is unaware of personal concerns but, in fact, we often are unaware of things that really are of concern to us. It's generally easier to be aware of external concerns than internal concerns. For example, as a student it may be relatively easy to be aware of concerns over performance on an examination but very difficult to be aware of concerns about one's ability to be a good friend. While some students may become aware of their concerns, there are far too few opportunities to express these concerns in an open, trusting environment. Some students have the advantage of being able to express concerns to their parents.

Self-science class can provide students with a place they can safely and constructively express both their external and internal concerns. Through the gradual establishment of the norms and goals of the curriculum, a feeling of trust and safety is established where students can express their concerns. By acknowledging student input on all levels from the beginning of the year, students learn that discussing their concerns has validity.

Discussion can be focused around the following kinds of questions: Have you ever felt as if you were the only person to be concerned about _____? Do others usually relate their concerns to you? What are the situations that allow this to happen? To whom do you feel you can tell your concerns?

These discussions following an experiential game help students realize that their fears and concerns are usually shared by at least a few others in the class. This facilitates their recognition of others' concerns as well as accepting the responsibility for their own. Becoming more aware of personal concerns prepares students for recognizing their typical reactions and behavior patterns.

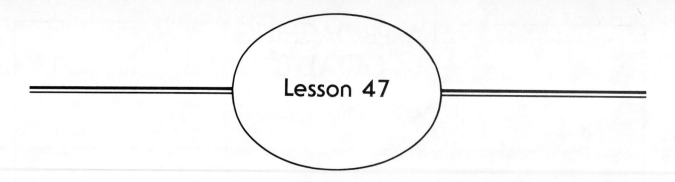

MATERIALS

Trumpet display, 3 x 5 cards (two for each student)

BEGINNING

Introduce the concept of "concerns for fears." (Use the preceding information in your own style.)

AFFECTIVE EXPERIENCE

• Play *Secret in the Hat* (following).
• Play *Fear in the Hat* (following).

COGNITIVE INQUIRY

Ask the questions for the *Secret in the Hat* experience and for the *Fear in the Hat* experience, as follows.

1. "What other fears could you have given?"
2. "Is it too risky to give all your fears?"
3. "Did you keep some fears to yourself?"
4. "When people disclose themselves, is this a sign of weakness?"
5. "Is it easier to disclose yourself in this class?"
6. "Are there other places where you would feel free to disclose your fears?"

ASSIGNMENT

Tell the students, "Write in your journal four fears you have; two you'd share and two you'd keep to yourself."

Teacher Comments _____

_____

_____

_____

_____

_____

_____

_____

_____

_____

_____

_____

Secret in the Hat Game

This exercise is designed to diagnose concerns and to promote self-awareness.

PROCEDURE

Have students write a secret they've never told anyone on a 3 x 5 card and give it to you. There should be no names on the cards. Shuffle the cards and read them aloud.

ACTIVITY

Each student gets a card and reads it aloud to the group.

Ask the following questions.

1. "How did you feel hearing others' secrets?"
2. "How did you feel hearing your secret read?"
3. "How do you suppose the others felt?"
4. "Were you surprised to learn others had fears similar to your own?"
5. "How risky were you when disclosing your fears?"

Fear in the Hat Game

Before beginning the game, restate the necessity for taking the fear seriously. (It is highly important that the teacher participate. This provides safety for the students as well as providing the teacher with the opportunity for subtly moving the discussion of fears from external to internal.) When students play this game for the first time, the fears presented are usually external, such as fear of the dark, snakes, etc. Gradually students move toward more internal concerns such as fear of not having a friend, being alone, etc.

This exercise is designed to diagnose students' concerns and to promote self-awareness. It's particularly useful because it permits anonymity; students consequently are free to reveal as much or as little as they wish.

PROCEDURE

Ask each child to write a fear on a 3 x 5 card and to give it to you. Shuffle the cards and pass one to each child. Have the students read the cards, one at a time, and act out the fears by exaggerating them.

ACTIVITY

Have the child acting out the fear put the fear in a chair and tell it why s/he is not afraid of it.

DISCUSSION QUESTIONS

Ask the following questions.

1. "How did you feel seeing someone else work on your fear?"
2. "How did you feel hearing others' fears?"
3. "Did you notice any patterns?"
4. "Has anyone else ever experienced the same or a similar kind of fear?"
5. "When are you most likely to experience such a fear?"
6. "Wouldn't most people experience that fear under similar circumstances?"
7. "How is one fear related to another?"

Notes from Nueva

Today we introduced a new game, Fear in the Hat. The children decided to act out nonverbally the card they drew. After each fear was guessed or read, everyone added to the experience by relating to the particular fear. Everyone was willing to admit a fear to the group and to explain why. We talked about how we felt revealing our fears, learning about other peoples' and in the discussion recognized several patterns. One was a fear that related to a similar, real-life experience in the past. The other was fear for our safety and well-being.

CAMILLE: *Camille could not think of anything she was afraid of at first. She finally thought of something as I sat by her and discussed possibilities (being alone, scary noises, people fighting, getting hurt). She was frightened about having to go to live with her father. She explained that her father had a new wife, who had two children. They were all mean to her. She worried about something happening to her mother which would cause her to have to live with her dad. Everyone was supportive and talked about who they'd live with if something happened to their parents. In the beginning, Camille was very tense telling us about her fear, but she relaxed as the group gave her support and shared their fears about the same problem. Today was one of the first times Camille participated actively.*

KELLY: *Kelly was afraid of doors. This related to an experience she told us about several months ago. A bomb had been left on the front porch and would have killed whomever opened the door. Fortunately, no one was home. She told about her fear of opening the front door, her bedroom door, and almost any door she couldn't see through. Kelly was able to recognize the pattern, and relate it later to Tim's fear, which also had to do with a real life experience.*

TIM: *Tim was afraid that a man in New York would shoot him in the head with a machine gun. He was able to see that this related to his experience during the riots in Chicago when a man with a shotgun went berserk in a hospital where Tim and his friends sought refuge. Tim witnessed a policeman shoot this man through the head after he had killed a number of people. Everyone agreed that they would be afraid, too, and there was considerable discussion about being shot, stabbed, attacked, etc.*

ARTHUR: *Arthur was afraid of cars driving up his driveway at night and stopping, and also strange noises at night. They live in a house with a long driveway on several acres of land. He explained that it's an old house and it makes lots of creaky, funny noises. He's afraid someone will come and try to rob them or hurt them if they know just the kids are at home with the housekeeper, who is Oriental, limps badly, but is a Black Belt in Samurai swords. There was a lot of joking about her abilities to protect them as well as keep them in line.*

BRUCE: *Bruce was afraid of going out alone to the barn at night to feed the animals. He explained that it's very, very dark and once you're out there, no one can see or hear you from the house if you need help. Arthur and Tim immediately agreed, and they both related their mutual experience of being down at a store at night, about a block from their house and then walking back. They had decided they were too scared to stay down there. Every sound scared them more, until they were running as fast as they could to get home. Bruce decided to take his dog or another person with him in the future.*

We had a very good group today with everyone revealing a lot about their own fears as well as their mutual fears.

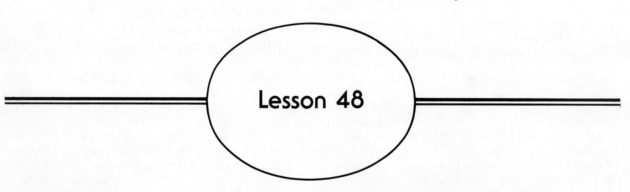

Lesson 48

MATERIALS
Trumpet display

BEGINNING
Discuss fears (journal entries) that are comfortable. Review concept of projection.

AFFECTIVE EXPERIENCE
• Complete the *Mother and Father Projection Game* (following).

COGNITIVE INQUIRY
Ask the questions to the *Mother and Father Projection* experience, as follows.

1. "Do many people have fears about their personal safety? Do you? What kinds?"
2. "Do you see how the Trumpet can be used with all kinds of patterns?"
3. "Is it any easier to talk about fears?"
4. "Which of your fears seems to be similar to the fears of others?"

ASSIGNMENT
None. Flow Lesson to follow.

_____

_____

_____

_____

_____

_____

_____

_____

_____

_____

Mother and Father Projection Game

This exercise is used to elicit and diagnose students' concerns.

PROCEDURE

Going around the room one at a time, ask each student to describe her/himself as if her/his mother were talking. For example: "Johnny's a nice enough boy, but he's kinda lazy. He never picks up his clothes. . . ." Repeat this procedure as if the student were the father.

ACTIVITY

Discuss "I learned . . ." statements in a large group. Have the class make the appropriate journal entries.

VARIATION

Do the projections in dyads or quartets rather than going around the whole room one at a time. Have the students exaggerate their parents' behaviors.

DISCUSSION QUESTIONS

1. "I discovered that I . . ."
2. "If I had it to do over, I'd . . ."

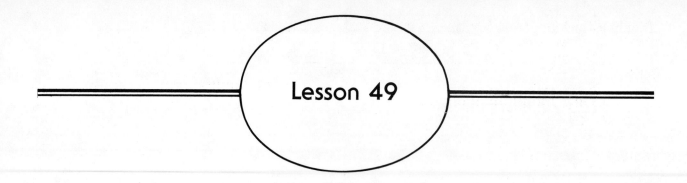

Lesson 49

FLOW LESSON
(See Appendix D, p. 161.)

Teacher Comments _____

_____

_____

_____

_____

_____

_____

_____

_____

_____

Notes from Nueva _____

We worked on projection again today. We asked everyone to think about someone they really liked and to write down four or five things about that person. We did the same with someone we didn't like, and also things we liked about our mothers and fathers. We shared the first two projections—on each set of negative projections about the person we didn't like. We did some brainstorming on what was good about one of the negative statements. The group really enjoyed doing this and we talked about removing our instant judgment and trying to be more objective.

We also talked about what projection means, and I think everyone in the group except Debbie and Darby understood the concept. (We will check this out next week when we finish up the mother and father projections.)

	LIKE	DON'T LIKE
PETER:	He understands me. He's a good "shrink." He likes the Rolling Stones.	Freaks out on typewriters. He has a flat top. He has a square personality. Flighty.
	MOTHER	FATHER
	Not crabby. Not overprotective. She sends me to Nueva.	Understanding. Good personality. Permissive.
	LIKE	DON'T LIKE
TIM:	He's cute. Good dancer. Loves rock and roll music.	Big baby. Stupid as a rooster. Hate his glasses.
KATHY:	Nice fun. She likes me. I like her.	Brat Stupid Lies Mean Socks me.

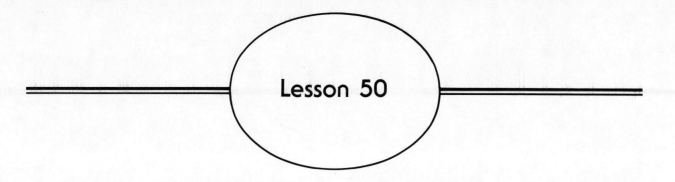

Lesson 50

MATERIALS

Newsprint, magic markers, Trumpet display

BEGINNING

Review the steps in the Trumpet. Review concepts of killer statements, confidential, projection, avoidance, etc.

AFFECTIVE EXPERIENCE

- Play the *Three Wishes Game* (following).
- Play the *"I wonder . . ."* Statements Game (following).

COGNITIVE INQUIRY

Ask the questions for the *Three Wishes* experience and the *"I wonder . . . Statements*, as follows.

1. "Were there any patterns in the experiences?"
2. "Are you willing to share your 'I wonder . . .' statements?"
3. "How similar are yours to others?"

ASSIGNMENT

Tell the class, "Write in your journal twenty words that express your positive feelings and ten words that express your negative feelings."

Teacher Comments _____

_____
_____
_____
_____
_____
_____
_____
_____
_____
_____

Three Wishes Game

This exercise can help students consider some of their concerns.

PROCEDURE

Ask the students, "If you suddenly were given three wishes, what would they be?" (Give the students a few minutes to think about this and then ask for "wishes" to be shared with the class.)

ACTIVITY

Students can discover similarities and differences in wishes by using the first two processing questions below. General areas of concerns can be noted on the board or newsprint. The class can then brainstorm ways to make wishes come true.

Have the group fantasize a magic wand or a magical elf that can grant wishes.

Ask the following questions.

1. "In what ways were your wishes like other students'?"
2. "In what ways were yours unique?"
3. "Do you feel your wishes could ever come true?"
4. "How could you make them come true?"

"I Wonder . . ." Statements Game

This exercise is used primarily to elicit students' concerns. It can also be used at the end of any exercise as a process procedure.

PROCEDURE

Ask students to make statements beginning with "I wonder . . ." (what, if, why, when, etc.). Examples: "I wonder why the teacher seems sad today," "I wonder if my parents will let me go out on the weekend."

To break through imitation patterns and to elicit deeper concerns, go around the class, one student after another, about three times. Watch for patterns of concerns emerging.

ACTIVITY

Ask students how they felt hearing others' statements. Ask if they noticed any similarity or differences in concerns.

VARIATION

Ask students to pick a partner and take turns making "I wonder . . ." statements to each other.

DISCUSSION QUESTIONS

Ask the class, "Have you any new 'I wonder . . .' statements to make now that the exercise is over? Any 'I learned . . .' statements?"

Notes from Nueva _____

We reviewed our projections from last week, such as people we liked.

We reowned that when we say things to other people, it may be something that's true about ourselves—good or bad.

We took a few minutes to review all the things the group remembered talking about during the year.

Boys and girls	*Trumpet*
Explode	*Hopes*
Robots	*Fears*
Trustfalls and walks	*Rumor*
Camera	*Telephone*
Consensus	*Killer statements*
Magic bag	*Imagination*
Likes	*Way you feel about your-*
Break in	*self and other people*
Being absent	*Projections*
Being confidential	*Bad times*
Dreams	*Personal things*
Nonverbal	*Learning about senses*
Birthdays	*Self-sciencing machine*
Good Times	*Lou Savory and the Music*
Reowning	*My birthday parties*

APPROACHING GOAL 9

Recognizing One's Present Behavioral Patterns; Learning About One's Own Learning Styles

Lessons 51–56

Lessons 51 to 56 use all the tools developed in self-science to show students how to identify their own learning styles and those behavioral patterns with which they feel comfortable and which they are able to perceive.

GROUP BEHAVIOR

Learning about learning is an exciting pay-off. The group will be feeling a sense of pride and accomplishment, using and sharing their self-science tools for relatively independent inquiry. (Help individuals in the group accept and apply their findings to their ongoing schoolwork. Individual conferences are good here, if possible.)

EVIDENCE OF STUDENT GROWTH

Growth toward the goal will be demonstrated by the students as follows.

AFFECTIVE EXPECTATIONS

- Demonstrating an increasing ability to identify and describe personal behavioral patterns.
- Identifying personal learning patterns.
- Demonstrating an increasing awareness of the consequences and functions of behavioral patterns.

COGNITIVE EXPECTATIONS

- Learning about one's personal learning patterns.
- Integrating and using the cognitive tools taught to date.

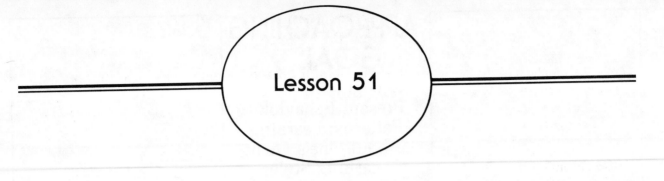

MATERIALS

"How Do I Learn?" questionnaires (one for each student)

BEGINNING

Remind the class about the Trumpet steps—observing, inventorying, finding patterns, evaluating patterns, and making decisions about their patterns.

Ask for patterns in the group (e.g., how boys sit on one side, girls on the other; how "everybody used to gang up on _____, but that now has changed." Use any material you can from group experiences).

Remind the class that very early on you promised you would show them something about learning patterns. At this point, the students should know something about learning patterns, too. Elicit the group's awareness of ways they have been learning (e.g., through games, discussions, inventorying, experiments, etc.).

AFFECTIVE EXPERIENCE AND COGNITIVE INQUIRY

Distribute the "How Do I Learn?" questionnaire (following). Explain that the questions should not be answered now. They should be answered a week from now, or when the group feels ready. Tell students, "Now, let's see if we can devise

some *experiments* to get the information needed to answer the questions." Brainstorm ideas with the group. Some possibilities are: each child could role-play a learning situation (such as C or D on the questionnaire); students could survey themselves for a week; or invent a game; or pair up with a friend and then watch each other.

As you brainstorm, indicate the name of the person giving the suggestion. When the brainstorming is finished, suggest that there are personal styles in the kinds of suggestions people make. For example, the person suggesting role-playing may have a learning style that works best through physical activity, using the entire self to learn.

Stress that no one learning style is "better" than another. We each learn differently. As with ball players, we each have our strong points (pitching, batting, running, etc.). Frankly discuss the point that many subjects in school are taught for only one kind of learning style. That may be why some people have trouble learning. (In the next few lessons, coping techniques and alternatives will be suggested.)

ASSIGNMENT

Tell the class, "Put in answers to the first three (A, B, C) items on the questionnaire in your journal."

Teacher Comments _____

_____

_____

_____

_____

_____

_____

_____

_____

_____

_____

How Do I Learn?*

Circle the numbers of the items you think are most like you. If you think more than one item is like you, circle more numbers.

A. I can learn best in the:
   1. morning
   2. middle of the day
   3. afternoon
   4. evening
B. I can learn something easily by:
   1. reading it
   2. hearing it
   3. seeing it in pictures
   4. writing it in my own words
   5. explaining it to someone
   6. drawing a diagram or picture of it
   7. talking about it with somebody else
   8. teaching somebody else
C. I dislike having to learn:
   1. in big group meetings
   2. in little group meetings
   3. in game situations
   4. with a partner who chose me
   5. with a partner the teacher chose for me
   6. with a partner I don't know
   7. by myself
   8. in team situations

D. While learning the things that bother me the most are:
   1. being in a quiet place
   2. being in a noisy place
   3. having a radio or television on
   4. being interrupted
   5. stopping before I'm through
   6. having to wait for others to finish
E. I seem to do homework *best* with:
   1. an hour or more to think
   2. short work sessions
   3. having a work routine
F. For learning by reading I like to:
   1. ask questions *before* reading
   2. skim before reading
   3. also ask questions after reading
My most difficult subject is: _____

The easiest: _____

Lesson 52

MATERIALS

"How Do I Learn?" questionnaire (students to bring in)

BEGINNING

Review responses to A, B, C items on the "How Do I Learn?" questionnaire. Work on items D through E and complete answers.

AFFECTIVE EXPERIENCE

- Continue with "How Do I Learn?" questionnaire (complete responses to items D through E).

COGNITIVE INQUIRY

Ask the following questions.

1. "Did you mark more than one possibility for item D? If you did, are they equally bad?"
2. "How did you mark item E? Do other people have the same responses? Is your pattern similar to the majority of others? Did you learn anything about this item from your Time-Diary study?"
3. "How did you mark items F and G? Have you ever thought about these questions before? When?"
4. "Do you sometimes get confused when you consider whether you like a subject or a teacher? Can you like a teacher and not a subject? Vice-versa?"
5. "What other questions might be asked as items to put on the questionnaire? Put four of these items on the chalkboard and the possible alternatives. Brainstorm other questions that are important for how you learn."

ASSIGNMENT

Tell the class to select any two of the items put on the board and enter them in their journals with answers to the questions.

Teacher Comments

_____

_____

_____

_____

_____

_____

_____

_____

_____

_____

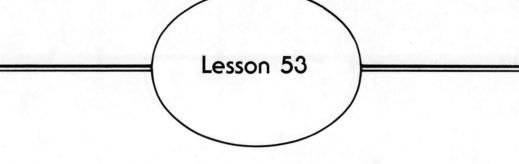

Lesson 53

MATERIALS
"How Do I Learn?" questionnaire

BEGINNING
Review the two additional items and have students discuss similarities and differences in groups of three.

AFFECTIVE EXPERIENCE
- Continue with use of "How Do I Learn?" questionnaire.

COGNITIVE INQUIRY
Complete the following: have students, one-by-one, develop out loud to the other students their individual learning patterns, based on the information they charted on the questionnaire. (This will probably take most of the class time. If more time is needed, the next lesson is a flow lesson and the first part of that period can be used.) In journal, have students brainstorm personal alternatives to their patterns.

Have volunteers discuss the new behaviors they feel they want to choose. Ask whether these new behaviors can be shared with other teachers.

ASSIGNMENT
Those unable to state their new behaviors to the class may write their responses into the journals.

Teacher Comments _____

_____

_____

_____

_____

_____

_____

_____

_____

_____

_____

Lesson 54

FLOW LESSON
(See Appendix D, p. 161.)

Teacher Comments _____

_____

_____

_____

_____

_____

_____

_____

_____

_____

_____

_____

Lesson 55

MATERIALS
Continuum to Look at Group Behavior (one for each student)

BEGINNING
Provide an opportunity for students who didn't talk earlier to give information regarding their patterns, behavior alternatives and possible choices.

Pass out the *Group Behavior Continuum*—one for each student.

AFFECTIVE EXPERIENCE
• Have the class complete the continuum exercises.

COGNITIVE INQUIRY
Ask the questions to the continuum as follows.

1. "What other kinds of continuum are applicable? Can you make up any?"

ACTIVITY

Agree with three other people in the class to mark their continuum as you perceive them, and have them do the same for you.

ASSIGNMENT

Tell the group to complete the marking of the continuum so there can be discussion at the next session.

Teacher Comments _____

_____

_____

_____

_____

_____

_____

_____

_____

_____

_____

Continuum to Look at Group Behavior

This exercise is useful for expanding the learner's capacity to look at personal behavior, to give and receive feedback, and to check perceptions of self with the way others perceive the learner. (Use names of both sexes so that sex role stereotypes will not be a variable.)

PROCEDURE

Explain what a continuum is. Draw a continuum on the chalkboard.

"Withdrawn Wilbur"   "Dominating
   "Wilma" |___|___|___|___| Dave/Doris"

Direct the students to place themselves on the continuum in terms of the way in which they behaved in the group today. Next, they are to place other members of their group on the continuum. This is done individually and silently on paper.

Give the class time to permit individuals to check out their perceptions of personal behavior with the perceptions of others.

ACTIVITY

Share in trios. Write everyone's continuum on the board for comparison. Journal entries; discussion.

VARIATIONS

Use other continuums.

"Silent Sam"   "Disruptive
   "Sally" |___|___|___|___| Roy/Ramona"

DISCUSSION QUESTIONS

Ask the following questions.

1. "Did others place you at the same point on the continuum as you placed yourself?"
2. "Did you see yourself as other members of the group saw you?"
3. "Did you see others as they saw themselves?"
4. "Is the way you behaved today your usual way of behaving in the group?" (Use "I learned . . ." statements.)

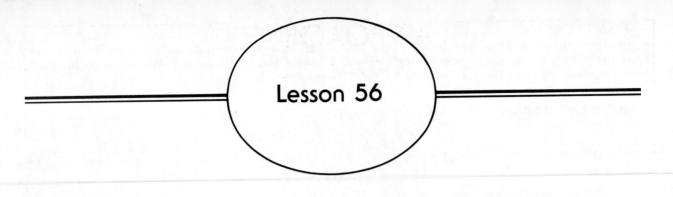

Lesson 56

BEGINNING

Divide the class into groups of four and discuss the continuum. See how closely the perceptions other people have match with those of the first person.

AFFECTIVE EXPERIENCE

- Use the continuums completed for the assignment.

COGNITIVE INQUIRY

Ask the following questions.

1. "How closely did the perceptions of others match yours? How were the perceptions alike? How different?"
2. "Were you harder on yourself than the others?"

3. "How closely did your perceptions of others match their perceptions of themselves? How were they different?"
4. "What value is there in getting feedback about how others perceive you? Is it helpful? Does feedback help you consider your patterns?"
5. "Are there times when you shouldn't change your pattern? Who has the power to choose one behavior over another?"

ASSIGNMENT

None

Teacher Comments _____

_____

_____

_____

_____

Notes from Nueva _____

Relating to Patterns and Discovering Patterns

A young boy who was in the fourth grade had been in self-sciencing one year before. About three months into the group, one of the other children confronted him with the fact that he always was disrupting the sessions, the discussions, and the activities by needing or having to be different. His usual pattern was either to sit on two or three bean bags or to sit on the piano or walk around the room or not to sit on the bean bags, etc. He would engage in these activities in an obviously attention-getting manner.

After being confronted with this, he was able to say that he did do this; that he disrupted the group and that he felt the need to be different from everyone else. As we probed this in detail, it became apparent that his need to be different was related to his fear that he would not be accepted by the rest of the group if he went along with the members. Consequently, he adopted a rejection model. We asked him to explore alternatives and he was able to at least think of the idea of behaving as the other children did at the beginning of the session by coming in and sitting down and preparing to engage in the activities and discussions. He was able to try on this pattern, and as the year proceeded many of the children began to feel more positively toward him as a group member.

APPROACHING GOAL 10

Experimenting With Alternative Behavioral Patterns

Lessons 57–60

Lessons 57 to 60 focus on the process of changing behavior. Students choose a pattern they wish to change. They observe and conceptualize the change process.

GROUP BEHAVIOR

This may be the most difficult Goal for the group to handle. Some groups may be unable to make progress here. Even so, becoming aware that changing one's patterns takes conscious awareness and effort can have value in accepting one's own limitations, tolerance for others, and development of realistic goals.

EVIDENCE OF STUDENT GROWTH

Growth toward the goal will be demonstrated by the students as follows.

AFFECTIVE EXPECTATIONS

- Showing an increasing ability to conceptualize alternatives.
- Experimenting with new behaviors.
- Starting to accept personal limitations.

COGNITIVE EXPECTATIONS

- Beginning to understand the process of making changes.

NOTE TO THE TEACHER

Trying on new behaviors or exploring alternative responses is usually the most difficult goal to attain. Surely it's unrealistic to expect all students to do this easily or often, without help. We all can see in our own behavior certain patterns (habits) which we seem to fully understand and yet are unable to change easily. Some of the most obvious patterns adults have in experimenting with alternatives includes: smoking, irritation with a boss or secretary, having difficulty getting up in the morning, etc. All of these are behaviors for which it's possible to think of alternative patterns. But actually experimenting with an alternative pattern is different from merely talking about it.

There are several different ways of introducing the notion of experimenting with alternative behavior patterns. It's a natural outgrowth of examining one's behavior patterns. Brainstorming alternatives in class is one way of coming up with a diversity of choices to a given behavioral pattern. Note that at first it is generally useful to focus on a class pattern rather than an individual pattern. Once alternatives have been explored, students can be asked to choose an alternative and try it.

Some discussion topics may center around such questions as: Is it hard to give up an old behavior pattern even for a one-time experiment? How will you feel if the new pattern doesn't work? What kind of person would you be if you never tried anything new? Activities such as role-playing and fantasy can often be helpful here.

If a self-science class has a pattern of boys sitting on one side, girls on the other, an alternative may be to sit boy/girl, boy/girl, etc. and then do some of the familiar activities of the class such as *Telephone Gossip, Indian Chief,* or *Trust Walk.* Trying on a group pattern provides students with the knowledge they are doing it together; this usually lends support for the trials.

Working on individual patterns is more difficult. *Patterns to Sell* (see Lesson 58) is one activity to employ to get students to experiment with new patterns. Role-reversal, a form of role-playing, can be used as a means of having students try on alternatives. For example, if each student identifies a typical way of responding in self-science class, the teacher can have each student assume the identity of another student. By playing a familiar game a student can experience what it's like to behave in another manner. Trying this kind of situation several times gives students some confidence about their ability to try on a new behavior in a more problematic situation.

Students need encouragement and support for trying on alternative behaviors. This support can be accomplished by overt praise from the teacher as well as by encouraging students to praise others and to express their feelings in relation to trying on alternative behaviors. Having the students express feelings about alternative behaviors is the beginning of the final and most important goal of evaluating behavior patterns.

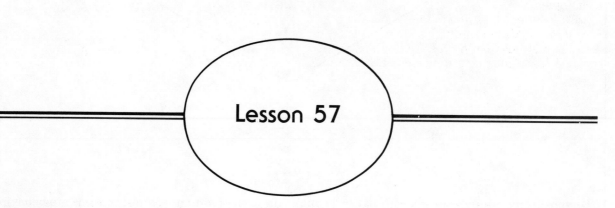

Lesson 57

MATERIALS
blank paper (for each student), Trumpet display

BEGINNING
Introduce and expand on the idea of alternative responses. (Read the introduction to this section.)

Review the parts of the Trumpet with special emphasis on alternative behaviors and choosing actions.

AFFECTIVE EXPERIENCE
• Complete the "Secrets" exercise.

COGNITIVE INQUIRY
Ask the questions to the *Secrets* experience as follows.

1. "Could you identify the secrets with the person who wrote them?"

2. "Did you think others identified your secret?"
3. "Was your secret consistent with your usual pattern of behavior?"
4. "Could you think of alternative behaviors for the secrets offered?"
5. "Were the secrets given more risky than those offered earlier in the year? Why do you suppose this happened?"

ASSIGNMENT
Tell the students, "Write two additional secrets in your journal and alternative behaviors you might have tried."

Teacher Comments

_____

_____

_____

_____

_____

_____

_____

_____

_____

_____

Secrets Game

This exercise is used for practice in trying on a new behavior.

PROCEDURES

Each person writes an unsigned secret on a blank piece of paper, folds it and drops it into a box. After the papers in the box are shuffled, each person draws a secret and keeps it folded until his turn comes.

The student then reads the secret aloud and continues talking/improvising as if the hopes, fears, aspirations, feelings of the writer were personal. If by chance a student opens his/her own secret, that individual may either pass or read it as if it were someone else's.

ACTIVITY

Discussion; journal entries.

DISCUSSION QUESTIONS

Ask the following questions.

1. "How did you feel when you heard your secret being read?"
2. "Did the reader react the same way you did?"
3. "How did you feel reliving someone else's secret?"

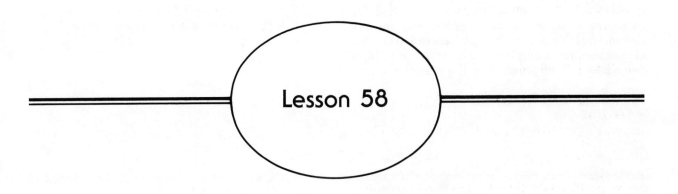

Lesson 58

MATERIALS

Trumpet display

BEGINNING

Discuss the *Secrets* and alternatives the students felt comfortable discussing in the group.

Have the students break up into triads and discuss with their friends less risky secrets and alternatives to their behaviors.

AFFECTIVE EXPERIENCE

• Play the *Patterns to Sell Game* (following).

COGNITIVE INQUIRY

Ask the questions to the *Patterns to Sell* experience as follows.

1. "How did your commercial compare to the others? Which commercials might you accept?"
2. "How do you go about considering alternatives? Is it easy to think about other options?"
3. "How does one choose one behavior over another? What is used when new behaviors are tried? Can anything be gained? Can anything be lost? What does it take to try a new behavior?"
4. "Can anyone help you do this?"
5. "How do you decide whether the new behavior is better than the old?"

ASSIGNMENT

None. Flow lesson to follow.

Teacher Comments _____

_____

_____

_____

_____

_____

Patterns to Sell Game*

This exercise is designed to be used for the "alternatives" and "choices" steps of the Trumpet, highlighting these steps.

PROCEDURE

Students are asked to make a commercial for their pattern similar to a Geritol commercial. Imagine your pattern as a medical potion. If someone were to take an amount of this potion, what would it do for them? Consequences of a pattern can be determined by listing dangerous side effects that must be written on the label of the potion.

ACTIVITY

Processing can be an integral part of writing the commercial if students answer for themselves the following process questions before writing the commercial. They can also get feedback from the class after presenting their commercial as to how people felt about purchasing the pattern.

*Lyn Wightman, graduate student, University of Massachusetts.

VARIATION

Students can design a commercial to present to the class in mock TV or radio presentations.

DISCUSSION QUESTIONS

Ask the students to think about the following questions when writing their commercials.

1. "What will this potion do for someone?"
2. "How much potion should be taken? How often?"
3. "What are its strongest selling points?"
4. "What would the warning label say?"
5. "What are some of the side effects of taking this potion?"
6. "How would the potion be packaged?"
7. "What would it sell for?"
8. "Is it cheap or expensive for someone to buy?"

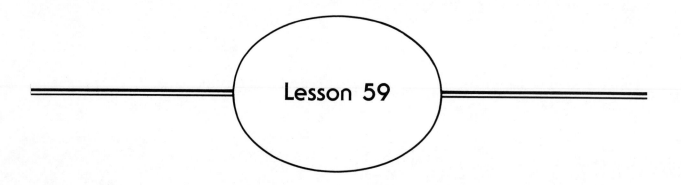

Lesson 59

MATERIALS
Trumpet display

FLOW LESSON
(See Appendix D, p. 161.)
(This is a good time to begin talking about disbanding the group.)

Teacher Comments _____

_____

_____

_____

_____

_____

_____

_____

_____

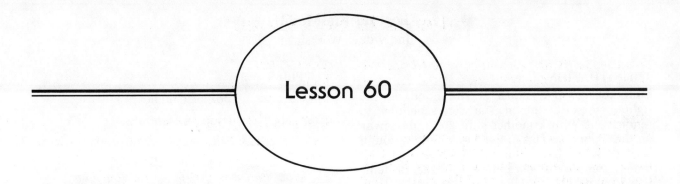

Lesson 60

MATERIALS

NASA Space Game (one for each student)

BEGINNING

Discuss idea of "choosing alternatives." Introduce the idea that sometimes it helps to talk with others about choices.

AFFECTIVE EXPERIENCE

• Play the "NASA Space Game."

COGNITIVE INQUIRY

Ask the questions to the "NASA Space Game" as follows.

1. "Does it help to talk over possible choices with other people?"

2. "When might it help? When might it not help?"
3. "With whom does a final decision or choice always rest? Who has responsibility for action? When do you think the best decisions are made?"
4. "How can the Trumpet process help in thinking through decisions?"
5. "Are some people reluctant to talk over problems with others? Why aren't all problems talked over with others?"

ASSIGNMENT

None.

Teacher Comments _____

_____

_____

NASA Space Game

This exercise is useful for expanding the learner's capacity to look at choices and to consider alternative actions. Further, the exercise is useful in helping the learner to at least consider talking over possible choices with others who may be helpful.

PROCEDURE

Pass out the NASA Game, one page to each learner (following). Direct the students to read, along with you, the directions to the game and then to complete the answer sheet on their own—individually and silently.

When they have completed the first part of the assignment, have them group into teams of five and then do their answers depending on the decision agreed to by the group.

ACTIVITIES

Read NASA answers (following). Have them compile their scores.

DISCUSSION QUESTIONS

Ask the following questions.

1. "Did you score as well when you made decisions by yourself as when you were working with other members of your team? How did you arrive at a decision for yourself? For members of the team?"
2. "Did it help to talk over possibilities with other people? How?"
3. "What did you do when as a team you couldn't agree on an answer?"
4. "Do all problems have a correct answer?"
5. "Was your behavior with the group similar to your usual behavior in groups?"
6. "What was helpful behavior on the part of others when group decisions were made?"

Lost on the Moon

Individual Worksheet

THE SITUATION

Your spaceship has just crash-landed on the lighted side of the moon. You were scheduled to rendezvous with a mother ship 200 miles away on the lighted surface of the moon, but the rough landing has ruined your ship and destroyed all the equipment on board, except for the 15 items listed below.

Due to technical difficulties the mother ship cannot come to you. You must go to it. Your crew's survival depends on reaching the mother ship, so you must choose the most critical items available for the 200-mile trip. Your task is to rank the 15 items in terms of their importance for survival. Place number one by the most important item, number two by the second most important, and so on through number 15, the least important.

SUPPLIES

_____ Box of matches

_____ Food concentrate

_____ Fifty feet of nylon rope

_____ Parachute silk

_____ Solar-powered portable heating unit

_____ Two .45 caliber pistols

_____ One case of dehydrated milk

_____ Two 100-pound tanks of oxygen

_____ Stellar map (of the moon's constellation)

_____ Self-inflating life raft

_____ Magnetic compass

_____ Five gallons of water

_____ Signal flares

_____ First aid kit containing injection needles

_____ Solar-powered FM receiver-transmitter

© 1978 Goodyear Publishing Co. from Karen Stone and Hal Dillehunt, Self-Science: The Subject Is Me.

Lost on the Moon

NASA Rating of Supplies
(To be completed by all group members)

Supply		NASA's Ranks	Your Rank	Error Points	Group Ranks	Error Points
Box of matches	No oxygen on moon to sustain flame; virtually worthless	15				
Food concentrate	Efficient means of supplying energy requirements	4				
Fifty feet of nylon rope	Useful in scaling cliffs, tying injured together	6				
Parachute silk	Protection from sun's rays	8				
Solar-powered portable heating unit	Not needed unless on dark side	13				
Two .45 caliber pistols	Possible means of self-propulsion	11				
One case of dehydrated milk	Bulkier duplication of food concentrate	12				
Two 100-pound tanks of oxygen	Most pressing survival need	1				
Stellar map (of the moon's constellation)	Primary means of navigation	3				
Self-inflating life raft	CO_2 bottle in military raft may be used for propulsion	9				
Magnetic compass	Magnetic field on moon is not polarized; worthless for navigation	14				
Five gallons of water	Replacement for tremendous liquid loss on lighted side	2				
Signal flares	Distress signal when mother ship is sighted	10				
First aid kit containing injection needles	Needles for vitamins, medicines, etc., will fit special aperture in NASA space suits	7				
Solar-powered FM receiver-transmitter	For communication with mother ship, but FM requires line-of-sight transmission and short ranges	5				
Totals			_____			_____

Error points are the absolute difference between your ranks and NASA's (disregard plus or minus signs)

© 1978 Goodyear Publishing Co. from Karen Stone and Hal Dillehunt, Self-Science: The Subject Is Me.

Winding Up Goals 6-10

The last four lessons are intended to consolidate the work done during the program and leave the students with an awareness of the tools they now possess and some sense of when the tools are useful.

GROUP BEHAVIOR

Now the group must make final preparation for terminating. You can aid this process by focusing on beginnings, middles, and endings, using the new tools. You may wish to schedule individual conferences for final evaluation.

EVIDENCE OF STUDENT GROWTH

Growth toward the goal will be demonstrated by the students as follows.

AFFECTIVE AND COGNITIVE EXPECTATIONS

- Moving toward a satisfying sense of accomplishment and closure.
- Lessons 61 to 64 are the culminating lessons for the self-science program. As with the end of Section 3, a party or some sort of informal get-together is a good way to end.
- The final lessons are flow lessons, left open to review and discuss program materials. Give special attention to those areas which may yet be unclear to the group.

NOTE TO THE TEACHER

This last and final step in the process of learning about self is in some ways the easiest goal, once the other goals have been internalized. In very simple terms this involves examining or comparing one's present and alternative behavior patterns through the use of the previous goals of self-sciencing.

Once a student has identified and examined current behavior patterns, explored the consequences and functions of these patterns, and experimented with alternative patterns, the learner needs to understand new behaviors in a similar manner. In this way, it's possible to enlarge the repertoire of available responses on any given situation. The idea, in many instances, is not to abandon one pattern in favor of another, but rather to increase the available responses. For example, let's assume a child's pattern is to hit her younger brother every time the brother sits in front of the television thereby blocking her view, and the consequence is to be denied television by her mother while the function is that she feels better. If she tries the alternative of moving her position (thereby being able to view the television and not getting into trouble with her mother) but not feel better in relation to her brother, she may decide to use her old pattern sometimes and the alternative at other times. She is able to choose and must choose, being aware of the alternatives available and the potential consequences of the alternatives.

This last goal of evaluation is primarily cognitive rather than experiential. That is, the last goal is to make the student conscious of how old and new behavior patterns serve.

In group discussions focusing on the evaluation stage, it is important that the teacher refrain from imposing personal value judgments; i.e., one pattern is better than the other. This is the job of the student. The teacher can facilitate this process using the kinds of questioning techniques described up to this point as well as some or all of the following: "How did your alternative pattern serve you? When you think back on your old pattern and the new one, was there any difference in the way they made you feel? What was the difference? Where did you feel it? Are there times when you think your old pattern might serve you better than your new one? Are there any other alternative behavior patterns?" All of these questions will generate discussions that help the student evaluate personal patterns of behavior.

When students are able to evaluate personal patterns of behavior and their alternative patterns of behavior, they are able to increase their own life direction. They have internalized the steps of the Trumpet process and are freer to choose how they will respond to others and to situations they encounter. The students have learned a tool, a tool which will help them better understand themselves.

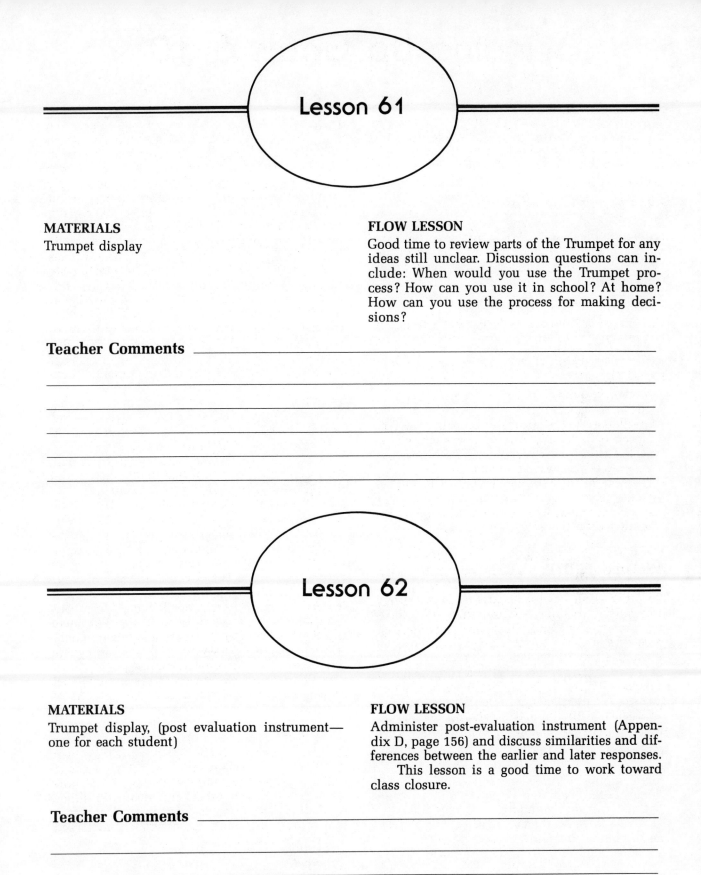

Lesson 61

MATERIALS
Trumpet display

FLOW LESSON
Good time to review parts of the Trumpet for any ideas still unclear. Discussion questions can include: When would you use the Trumpet process? How can you use it in school? At home? How can you use the process for making decisions?

Teacher Comments _____

_____

_____

_____

_____

_____

Lesson 62

MATERIALS
Trumpet display, (post evaluation instrument—one for each student)

FLOW LESSON
Administer post-evaluation instrument (Appendix D, page 156) and discuss similarities and differences between the earlier and later responses.

This lesson is a good time to work toward class closure.

Teacher Comments _____

_____

_____

_____

_____

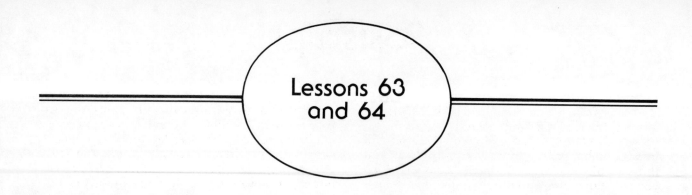

Lessons 63 and 64

MATERIALS
Trumpet display

FLOW LESSON
Final evaluation and informal activity.

Teacher Comments _____

_____

_____

_____

_____

_____

_____

_____

Notes from Nueva _____

Today we had a party. While we were eating we asked how everyone was feeling about ending self-sciencing. One reply was:

"Sob, don't put me in a bad mood. Wish we could keep on. It's the last time so it seems important. We can do it next year with the same group. I really like it."

We asked, "What have we done in here? How would you describe self-sciencing?"

The students replied, "We can discuss things—brainstorm. Neat when we could talk and play games—truthful—confidential. Things we did were exciting. Worth it because we did lots of different things and talked about lots of things. In the beginning we played a lot of games but now we can really talk with each other."

We said, "Would you like to have self-sciencing in the summer?"

Everyone said, "Yes."

We kept bringing up the ending of the group as there was a lot of resistance and denial. We stressed that this group is unique and although we will be a part of many groups, this particular group with these particular people is ending. The group reminded us to give "appreciates."

What are some words to describe self-sciencing?

fun	*killer statements*
body talk	*make friends*
explosion	*families*
truthful	*interesting*
interesting	*learning*
S.S. machine	*fears*
hearing/seeing	*friends*
appreciates	*embarrassing*
sciencing	*nonverbal*
education	*trusting*
Trumpet	*scary*
happy	*touching*
feelings	*great*
senses	*communication*
secrets	*consensus*
confidential	*daydreaming*

Postscript

How do you evaluate a student's skill in transforming internal data into cognitive concepts? If you think of a student as a computer, you can judge him/her solely by his output. Or, if you think of him/her as a bundle of behaviors, then you can judge him/her entirely in terms of behavior changes.

If you think of each student as a very special human being—a complex collection of feelings, thoughts, behaviors, experiences, information, and unknown qualities—then you're faced with a real problem. You can't very well write on a report card that you know a student is on the verge of being an independent learner because his/her eyes sparkle—or can you?

What about the music s/he hums while fiddling with an experiment? Or the day s/he forgot s/he was afraid to speak in front of the group?

In a way, evaluating these transformation processes is like evaluating a kindergartner's progress. You'll have to accumulate evidence in a variety of situations and in a variety of ways.

But then as teachers of self-science we are also learners. As the authors of self-science, we are opposed to giving grades for the program. Grades don't seem to be consistent with the goals of the program. If specific evaluations are required, however, we suggest the following criteria:

1. Did the learner come to know and understand the cognitive process of the Trumpet?
2. Did the learner participate actively in the course experiences and discussions?
3. Did the learner demonstrate changes in behavior?
4. Did the learner complete outside-of-class assignments?
5. Did the learner maintain confidential information?

Based upon the above criteria, the quality of individual student performances can be assessed by the teacher. A minimal response to these criteria should be satisfactory to parents. We suggest, however, that one additional input be considered—that of the student. Have each student write a half-page, personal evaluation on what was learned in self-science and append those comments to the teacher evaluations.

Appendixes

APPENDIX A
Values Clarification Exercises
(Should I or Shouldn't I?)

The experiments, discussion, and exercises in this appendix will help you to decide if you should choose to participate as a teacher of self-science. The values clarification forms which follow should be filled out now.

The purpose of values clarification is to help you capture your deepest, most immediate "gut" feelings, instead of giving a careful, studied response. Completion of these forms should take ten to twenty minutes.

Value Clarification Form 1

Are the Goals of Self-Science Philosophically Consistent With My Personal and the School's Values?

DIRECTIONS

Consider each of the four statements in support of self-science education. Answer each of the questions by circling the number on the continuum that most closely represents what you believe.

Continuum Key

Not at all.	If it wouldn't interfere with basic teaching-learning.	Might agree if more were understood.	Would agree as an ideal framework.	Would agree and wish to do something about it.
1	2	3	4	5

STATEMENT 1: Teaching-Learning About One's Self (Thoughts, Feelings, and Behaviors) is Legitimate in School.

Do I believe:

a. that teaching-learning about one's self is legitimate in school?

    1   2   3   4   5

b. students believe that teaching-learning about self is legitimate in school?

    1   2   3   4   5

c. other teachers in the school believe that teaching-learning about self is legitimate in school?

    1   2   3   4   5

d. the administration believes that teaching-learning about self is legitimate in school?

    1   2   3   4   5

e. parents believe that teaching-learning about self is legitimate in school?

    1   2   3   4   5

f. the Board of Education in the district believes that teaching-learning about self is legitimate in school?

    1   2   3   4   5

STATEMENT 2: Learning Words and Concepts for Negotiating Emotions is Important.

Do I believe:

a. that learning words and concepts for negotiating one's emotions is important?

    1   2   3   4   5

b. students believe that learning words and concepts for negotiating one's emotions is important?

    1   2   3   4   5

c. other teachers in the school believe that learning words and concepts for negotiating one's emotions is important?

    1   2   3   4   5

d. the administration in the school believes that learning words and concepts for negotiating one's emotions is important?

    1   2   3   4   5

e. parents in the school believe that learning words and concepts for negotiating one's emotions is important?

| | 1 | 2 | 3 | 4 | 5 |

f. the Board of Education in the district believes that learning words and concepts for negotiating one's emotions is important?

| | 1 | 2 | 3 | 4 | 5 |

STATEMENT 3: Learning Through Experience is Important.

Do I believe:

a. that learning through experience is important?

| | 1 | 2 | 3 | 4 | 5 |

b. students believe that learning through experience is important?

| | 1 | 2 | 3 | 4 | 5 |

c. other teachers in the school believe that learning through experience is important?

| | 1 | 2 | 3 | 4 | 5 |

d. the administration of the school believes that learning through experience is important?

| | 1 | 2 | 3 | 4 | 5 |

e. parents in the school believe that learning through experience is important?

| | 1 | 2 | 3 | 4 | 5 |

f. the Board of Education in the district believes that learning through experience is important?

| | 1 | 2 | 3 | 4 | 5 |

STATEMENT 4: Affective Awareness Can Contribute to Cognitive Growth.

Do I believe that:

a. affective awareness can contribute to cognitive growth?

| | 1 | 2 | 3 | 4 | 5 |

b. students believe that affective awareness can contribute to cognitive growth?

| | 1 | 2 | 3 | 4 | 5 |

c. other teachers in the school believe that affective awareness can contribute to cognitive growth?

| | 1 | 2 | 3 | 4 | 5 |

d. the administration in the school believes that affective awareness can contribute to cognitive growth?

| | 1 | 2 | 3 | 4 | 5 |

e. parents in the school believe that affective awareness can contribute to cognitive growth?

| | 1 | 2 | 3 | 4 | 5 |

f. the Board of Education in the district believes that affective awareness can contribute to cognitive growth?

| | 1 | 2 | 3 | 4 | 5 |

Now enter your answers on the following *Profile of Beliefs.*

Value Clarification Form 2

Profile of Beliefs

	Continuum				
	1	2	3	4	5
My Beliefs:					
Statement 1-a					
Statement 2-a					
Statement 3-a					
Statement 4-a					
What I Believe Students Believe:					
Statement 1-b					
Statement 2-b					
Statement 3-b					
Statement 4-b					
What I Believe Other Teachers Believe:					
Statement 1-c					
Statement 2-c					
Statement 3-c					
Statement 4-c					
What I Believe the School Administration Believes:					
Statement 1-d					
Statement 2-d					
Statement 3-d					
Statement 4-d					
What I Believe Parents Believe:					
Statement 1-e					
Statement 2-e					
Statement 3-e					
Statement 4-e					
What I Believe the Board of Education Believes:					
Statement 1-f					
Statement 2-f					
Statement 3-f					
Statement 4-f					

DISCUSSION

When the profile is completed, pause for a moment to consider how you felt as you were reading the statements.

Did you feel the questions surfaced any observations of value?

Did you feel silly?

Did you feel you were wasting your time?

Did you enjoy being a "Self-Scientist"?

There are, of course, no right answers to these questions. The questions were intended to demonstrate a fifth statement about Self-Science education; e.g., observing the process of an experience is an important tool for affective and cognitive learning.

ANALYZING THE PROFILE

Your profile gives you visible evidence of personal beliefs about self, as well as your perceptions about the beliefs of students, other teachers, the school administration, parents, and the Board of Education.

Statement 1 was intended to elicit your general feelings about including affective learning in school. Statement 2 was meant to elicit the weight you give to the need for affective awareness, whether in school or not. Statement 3 was intended to help you analyze your views on teaching methods. Statement 4 was meant to assist you in determining how you see the relationship between the affective and cognitive domains. An analysis of the Profile should help you both determine your course of action and identify problems to tackle.

If, as often happens, you charted your own beliefs at 3, 4, or 5, but charted the beliefs of *others* at 3 or below, this means you believe the environment for accepting self-science is less than totally positive. Respect this! Your perception is an important reality. We recommend against attempting self-science classes until you have reason to believe the climate will be supportive. Before "going ahead" you may wish to spend energies sharing the ideas of humanistic education with others in a nonjudgmental and respectful manner, perhaps helping them reconsider.

If most of your answers were charted at 3 or above, you probably have a favorable environment for introducing self-science. Perhaps you identified one group (e.g., board of education) at the 1 or 2 spot with the rest of your chart at 3 or above. This should indicate to you where some energies might be spent in "consciousness raising" as you proceed. If most of your answers were charted at 3 or below, you probably should not attempt self-science at this time.

The Profile also helps you evaluate your beliefs. If you charted a 2 or 3 to any statement, you may want to do further thinking, reading, or discussing in an effort to strengthen your value on that assumption.

Do I Have the Leadership Qualifications to Teach Self-Science?

Probably! This activity, though, is designed to have you experience the conscious process of identifying your patterns, just as later you may help children find some of their own patterns.

Step 1: List the personal qualities or characteristics you believe a good teacher should have. List as many as you think are important, up to 9.

1. _____
2. _____
3. _____
4. _____
5. _____
6. _____
7. _____
8. _____
9. _____

Step 2: Read the discussion of leadership qualifications on the following pages. As you read, check off any duplications which also appear on your list. (NOTE: This is not meant to be a "test," nor to create anxieties. Try to postpone your conclusions until the exercise is completed.)

LEADERSHIP QUALITIES

These leadership qualities were evolved from a series of brainstorming sessions with children and teachers alike at various workshops sponsored by the authors of the self-science curriculum. We specifically asked, "What are the qualities or characteristics needed for a good self-science leader?" The qualities seemed to divide into two main categories: qualities pertaining to self, and qualities of self with others.

A. Qualities Pertaining to Self
  1. *Liking Children*—interested; experiencing joy in children's learning and growing; being child-centered rather than subject-centered.
  2. *Self-Knowledge*—the more you know about yourself, the greater your ability to help children learn about themselves. Knowledge of self leads to deeper personal understanding about the "essence" of life, personal needs, and perhaps the tricks you play on yourself.
  3. *Openness*—the willingness to share your feelings and thoughts; the willingness to say, "I don't know." Children take many cues from their leader. If you share only on a superficial level, so will children. Being open fosters a sense of trust because there are no hidden surprises. Being open also implies being open to new learning for self.

B. Qualities of Self with Others
  4. *Warmth*—friendly, having a good sense of humor. Obviously it would be unrealistic to feel warmly toward all people. What is meant is a basic approach toward others in a warm, caring manner; being relaxed in most situations, helping others feel relaxed.
  5. *Acceptance*—accepting oneself and others; acknowledging the feelings of self and others as valid; accepting the good and bad in all of us; possessing a willingness to stand up for the child; having the ability to listen. This does *not* mean approving the behavior of a child who is disrupting a class.
  6. *Supportiveness*—being nondefensive, trustworthy. A teacher helping children learn something new, particularly about self, must be free to give support. A child needs to feel the support power in order to gain the security to venture into the unknown—a truism for people generally.

7. *Flexibility*—being able to alter a course of action is highly important. In part this means being able to flow with the mood of the class, being able to respond constructively to the unexpected. Imagine, for example, that a class is progressing smoothly toward a positive group feeling, a cohesiveness. The teacher has planned several activities to enhance this. Just before the class meeting two members have a fight. A teacher who is flexible enough to alter plans and deal with the problem of the fight will help the students to proceed positively. Being flexible allows the teacher to modulate the fine line between directiveness and nondirectiveness.

8. *Sensitivity*—being perceptive to what is going on with individual members of the class and to how their behavior is affecting the class. Sensitivity also implies being perceptive to self, your own feelings, and how they may be affecting the class. Sensitivity allows one to be a keen observer of the moment, the "here-and-now."

9. *Respect*—letting kids figure things out for themselves, listening to children. A basic respect for the individual frees the leader both to better examine self and to help the children examine themselves. This is an earned quality resulting in a mutual positive trust between students and teacher.

Step 3: After you have read the self-science qualities suggested, compare them to your original list. How many qualities showed up on both lists? At this point, we ask you to refrain from being judgmental about self-science *unless* you found *no* similarities between the two lists. In this case, it may be that you are subject-oriented and obviously committed to other aspects of education which you enjoy. This is one instance where we believe you would not enjoy teaching self-science and therefore should not proceed.

Step 4: Up to this point, you have experienced the process for identifying teacher qualities in self-science teachers in general. There are, in addition, steps to permit you to examine yourself more closely. (In case you may be wondering why there was no further discussion of the comparison at Step Three, it's because more generalizing wasn't necessary then.) Whether your list matched many or few items, or whether your list was particularly short is less important than how you now evaluate yourself on the basis of all the qualities mentioned.

A. On a separate piece of paper, make a list of the leadership qualifications from your list plus any additional items from the Nueva list: i.e., list the items which compare similarly only once. You may have a list of approximately nine to seventeen items. On a continuum of 0 to 10 (0 = poor; 10 = best) rate yourself in terms of the qualities listed.

B. Choose the item with the lowest rating and list five conditions or things you think you could do to improve that quality in yourself.

C. Of those five things you listed, ask yourself, "Over which ones do I have power?" You, too, will grow from your involvement in the self-science curriculum. Should you decide to proceed and after you've worked through the curriculum, reevaluate your own personal qualities, using the same check sheet, to see how much growth you've made.

D. Plan to work in those areas where you feel you have power.

DISCUSSION

Were you surprised in any way at your findings? Did you notice teaching qualities usually listed, such as ability to control and discipline the class, were omitted from the Nueva list? (In a self-science group, control and discipline techniques are rarely needed. They are discussed simply as "tools" in Appendix C, Useful Teaching Techniques).

Did you feel discouraged if few of your items matched? Are you willing to open yourself to expanding those qualities on which you rated yourself lowest? These are samples of questions to consider as part of your quest for self-knowledge.

We urge you not to feel discouraged or judgmental with your own ratings. Try to accept the view that previous expectations (e.g., of "perfection") can often cloud the self-science understandings of "This is who I am (in a specific situation) . . . this is what I think I know how to do . . . this is what I don't think I know how to do . . . this is what I *want* to do."

Now you should be able to make a more thoughtful decision about your next action; i.e., go . . . no go!

APPENDIX B
Getting Started

GAINING ACCEPTANCE FOR THE SELF-SCIENCE CURRICULUM WITHIN THE SCHOOL

The approach one takes in initiating a self-science curriculum naturally depends upon the particular structure and limitations of the school and/or school district. Needless to say, introducing an affective curriculum can and often is a risky endeavor. You must intuitively assess the potential level of acceptance by the superintendent, principal, fellow teachers, other staff, parents and, of course, students. Depending upon the particular situation, it is probably best to do some informal surveying of colleagues before making any formal presentation.

There are two kinds of support to be looked for in terms of informal surveying of colleagues; both are important and necessary for the success of the program and your sense of well-being. The first support to be assessed relates to colleagues' general awareness and feeling of importance for affective development. Find out both who thinks affective education is important and who thinks it is not important and who thinks it should not be taught in school. There are shades of grey between these poles: you need to find out where the greatest opposition as well as support rests. You should, for example, consider carefully whether or not you can carry through with self-science if the principal is opposed, or if other staff members are opposed.

The second support to be assessed relates to who else on the staff is willing to try such an endeavor. This support is very important, as it will likely influence the success of the self-science classes with the students and parents. Be sure to talk with the school psychologists; they often possess valuable skills, as well as status, and can be very helpful in insuring a fair test of the curriculum.

Assuming that you receive sufficient support to proceed, plan to make a formal presentation about self-science. There are several alternatives for doing this.

One alternative is to bring in an outside expert in self-science to do the presentation. This provides you with some degree of psychological safety, as well as opening up a relationship between the staff and a recognized authority in the field.

If you can't manage this, give a joint presentation with other interested teachers. Structure your presentation around the ideas presented earlier in the book, bearing in mind:

1. That you need to adopt a nondefensive, open attitude toward colleagues in the school. If you know where criticism comes from, you may be able to do something about it.
2. That much criticism of humanistic education as too open-ended and meaningless is legitimate. Understand and communicate that self-science uses humanistic, experiential materials at the beginning of lessons to generate data, but that the program moves on to provide cognitive inquiry and closure, unlike most other affective programs. Self-science has a structure and a sequence, with evaluation procedures built-in. Self-science provides a genuine educational experience in learning about learning.
3. That you let colleagues know you will welcome feedback as you go along, setting aside times for input, such as information about a student's eagerness or resistance to attend self-science.
4. That homework assignments are of an interdisciplinary nature, involving reading, writing, math, research, drawing, etc. Invite interested teachers in the core subjects to coordinate with you on these assignments.
5. That confidentiality is one of the self-science ground rules because confidence builds trust. Within this framework, solicit input from your colleagues.

INTRODUCING SELF-SCIENCE EDUCATION TO PARENTS

When you have gained the support of your school's administration and faculty, inform parents about this new subject, self-science.

Understand that in most school settings, the introduction of a new subject matter to the curriculum is always greeted by parents with a variety of responses: those totally opposed; those mildly curious or apprehensive; those strongly supportive and enthusiastic.

Knowing this, you will want to determine how to communicate about self-science as clearly, nondefensively and persuasively as you can. Points to be made are that self-science:

—is an elective (option);
—offers students a chance to develop basic skills and tools for learning beyond the basic subject matter skills of other classes;
—is concerned with preparing students to use their existing skills in situations that concern them now, as students, and which will be of concern all their adult lives; e.g., solving problems, taking responsibility for their own learning and behavior, communicating with others, coping with changes, making vocational and personal choices;
—uses the methods of scientific inquiry to teach students to see themselves both as individuals and as parts of a group, including opportunities to learn about their own learning styles and study habits;
—is *not* a course in psychology, nor a place to bring emotional problems;
—*is* derived from a wealth of proven information in educational theory, learning theory and child development, as well as from several years of testing and application within school situations.

These ideas are best communicated face-to-face; an evening meeting with twenty to twenty-five people attending is ideal. A group which is too large makes it difficult to have good discussions.

If a small meeting isn't practical, consider scheduling a series of meetings, or making a brief introduction at a large meeting, such as the usual PTA evening early in the semester; invite interested parents to a subsequent workshop.

Meetings can be called by letter or telephone. Mentally assess the attitudes and interests of your parent community to determine what presentation style will be most effective for them.

If you decide to send a written invitation, we suggest you describe the course briefly and invite feedback by enclosing a short questionnaire and a self-addressed stamped envelope. We have used the questions below and have found them useful.

---

1. Would you be willing to meet and discuss self-science in greater detail?

   _____

2. Which of the following dates would be best for you? (Circle best date)

   _____   _____   _____

3. What, if any, are your concerns about this new class? (Any questions raised will be answered at the meeting and discussed anonymously.)

   _____

   _____

This last question is open-ended and gives you an opportunity to assess the general parental attitudes and concerns. Parent responses should help you prepare answers for the meeting.

If having parents write questions seems too impersonal to you, or if it would contradict the teacher-parent climate of your school, have paper and pencils available at the initial presentation so parents can write anonymous questions.

The meeting itself will take shape according to your assessment of the parents with whom you are meeting. Some groups of parents will want only a formal presentation with a question and answer period; others will welcome participation in an experiential learning situation, such as one of the games in the curriculum. Most important: parents should feel comfortable and nonthreatened by your presentation.

One of the major things to accomplish at the presentation is to let parents know you are on their side, that you understand their concerns. They want to be reassured that this new subject will not be threatening to them personally, nor to their value systems and life styles. Answer any questions raised on the parent questionnaire. Here are our answers to four common questions:

Q1. Is self-science really important to the education of my child?
A—Yes. In the teaching-learning process, there are not enough chances to focus on the learner and the learning processes. By setting aside a small amount of time each week to help students study themselves, there will be short-term and long-term benefits. We believe that children who take self-science will show more active participation in school life, a greater sense of responsibility, and greater self-confidence.

Q2. What happens if my child reveals personal family matters?

A—All of our games and experiences are designed to help the learner become aware of personal patterns and responses, how they serve him or her, and what the consequences are. We discuss similarities and differences within the peer group. We guide discussions in such a way that we do not talk about people who are not present. We might, however, discuss how our mother or father responds to us when we hit our brother or sister in anger. This helps children understand that behavior and responses have consequences.

When we are learning about our patterns for expressing anger or happiness and exploring alternative ways of being, we might discuss how we've observed our friends, our teachers, members of our family responding. Through these kinds of observations we can enrich our own alternatives. But the real focus on self-science is "self," and we focus our efforts toward understanding ourselves and our own behaviors.

Q3. Why can't I as a parent observe? Why is confidentiality a part of the class?

A—Crucial to the group are the feelings of mutual respect, acceptance and trust. Without these feelings, there is little, if any, chance students will feel comfortable enough to participate fully.

Confidentiality is important to the children. Few children are willing to reveal that they are afraid of the dark, have a nickname they hate, the fact that they still have stuffed animals they love, or a problem with a friend, unless they know all other members of the group will keep this information confidential. Few children are willing to try new ways when someone strange is watching.

There is certainly no objection to your children telling you all about the experience and activities *they* have in self-science class and their *own* responses. We only request that they keep others' responses confidential. Children enjoy knowing they are trustworthy and able to trust others.

Incidentally, as the group matures, at a later point, the group may come to a consensus about visitors—yes or no. If you wish to attend the class, ask your child to take the matter up with the group.

Q4. What happens if a child reveals deep personal problems?

A—Self-science is not designed as therapy and is not intended to deal with serious emotional disturbances. In the experience of the people who have written this curriculum, deep-seated personal problems have never been revealed.

The focus of self-science is to teach cognitive processes for recognizing and coping with internal states, and not the revelation of unconscious conflicts.

If such a situation were to occur, the teachers would attempt to work with the child individually in the immediate situation, as well as consult with the principal, school psychologist (if any), and parents, following essentially the same procedures if the concern were noted during language arts, math, or recess time.

INTRODUCING SELF-SCIENCE TO STUDENTS

Self-science is usually a voluntary elective for students, whether offered as a separate course or included as a mini-course within subject-areas.*

Before a student can volunteer to take the course with any degree of understanding, it is important to provide some kind of introductory explanation. This can be done in several ways—through a presentation in the student's homeroom, during another class time, or by invitation to the self-science classroom at noon or after school.

When visiting another classroom, ask the core teacher to give you twenty to thirty minutes for a demonstration lesson. (You might also consider bagging two birds with one stone by inviting a few "reluctant" teachers to sit in.)

As with the presentations to other teachers and parents, your tone should be as low-key and easy as possible. You are not trying to "sell" the course, nor are you trying to attract the more difficult students who may think this is an invitation to "goof-off."

Again, as with the other presentations, determine the style of presentation by the attitudes and interests of the students, and, in this case, a recognition of the students' ages and class level. With older students you may want to make some of the same points you made with the parents; such as that self-science is a laboratory of the world they live in, where people must solve problems, deal with change, and communicate.

The presentation should offer the students some degree of involvement. It should be fun and low in risk. Explanations should be simple and direct, enhancing as much student participation as possible.

SAMPLE SUGGESTIONS FOR PRESENTATIONS TO STUDENT

Begin the presentation by introducing yourself and then playing the "Bumpety-Bump" game (p. 20) from the program. Start the game with names. Play the variations if the climate permits. This game is usually viewed as fun, provides movement and involvement among the students and allows everyone to participate. (Allow about ten minutes.)

---

*For classroom management where self-science is given as a mini-course within the subject area: students electing *not* to take self-science might do individualized work (e.g., research, skills development) in the library. Students should not feel penalized or rewarded in any way for making or not making a voluntary choice to take self-science.

Once the game is completed, have the students sit down, preferably in a circle, or comfortably within hearing distance. Begin the more formal aspects of the presentation. Ask the students if they enjoyed the game. Ask them if they observed anything about the way they, or others, played the game.

If the students resist the discussion or indicate that they thought the game was silly, agree with and support their perceptions. One of the major things to be accomplished in this presentation is to let the students know that you are on their side—that you see the world as they do. If the game seemed silly to them, use this information to support self-science; Point out that they just used one of the tools of self-science—observation—to find out what they felt and thought about something.

Knowing what *you* think or feel about something is important in forming judgments and making decisions.

If somebody *didn't* think the game was silly but went along with the group anyway, *that* would be an important thing for that person to know. Doing things and then talking about them is one of the things we do in self-science.

If the students get into a positive discussion, follow up with a "closure" by pointing out the action of doing something and then talking about it.

Present the basic ideas of self-science to the students; i.e., that it is a study of self, we are the subject matter; that we learn about how we act and react as people, how we feel, how we learn. To do this, a variety of games and experiences is used. As with the "Bumpety-Bump" game, games and experiences give us information for knowing and understanding ourselves better.

Some students may have difficulty conceptualizing a course in which oneself is the subject of investigations. If this seems to be the case, use the brainstorming technique to elicit a list of what might be studied about "self."

Ask, "What could we learn about ourselves?" A list might start with externals such as height, color of hair, eyes, or skins; move on to learning how we are alike and/or different; what we like or don't like to eat, wear, see, smell, hear; feelings we all share; what we do when we're happy; what we think when we're scared; how we behave when we feel good about ourselves; how others react when we're nice or angry.

A long list on the chalkboard demonstrates to the group the endless possibilities self provides as subject matter. *How* we learn these things and *why* they are important are parts of the self-science course.

Finally, the presentation should describe the particulars of the class; e.g., time, place, length, homework assignments, etc. Students may feel more comfortable about enrolling if they are allowed some time before making a commitment.

Students need an opportunity to ask their questions and express concerns about the course. You may wish to make note of their concerns and use the material as topics for the unstructured flow lesson, discussed in the section prior to the actual lessons.

Close the presentation with one of the games from the program, such as the "Telephone Gossip Chain" (see p. 29).

APPENDIX C
Useful Teaching Techniques

GROUP BEHAVIOR

Self-science involves a group; it is a people-centered curriculum. Much of the content comes from the members of the group and, in order to attain the curriculum goals, the collective individuals must progress through various states of group growth. Progressing through these stages —with constant awareness and discussion— is part of the self-science learning.

The stages are indicated as much as possible in the lesson plans, but your general awareness *that* a group develops and grows helps you in terms of your own expectations and demands.

Formal groups usually have beginnings, middles, and endings. With self-science there is also a preforming time when you will be communicating about the subject of self-science to potential students, other teachers, parents, and administrators. Suggestions for the pre-session time are given in Appendix B.

The beginning stage of the group is a slow, maturing process. Members are usually anxious. They question; they do not immediately feel a group solidarity; they are discovering the purposes for their meetings.

Students feel each other out, building a feeling of security in their relationships with one another. During this time, students begin gravitating toward particular other students, forming alliances or subgroups.

This is a critical stage of growth; children need to feel the support of at least one other student to begin exploring themselves. Alliances should be allowed to develop. Alliances, however, can become detrimental to the group's work if they are allowed to become exclusive over long periods of time.

Encourage members of the alliances to relate to other members of the group, once security has been found. Ask students to choose different partners in various games and activities.

Our experiences have shown that the strongest alliances develop among children of the same sex. Bridging these alliances is often difficult; we have been most successful when we have attempted to make the bridge approximately midway through the program.

Rely on your intuition as to the best time to begin bridging the alliances between sexes. You can early on make an effort to choose partners from both sexes. Also choose leaders from each sex to work with you as partners in some of the activities. Children you identify as leaders can be extremely helpful! These children are usually the most likely to cooperate; they are probably the most secure within their peer group. Shy or retiring students are more likely to cooperate once peer leaders have agreed to participate.

Group cohesiveness, a group life, and group work will emerge when students are relatively secure.

Part of establishing cohesiveness is establishing trust. Trust is dealt with quite consciously in the lessons (6 to 11) of Goal Two, where specific ground rules for confidentiality are discussed quite thoroughly. Seeking trust, however, is a never-ending effort. You will be dealing with the building of trust from start to finish. After all, the deeper levels of trust permit deeper and deeper personal exploration, the essence of self-science.

The middle stage of the group process proceeds, roughly, through two levels:

1. At first, students will explore similarities and differences among themselves, focusing on similarities. Students find out if other members of their group have similar family backgrounds and experiences, similar fears, similar hopes, similar tastes in food. Emphasize similarities at this point because "similarity" sharing is safer emotionally.

You can strengthen your "pilgrims' progress" at this point by focusing on positive attitudes expressed by one student for another; i.e., encouraging students to work in a supportive constructive manner rather than a competitive-destructive manner. Again, lessons and games will help you accomplish this.

2. Students, after they feel relatively safe in the group, are then ready to move to the next level, which involves greater self-exploration. Focus is on the differences among group members and the personal meanings of these differences. Here, you assure and reassure the group that we are all positively and uniquely different from others in at least some ways. You will point out the "similarity of our differences."

During this middle-stage, your sensitivity to the students' needs for belonging helps keep the group in balance. Guide discussion and activities so that each member reveals a similar degree of information about self. This procedure avoids the possibility of one student's feeling s/he revealed too much, or another student's feeling inadequate because s/he couldn't reveal as much.

Somewhere during all this, there is a point when members need to rebel and test, either you or others. Be listening for expressions of hostility and expect that with some openness and support from you, it will pass. Hostility provides a safety valve. In some ways, it's your clue that the process is working. Indifferent people don't usually waste time testing. A "storm before the calm" can be read as a need to feel accepted in all ways, and thus safe.

When we say accept the testing and don't reject the students doing the testing, we do *not* mean to allow a few to disrupt the group. (Some specific tactics are suggested in the next section on group dynamics.) Recognize that the feelings generated are real without escalating or counterattacking on your part. You may want to try to discover the causes of the rebelling and confront them consciously at a later point. You may decide to ride it out. If your communication with the group seems relatively open (and only you can be the judge of that), you may want to propose that the group become aware of and deal with the hostility, with your guidance.

As all these diverse explorations take place, the major work of self-knowledge is occurring. Students are acquiring the tools for examining themselves, their feelings, their patterns of response to others, their study and learning styles.

The final stage of the group is, naturally, termination. It is the ending, symbolically representing death. Children as well as adults usually have difficulty dealing with endings. Our experience has been that children in self-science classes resist talking about the end of the class. Although you shouldn't force it, you would be wise to begin mentioning ending at least one month before the last meeting. We discuss endings in other situations and how they are like beginnings in some ways, to help the group deal with the termination of their class and recognize their own response to the ending.

This then is the developmental growth you may expect from your group. Be aware, not every group proceeds to the same level or at the same rate. Nor is the progression even. Expect to spend at least half of a year's course establishing the climate and trust described.

GROUP DYNAMICS AND "DISCIPLINE"

How the group flows in stages—the group growth—is one kind of awareness you need to know. Another is understanding how to deal with the various kinds of interactions within the group on any particular day—group dynamics.

In a more traditional setting, we might now be talking about "discipline"; indeed, group dynamics can include discipline, but what we're after here is a style of classroom management that can demonstrate the spirit of self-science.

The discussion here goes beyond the concept of teacher as role model. The spirit of self-science means executing the ideals of respect and trust in very specific ways.

> We must make sure we help the kids feel their experiences, ideas, and what's happening to them is important . . . to build self-awareness and self-esteem, they must value their experiences.*

One way to help children feel important is to share problems with them. So, in general, the daily logistics and squabbles and interruptions might best be ping-ponged to the group for solutions. They may or may not be able to handle this, but then you are there to help "rescue" with suggestions.

> Before the game began, Henry created a diversion by leaving the circle. We discussed his want to sit next to Andrew, and the group offered alternative ways to have this happen. When Henry finally joined us, he was upset that we seemed to show anger towards him. We talked it out and then went back to the game.*

Reassurance is another way. You will spend the first several lessons establishing ground rules with the children, both to make them seem comfortable and to establish limits. These are spelled out quite thoroughly in the lessons, but they will need reinforcing as you go along. The ground rule of being able to "pass" if you don't feel like participating in an activity is, for example, important to encourage shyer children. Group consensus is another ground rule that removes you from being the constant "authority," putting responsibility on the children, reassuring them by involving them.

> Millie wanted to play *Explode*. Several others said, "No." I suggested that anyone who wanted to play should get up, and the rest of us would watch. Only Millie and Jenny got up, so they decided not to play.*

Challenge is another tool to use. "Don't agree (to do something) unless you really want to listen!"

These are general approaches. There may be times when you'll be faced with a great deal of attention-getting, bossy or disruptive behavior, or when the group mood (high, low, intense, noisy) is such that the children are really asking for

---

*The excerpts in this chapter noted by (*) are examples of the authors' and other teachers' experiences who have used the self-science curriculum with their students.

some kind of direction. We have found the following techniques to be extremely useful:

What are you doing right now? This is asking the students to observe their own behavior, and in the observing to come to the conclusion that there might be another way to behave.

Throughout the group Bill and John were at each other (poking, touching, pulling, wrestling). I frequently asked them, "What are you doing right now? How does it make you feel?" They'd get in touch with their disruptive behavior and stop fooling around; two minutes later they'd be doing it again. I decided to spend the last ten minutes talking with everyone about this. I asked the boys if they often did this, and they "didn't know." The group agreed that they did. We talked about patterns and they finally agreed that it was a pattern. We agreed to talk about their pattern at our next Flow Lesson.*

Be Somebody Else. Whenever there is a conflict or difference of opinion in the class so emotional or involving that the participants find it hard to be rational, ask them to imagine ("See in your head." "Hear in your head.") being the other person. Ask yourself the question (as the other person), "What do I need right now?" If the arguers can, have them take the role of the other person. See if they can see themselves and the situation from the other side.

The Freezing Game. This is a stronger version of, "What are you doing now?" for any kind of intense group behavior. You call out, "Freeze!" Insist that everyone stop and stay frozen in position. Then direct the children to observe themselves, asking them to think about what was happening. When you say, "Unfreeze," generally the group will be calmer and willing to reflect.

Maurice, Jack, Art and Tom have problems. Art refuses to play when we switch and have boy/girl partners. He goes inside. There was a lot of fooling around today (during the *Trust Walk*) from the four of them. At the end of the Walk the boys were (in my opinion) expressing a lot of their anxiety in aggressive, fooling-around ways. I asked them to "Freeze!"

Sit down and think. Was it hard to Trust?
    Yes? Sometimes? A little?
What were you just doing?
    Fooling around? Pushing? Not listening?
How do you act when you're anxious about something?
    Silly? Afraid?
Do you think you felt anxious about the *Trust Walk*?
    Yes?
What do you get from self-science?
    You learn about yourself and other people?

Let's talk about this more next week. We need to go now. I want you to remember what we do in self-science. We don't just play games. We also talk and think about the game we play. Okay, Unfreeze.*

Labelling the Behavior as Unacceptable. Sometimes just your labelling is enough to deal with the behavior. As with any other kind of labelling,

name the specific behavior; avoid generalizing. If the disruptive behavior continues, ask for group consensus on how to handle it. Negotiate, using your own feelings; e.g., "I don't like it when Sam keeps interrupting. I appreciate it when others respect my feelings. What will you do about it?"

Games to Blow Off Steam. Sometimes the energy level of the group is so high, trying to work against it is counterproductive. Energy-reducing games help clear the air. They also serve the purpose of helping students become more aware of their feelings, and as such, are used formally in some of the lessons, i.e., Approaching Goal 3.

The Screaming Game. Sit, stand, or look in a mirror. Ask the students to scream as loud as they can . . . scream without sound . . . scream with a whisper . . . scream with their bodies . . . scream like their teacher . . . scream because they are mad, excited, scared, happy. If a child can't participate, reduce the risk level until s/he can . . . scream silently . . . scream like a mouse . . . scream in the littlest voice you have.

Explode. This is a tag game. You or an appointed leader are It. Whomever the leader tags must "explode!" . . . i.e., scream, jump, fall, growl, whatever; to the degree the student wants to ventilate feelings.

Choose these techniques as the situation seems to demand. By accepting the premise that a great deal of learning goes on through these techniques, you may feel less frustrated if a planned lesson gets interrupted. You don't have to "go" with the group feeling at all times. Sometimes ignoring it will help it to pass; this on-the-spot decision is much like taking mental temperatures.

USING AFFECTIVE EXPERIENTIAL TECHNIQUES

Certain psychological techniques are extremely useful for the affective experience which is part of every lesson. These are simple to learn and practice: retain them in your bag of self-science teaching tools until needed. (Lesson plans tell you when to use the techniques for specific purposes.)

Brainstorming. This technique is used to elicit spontaneous ideas from the group. It is used throughout the curriculum to generate data, to catalogue, and to problem-solve.

When brainstorming, you and/or a volunteer should stand at the chalkboard and invite the group to call out ideas as quickly as possible. Write them down. Stop when the group appears to have exhausted their responses. An occasional idea from you from time-to-time may respark the group.

When you first present the concept of brainstorming, stress that any thought, no matter how wild or harebrained, is important. Let the group experience the surfacing of ideas without prejudging them. Accepting and praising will help reinforce the point that there are no right or wrong suggestions.

An interesting byproduct of brainstorming is the group's strong sense of satisfaction and amazement at their own creativity.

"We didn't know we knew so much!"*

Role-Playing. This technique is used to create a safe (relatively anxiety-free) tool for self-awareness and sensitivity to others; seeing the other's point of view; spotting patterns.

Role-playing is a dramatic situation in which two or more children enact by taking "roles," by pretending, by improvising the situation. Topics which lend themselves best to role-playing are visually controversial and/or emotionally laden areas which can be examined with less threat in a play-acting situation.

Role-playing provides valuable grist for follow-up discussions. Topics for role-playing and discussion are suggested throughout the self-science program. The unstructured Flow Lessons also offer opportunities for role-playing.

These simple approaches often help role-playing to be stimulating experiences:

> Start by choosing the players and structuring the situation. "Jimmy, you be yourself at breakfast this morning. Vicky, you be Jimmy's mother. Show us how you two get into a fight because Jimmy hasn't cleaned his room." Or, "Tony, you be me. Billy, Jenny—you two don't feel like doing anything in the group today. As a matter of fact, you're sitting around making faces at the rest of us. Tony, you handle it. Go."

Keep the period of role-playing brief. You may at times want other teams to role-play the same topic.

Effectiveness is also aided by how you cast the players. When the goal is to generate self-awareness, a student might best play him/herself and then have the opportunity of seeing other students playing that role, too. When the goal is to aid students in seeing other points of view, cast a student in a role directly in conflict with his/her own position—i.e., *role reversal.*

Labelling situations as "role-playing" is not important. Often the group finds a favorite situation, such as role-playing an authority figure, and refer to the technique as a game; e.g., *The Mr. Alberti Game*," "*The Mad at Dad Game*."

Fantasizing. This resembles role-playing because it requires using imagination. But rather than acting out with others, fantasizing is generally a quiet activity, inner-directed, a useful technique for generating imagery and an awareness of internal states.

The value of fantasy is not to be underestimated.† A child's ability to discriminate between real and unreal states is heightened by experiencing fantasy in an accepting climate. The television-conditioned student, particularly, has been exposed to other people's imagination and imagery, usually at the expense of his/her own. Thus fantasy is encouraged in self-science both as a developmental skill and as a technique for awareness.

Topics for fantasy are suggested throughout the program. Sometimes students are asked to imagine themselves, "Get a picture in your head of . . ." Sometimes students are asked to picture and then report their fantasies out loud.

Start fantasy sessions with a period of quiet relaxation, i.e., listen to soft music with eyes shut. Or, experiment with conscious relaxation techniques. A simple one is to count backwards from ten to one. Ask the students to close their eyes as you count, and to take a deep breath on each number. Count slowly, allowing for genuine deep breathing. When the countdown is complete, quietly introduce the fantasy situation.

Fantasy sessions may be ended by a quiet reminder of the difference between fantasy and reality. Say to the group:

> "Now it's time to come back into the room. When I count to three, everybody come back into the room. When I count to three, everybody come back to the here-and-now. One, two, three!"

A stretching time or a brief physical activity following the fantasy helps with the transition.

Boasting. This is a technique used to create positive reinforcement of a particular behavior. If the children have trouble listening to each other, instead of confronting them with a negative approach ("You have to listen better, children!") we suggest having them boast and brag and exclaim how good one is at that particular thing. "I'm a good listener!" Direct the group to boast in different ways—whisper, shout, laugh.

Children may boast about their abilities. "I'm the best boxer in . . ." "I can play the violin!" "I'm the best in math." Or, children may boast about difficult areas: this serves to desensitize and often helps to create a sense of humor or perspective.

> From a Nueva Journal entry: "Harry couldn't think of anything good about himself, even though the other children tried to help him. He does not feel capable at school or at home. We started boasting. During the boasting, Harry began, 'I'm terrible.' I got him to do it more—louder—standing up and doing it. 'Shout as loud as you can!' Finally the other children were laughing and telling him he was the best at boasting that he was terrible. Harry started laughing, too,"*

---

†An excellent discussion of the value of fantasy may be found in *Put Your Mother on the Ceiling* by Richard de Mille, Viking Press, 1973.

Resents and Appreciates. Learning to express resentment or appreciation is an important tool, used as the group climate demands. Suggestions are given in the Flow Lessons for using Resents and Appreciates. You may want to use the techniques as general tools.

> We discuss what the two words mean, who has given us a Resent or an Appreciate, who have we given them to, what's the best one we ever got, which is easier to give. We might go around the group and give everyone an Appreciate—or we might imagine giving our parents, brothers, sisters, or teachers an Appreciate or Resent—how they might feel and how we feel when we get one. We're trying to get across the idea that this is a tool for communication. We can tell other people specifically what we appreciate about them or specifically what we resent. You never say unfinished statements such as "I appreciate/resent you." You always add, "I appreciate/resent you for making me my favorite cake, for pushing me and walking away."*

USING COGNITIVE INQUIRY TECHNIQUES

The opportunity to really learn in self-science pivots on the *Cognitive Inquiry* part of each lesson. By "learn," we mean to make conscious appraisal of the ideas generated during the affective-experiential activity, using the many cognitive tools at our disposal.

Each lesson suggests the specific cognitive follow-up and, in most instances, provides *Discussion Questions* appropriate for the activity.

DISCUSSION QUESTIONS ARE YOUR KEY COGNITIVE TEACHING TOOLS

Asking questions elicits responses and involvement in an ideal way; asking questions puts the focus on learning rather than teaching.

The self-science approach to asking effective questions is to ask *what?*, not *why?* It may take you a while to decondition yourself to the automatic "why's," but we have found that "why" questions lead to nonproductive, defensive, and circular responses, whereas, "what" questions encourage precise observation in a nonjudgmental way, permitting open discussion.

What do you see?
What do you hear?
What do you feel?
What are you thinking?
What just happened? What did you just do?
What were you feeling about that?
What do you appreciate?
What do you resent?

These are the kinds of questions to use over and over. Not only will you help students sharpen their cognitive faculties, but you will model appropriate and healthy modes of coping and analytical behavior.

Raths, Harmin and Simon suggest more clarifying questions in *Values and Teaching*.†

Is this something that you prize?
Are you glad about that?
Did you consider any alternatives?
Can you give me some examples of that idea?
What do you mean by . . . ? Can you define that word?
Where would that idea lead? What would be its consequences?
Would you really *do* that or are you just talking?
Are you saying that . . . (repeat the question)?
What other possibilities are there?
Is that very important to you?
Do you do this often?
Would you do the same thing over again?
Do you value that?

Our second general questioning approach is to constantly use the expectations of the lesson to focus on similarities and differences in response. Does anyone else in our group feel the same (different)? This kind of question drives home many points. It creates awareness of self and others; it builds reassurance by sharing similar thoughts and feelings; it enhances self-esteem by permitting recognition of differences. There is an underlying premise of respect for the thoughts and feelings of others; again, a demonstration in action of the goals of self-science.

---

†This book is highly recommended for related reading in teaching self-science. Raths, Harmin, Simon. *Values and Teaching*. Charles E. Merrill, 1966.

APPENDIX D
Classroom Management Techniques

LESSON PREPARATION

Each lesson plan gives you a step-by-step format; review it just prior to teaching. Try keeping rough notes on the dynamics of each lesson. These notes, kept in the form of a journal or diary can be very useful. (The notes in this handbook are from our journals.) Keeping notes helps focus thinking, makes you more aware of what's happening, and lets you see progress. Ten or fifteen minutes immediately after a class will do. Often something will come up—a topic for future discussion or an individual problem—which you will want to note for planning a subsequent Flow Lesson. Use the Teacher Comment space in each lesson for this purpose if you wish.

DECISIONS TO MAKE

How Voluntary Should the Self-Science Class Be?

We strongly believe that self-science should be offered as an elective, with a two-week trial period where students decide for themselves how they feel about the new and unfamiliar course. After two weeks, students are asked to sign a contract as a commitment for staying in the group.

How Should Student Progress Be Reported?

We prefer not to give grades; rather, we help students develop techniques for self-evaluation.

It may not be possible, however, for you (or you may not wish) to adopt this suggestion. You may work out a Pass/Fail system based on attendance and completed assignments. Whatever you decide, discuss your expectations quite clearly and openly with the group at the onset. (See also page 156.)

Should I Teach With a Co-Leader?

An important decision! We have found that two leaders (preferably a man and a woman) can provide certain supports not possible with one. Two leaders can check each other by following up discussions, observing each other's teaching techniques, correcting any possible biases or omissions, etc. Two leaders can also provide a communication model by the way they talk to each other during group meetings. Consider the advantages, particularly when first teaching self-science, to sharing leadership. The arrangement isn't always practical, but the suggestion is worth your consideration. Don't forget parents as possible co-leaders.

How Can I Share Self-Science Information With Other Classroom Teachers?

There is a delicate balance to keep in mind as you try to create a favorable climate with other classroom teachers. A reasonable degree of sharing can be of mutual assistance to you and other classroom teachers. Feedback can tell you whether some of the techniques taught are carried over, whether classroom behavior is changing in any way. Feedback from you can give the classroom teacher a second pair of eyes to consider what is happening in the classroom.

Your problem is one of respecting the group's confidence. Privacy and confidentiality are so important for creating a climate of trust, they are an entire Goal (Goal 2). Before you disclose any personal material, check with the individuals in the group and ask how they feel about discussing the matter with others.

SOME COMMON QUESTIONS

1. *"Don't I have to be a therapist to handle a group talking about themselves?"*

NO! Self-science is education—using cognitive methods to perceive affective states, patterns, group relationships, learning and study stules. Self-science is *not* group therapy. True, you may want to "work" with a child on a particular problem, but this is education work, not therapy. As trust grows, children *will* come to you with problems about their home or problems they are having with other teachers or friends. Your role is that of any interested advisor; encourage the child to talk over the problem directly with whom s/he has the problem. Help identify the problem and help the child develop a plan of action.

In some very few instances, you may spot a child in true trouble; refer the child to a guidance counselor or to your school psychologist—the same action you would take in any classroom.

AUTHORS' NOTE:

We never had a child have any kind of serious emotional breakdown. In a self-science class we have had children cry on occasion and become upset; however, we did not feel this inappropriate when dealing with important material. If a child does seem to become very upset, we may remove the child and work with him/her individually. That is, I may take the child out of the room while Karen continues with the group or vice-versa. We had only one instance where a child became so upset that this kind of attention was needed. I took the child to my office and let him cry and relax and then we discussed the situation. This was a child whose parents were in the middle of a divorce, and he was experiencing a great deal of difficulty with his father during the course of the divorce.

A few children seemed to need a little extra time; Karen and I would make ourselves available for this. If we happened to have two groups back-to-back, one of us would take the child aside and work with him/her while the other began the second group. This is an advantage of having two leaders.

Occasionally we have had children complain about their parents. What we have tried in these cases is to encourage the child to talk directly with the parent, usually offering, if it would be easier, for one of us to be there. We have never had a child arrange this kind of situation, even though a child may have initially responded favorably to the idea; usually, the child is able to deal with the parent. We try to anticipate the alternative responses from the parent. The child is then somewhat prepared for the way the parent responds.

There have been several situations which have occurred with various adults in relation to the children. These matters, when the child was displeased with a particular teacher or other adult, often came up in the self-science class. We attempted to find out as much information as possible from the children; possible solutions were explored. We did not talk to teachers unless we had permission from the children. I can think of one instance where three or four adolescent girls were critical of a faculty member (female) who they felt was wearing very, very short skirts. As we explored the matter, it was probably the kids' problem rather than the teacher's. To have dealt with the matter negatively would have been to say to the children, "You're not okay. Your problems are not worth consideration." What we did was talk with them and finally ask them if they felt free to talk to the teacher. They didn't feel comfortable doing that. So we asked them if one of us could speak with her. They said, "Yes," to that.

I had a conference with the teacher; rather than telling her that it was her problem, I indicated to her that it was the kids' problem, that they could not deal with the fact that she wore very, very short skirts. The teacher began wearing pantsuits and some of the attitudinal problems between the teacher and the students seemed to dissipate.

Another situation was one in which a group of students (these were younger children) were dissatisfied with the teacher, who they perceived as being quite strong in the disciplinarian role (with some reason). At the time, we utilized the "Mr. Alberti" game. This basically is a game of role-playing, giving the teacher a voice—a child role-plays a particular teacher, and the rest of the children act as they usually do. It became clear that much of the reason for the teacher's disciplinary actions was because of the children's actions. Through the use of the game they gradually understood how frustrated the teacher was when the children were "messing around," not attending to what they were supposed to be doing.

Our general philosophy, I suppose, in dealing with conflictual problems with children is to encourage them to speak for themselves and to try to prepare them so they can approach another child or an adult in a way that does not lead to defensive reaction.

Consequently, we try to teach them a number of communication skills. We encourage them to handle their own problems, rather than for us to do it. We have yet to run into a situation where children were not open to this kind of approach, except when they intuitively knew their reaction to a particular person was a defensive reaction. When we encountered this, we tried to circumvent it in some way. An example is the preceding case of the adolescent girls and their teacher. We tried to zero in with them specifically on what it was about the teacher that bothered them, and we decided to try a reowning technique (repeating what has been said about someone or something else as though it were true of oneself, taught by lessons in Goal 6). They did it. They gave several general characteristics about her, something like, "She thinks she's sexy but she's not." We had them reown the statement. We had to do this with a certain amount of humor or the children wouldn't have entertained the notion.

2. *How Will I Know I'm Successful in Teaching Self-Science?*

Be clear on what to expect from teaching self-science. "Success" and "failure" are really nonoperative. What you can expect are minimal to maximal outcomes. But in these days of educational accountability, it behooves one to answer the question, "What evidence will I accept that the program is having benefits for the students I serve?"

The answer depends upon the level of evaluation sophistication desired. Those who decide to rely on specific instruments may wish to give "pre-" and "post-" administrations of the Coopersmith *Self-Esteem* tool. In addition, Meyer and others at the Educational Research Council of America have found the use of sociometric devices to be quite effective for determining how students extend their sphere of positive relationships.

Less sophisticated measures include the decision on the part of the student to voluntarily participate in and complete the course of study. A place somewhat in between these two extremes, perhaps, is the most acceptable assessment position. Evaluation at this level can be completed by analyzing the anticipated affective and objective outcomes as stated in the program. The teacher can identify a series of questions that, when answered affirmatively, give evidence the program and the teacher are doing what the program was designed to do. Additional ideas can be obtained by writing the Nueva Learning Center (6565 Skyline Boulevard, Hillsborough, California 94010).

Unlike a traditional course, learning in self-science is really measured by what the student carries over into classrooms and social situations. Students check their own self-growth by looking at themselves through their journal entries. Moreover, a parent survey to ascertain changes in student behavior at home, with parents, siblings, and others is a good index for evaluation purposes.

"Seed planting" now doesn't always produce immediate results. Even with this in mind, the self-science teacher can often obtain valuable evaluation information through questionnaires and surveys regarding actual changes in student behavior in other parts of the school. Behavior changes should be apparent if the learning program is working well.

When personal expectations are clarified, worries about failures diminish. No single program or teacher is likely to resolve all problems. Field testing of self-science has been so positive, however, that the teacher should be assured that a high degree of success is possible. Even if results are somewhat less than anticipated, the analysis of "mistakes" is in itself a powerful learning opportunity.

The teacher seriously interested in assessment will take a hard look at personal performance; i.e., is the teacher modeling expected behavior? Are the teaching strategies built into the program being carried out accurately? Is the necessary planning for program implementation being accomplished? The question of personal competency is always with the professional, requiring periodic serious examination.

To help the neophyte self-science teacher evaluate the program, we have briefly outlined evaluation tools useful to us. A statement about each is made and the forms are illustrated in subsequent pages.

RECORD-KEEPING TOOLS

These forms help you and the group sharpen your observations and evaluations, the cognitive aspects of self-science. The lessons indicate when and how to use the forms. The samples may be put on duplicating masters for multiple use.

THE STUDENT JOURNAL

Starting with Lesson 3, students are asked to keep journals; they are used to sharpen powers of observation and awareness and to create a sense of progress. Journals may be either spiral-bound notebooks, or looseleaf. Information in the journals is private. Students don't share unless they want to. Find a private place to lock up the journals between classes.

THE STUDENT PROFILE SHEET (ANECDOTAL REPORT)

This is a tool for determining individual and group progress. The sheets are used twice for each student—at the end of Section I and also at the end of Section II.

Lesson Plans give further suggestions for evaluating progress at specified times.

THE TEACHER-RESPONSE FORM AND THE STUDENT-RESPONSE FORM

These are administered at the end of the course; they are self-explanatory.

THE PARENT RESPONSE FORM

This is mailed to parents at about the three-quarter point; it, too, is self-explanatory.

Student Profile Sheet
(Anecdotal Record)

1. Student's understanding of what s/he is learning about her/himself and how s/he uses the knowledge.
   (J. learned that expressing anger did not always push people apart but sometimes brought them together.)

2. Student "sharing."
   (J. came to the group and asked to talk about having no friends. He wanted to know what to do. The group shared his concern and offered their ideas and feelings.)

3. Student shares a description of personal feelings, thoughts, or actions.
   (J. shared that he was afraid to be home alone.)

4. Student initiates game, fantasy, role-playing, etc.
   (J. asked to use role-playing to work through a conflict.)

5. Four areas student feels comfortable talking about in the group.
   a. Problems with people in the group.
   b. Fear of not being liked.
   c. Boy-girl relationships.
   d. Trust—both in the group and outside.

6. Student is able to describe strengths and weaknesses.
   (Strength: I really care about other people's feelings.
   Weakness: I care too much about how other people see me. I'm not sure of myself.)

7. Explicit statements. "I want, need, feel, think . . ."
   (M. doesn't like me because I tease him. I feel bored.)

8. Student's ability to state personal concerns and relate to concerns of others.
   (J. "I'm afraid my mother will die. I know D. is feeling unhappy because he does not like being called names by the other students and they've been doing that all day.")

Teacher's Response Form

(For Other Teachers Who Have Self-Science Students)

1. What have you observed to be the effect of self-science upon your students? (Where possible, give specific examples of the effect on particular children. Do not use their names.)

_____

_____

_____

_____

_____

2. In addition to whatever effect self-science has had on the students' social and emotional development, has there been any effect in academic areas? Do they seem to apply any of the self-science techniques to academic areas?

_____

_____

_____

_____

_____

3. Have you incorporated self-science concepts in your work? If so, how? With what affect? What problems, if any, have you encountered in doing so? If not, why not?

_____

_____

_____

_____

_____

4. Do you think self-science should be a part of the regular curriculum? If so, as a special topic? As part of other subjects? If so, how should this be done? How should teachers be prepared?

_____

_____

_____

_____

_____

Student Response Form
(For Self-Science Participants)

1. What did you like most/least about self-science?

_____

_____

_____

2. Did it have any effect upon you? On how you related to others in the group outside of our sessions? To others at school? To friends outside of school? To your relations with your parents? With brothers or sisters? (Where possible, please try to give a specific example of how self-science affected you and your relations with others.)

_____

_____

_____

3. Do you think self-science has had any effect on your academic work at school? If so, how?

_____

_____

_____

4. Should more/less time be devoted to self-science?

_____

_____

_____

5. What changes would you want to see in self-science?

_____

_____

_____

6. In two or three sentences each, how would you describe self-science to:
   A new classmate at school?
   Your parents?
   The principal of a new school you transfer to?

_____

_____

_____

Parent Response Form
(For Parents of Children Participating in Self-Science)

As you know, your son/daughter _____ has been participating voluntarily for the past _____ year(s) in our self-science program. We are interested in its effect on children and would appreciate your taking the time to answer the following questions. As we are interested in the program's effect on the children as a whole, please feel free, should you wish, to tear off the top section and not use your child's name in your answers. Thank you.

----

1. Has your child discussed self-science with you? What has s/he said about it? What it is? What we do in self-science? How they feel about it?

_____

_____

_____

2. Have you noticed any changes in your child's behavior since s/he has been participating in self-science? In how s/he relates to friends? Siblings? You? Please be as specific as possible.

_____

_____

_____

3. If your child at _____ (school) has siblings at other schools (or at _____ (school) but not in self-sciencing), do you notice any difference in how they deal with their emotions? Other people?

_____

_____

_____

4. Has self-science had any effect on your child's academic work?

_____

_____

_____

5. Do you think self-science is a valuable part of the _____ (school) curriculum? Would you want to see it expanded or reduced? For schools other than _____ (school) do you think a program such as self-science would be desirable?

_____

_____

_____

© 1978 Goodyear Publishing Co. from Karen Stone and Hal Dillehunt, Self-Science: The Subject Is Me.

About the Flow Lessons

WHAT ARE THEY?

Flow lessons are suggested at ten different times in the curriculum sequence. These are unstructured to allow for group flow and specific group needs. Though the subject matter is open, the process of self-science is reinforced through these lessons.

Flow lessons are opportunities to deal with group-initiated topics: areas the children have said they'd like to talk more about. Flow lessons often resemble rap sessions.

Flow lessons may also be used to focus on individual patterns or problems you may have observed.

Often planned lessons will turn into a flow lesson, simply because the group spirit that day will demand dealing with the children's concerns. In this case, it's usually better to go with the group, dealing with whatever evoked the concern; come back to the lesson plan the next time. As you become more familiar with the goals of the curriculum and the Trumpet process, you will use flow lessons more frequently. These nonstructured sessions, initiated by students, indicate an openness and trust that allows them to deal with personal concerns.

SUGGESTED TOPICS

Undoubtedly, your own group will provide a wealth of topics for flow lessons, but some of the topics we have addressed are:

- Just plain talking
- Birthdays
- Halloween
- Thanksgiving
- Adoption
- Christmas
- What happened during vacation
- Divorce
- Sex
- Personal problems
- Illness
- Death

We have also used flow lessons for parties or for taking a special field trip.

The subject matter of flow lessons is far less important than the affective study and the cognitive awareness you bring to the lessons.

Use any of the techniques suggested to get the ball rolling: role-playing, brainstorming, fantasy, or just plain conversation and question asking. Let the group suggest and play any of the favorite games they have learned.

The *Notes From Nueva* which follow give you the flavor of the flow lessons we have encountered.

Notes from Nueva

JUST PLAIN TALKING

The kids came in, sat down and started talking. They were talking about a new student who is "weird." We had a lengthy discussion about what "weird" meant to them. Hal said that we think people are weird when we don't know anything about them and they seem different to us.

We remarked that Kay was not with us. She was not at school. We talked about Kay's role in the group.

"She never says anything."
"She's shy."
"She's quiet."
"She didn't come today because Helen isn't here."

We asked if they could think of ways they could help Kay become more a part of the group. We can try to include her more and ask her questions.

BIRTHDAYS

The Birthday Game can be introduced either because someone is having one or as a special treat. All children love to talk about their birthdays. We usually have a brief discussion about why birthdays are important (they are our own special day—a celebration of "me") and what they like most about birthdays. We may then act out our favorite birthday, our favorite cake, the earliest birthday we can remember, the worst/best presents, or we fantasize about the perfect birthday—when it would be, who'd be there, what we'd do, etc. A group of 12 year olds discovered that they still liked to get certain toys for their birthday, even if they were childish. They were amazed to discover they all have stuffed animals they enjoyed playing with occasionally.

THANKSGIVING

We opened by talking about Thanksgiving. They were thankful for not having school, homework, friends, parents, etc. They told about Pilgrims, the Mayflower, the Indians and the Thanksgiving feast.

We suggested that we might make family appreciation cards for Thanksgiving. This is a good time to introduce "Appreciates." We have the children make a place card for each member of their family and write one thing they appreciate about that person on the card. These are taken home and placed on the table. We follow up with discussions about the feelings and responses of their family. This is a good time for the leader to give each child an Appreciate. This often leads to dealing with Resents, which we don't write on place cards to be taken home. The use of Resents and Appreciates as a technique helps children become aware of their attitude toward others.

Mark made cards this time for his mother and father. Paul didn't want to make any. While we were doing this, we talked about what we would be doing for Thanksgiving. We all agreed it was a special time to be with our families.

ADOPTION

Jill started talking about her birth certificate that said she was Norwegian and German but that they could put anything they wanted on a birth certificate. Her sister, Alice, was a combination of lots of things. She thought it was better to just be from two nationalities. Hal asked why hers was different from her sister's, and she told everyone she was adopted. I asked Jill if she would like to talk about how it felt to be adopted. She said, "Yes." It didn't bother her a bit (very defensively). Terry said he used to think he was adopted because his older brother used to tell him he was when he was mad at him. Art and Doris said they'd thought about it sometimes and I told Jill that I used to think I was adopted when I thought my mother was mean to me.

Terry said he thought Jill didn't want to talk about being adopted, but she insisted that she did. I suggested that we talk about this after Christmas vacation. I felt Jill had revealed as much as she was comfortable with at the time. I suggested that we talk about our favorite Christmas present.

Notes from Nueva

CHRISTMAS

I mentioned that everyone in school seemed very excited, and several children mentioned it was because of Christmas. I asked everyone, "What was your favorite Christmas?"

"This year because I'm getting a large box that might be a drum set."

"Last year because I got a bow and arrow."

"Next year because I don't know what I'll get."

"This year because I found some presents and I think they're for me."

"This year because my grandmother is going to get me a Spanish doll."

"When I got a Raggedy-Ann."

"Last year, I got a bike."

"Every Christmas."

"This year because I got a desk with a locked drawer."

"I never had Christmas. We have Hanukkah. I like every Hanukkah."

"Can't decide. Last Christmas I went to my friend's house on Christmas Eve and this Christmas, we're going to Jamaica."

"Last Christmas. I got a spinning wheel."

We talked about what we did at Christmas and about some of the customs we had in our families.

CUSTOMS:

We have a tree and decorate it.

We open our presents on Christmas Day.

Some people open one on Christmas Eve.

Read "The Night Before Christmas."

Have to wait until everyone's awake.

At some houses, they decorate the tree on Christmas Eve.

Hunt for presents that are hidden on Christmas Eve.

Jack had a pattern of sneaking candy out of his sister's stocking.

We asked if there ever is a time when Christmas isn't fun.

"Don't get what you want. You get disappointed."

The children asked to play Explode. (We were talking about unhappy Christmases.)

Why do you need to explode?

"Need to waste energy. We have too much."

"Because we're always inside."

"Because I don't get to go outside."

"Because we saw a ballet yesterday and we had to sit around a lot."

"Because I like to run."

How does Christmas make you feel?

Happy; good; makes you sad when it's over because you have to wait another year to get more presents.

Mary reminded us that we said we'd play Tape Recorder Game today; so, we introduced the tape recorder game. The Speaker told what s/he wanted for Christmas.

"All my wishes to come true; a GI Joe; helicopter; electric football; machine gun; tape recorder."

"Puppy; watch; camera."

"Puppy; watch."

Mark said his favorite present was a stuffed Teddy Bear that he had wanted for months. As a matter of fact, he still had it. He had about three stuffed animals. Billy was laughing. Mary turned to him and said, "What are you laughing about? There's nothing wrong with having stuffed animals." Billy said, "I know, I have some."

For the next half hour everyone in the group had a wonderful time reminiscing about being a little child. Sean told about the blanket he'd had since he was a baby. It had so many holes in it, it was a rag. When he was six he "acted like a big man," and told his mother he didn't want it any more and she could throw it away any time. About a week later he came home from school and ran all over the house looking for his blanket because he needed it. He finally asked his mother if she knew where it was. She had thrown it away. He ran up to his room and cried because he still needed it, and it was gone.

Billy said he didn't have a blanket but he had a rubber Snoopy dog. He used to chew on the dog's nose instead of sucking his thumb or a pacifier. He recalled that he went through a number of Snoopies.

Jack told about his stuffed animals. He has a lot of them and one day he decided to give them a bath and they were ruined. He had a kitten with real fur and all the fur fell off and he felt really bad.

Mark remembered that he'd always wanted a little plastic lawn mower and he was so excited when he got one. All the boys had wanted this particular toy and they had great fun laughing together and remembering the lawns they pretended to be mowing. Mark also liked the GI Joe that he'd gotten even though the foot and hand fell off. At this point they all had a very lively discussion about GI Joe dolls, all of their equipment, how hard it was to dress them, all the imaginary games they played with them, and general relief that they all enjoyed this, including Karen who played with her brother's toys.

Karen recalled some dolls she had that she liked very much, but she talked a great deal with the boys about playing with toy soldiers and GI Joe men.

The entire group was very close today and really enjoyed reminiscing about earlier holiday seasons and being little children. We all wished each other happy holidays.

Notes From Nueva

SEX

It was mid-way through the year, this was a group of 11 and 12 year old students. The occasion was Valentine's Day. We asked the children what the meaning of Valentine's Day was, whereupon we heard a great deal of snickers and giggles from the students. With some continued prodding from the leaders, it became quite evident that their giggles were related to the topic of sex. No one, however, referred to it. "Well, you know what we're talking about; you know what it is." But no one was willing to talk about it.

As leaders, we decided that we would all whisper the word sex, together silently. Then we said it softly, loudly, lowly, quickly until we were able to say the word without too much embarrassment.

We asked them if there were things that they wanted to know about sex. They all indicated that there were some things—but that they knew almost everything. By their demeanor, it was quite apparent that they were embarrassed to ask the question they wanted to for fear of appearing unknowledgeable in the area. Consequently we used the technique of having everybody write down a question about sex on a piece of paper. The questions were mixed in a container, passed out, and read anonymously. The total group participated in answering the questions.

Although there was some nervous laughter, most of the children—in fact, I believe all of the children—expressed relief in being able to frankly ask the questions that were of concern to them. The discussion of sex continued often after that, relating to such topics as kissing, masturbation, dating, and feelings and values about sex.

ILLNESS

We had an interesting session talking about illness—our own and our parents'. Everyone told about their parents being ill and as they did, we asked them to show how they felt.

Dane said his mother was sick for three months and he stayed with his father. He saw her once a week and that helped, but he was lonesome for her and worried. He would have been worried to death if he hadn't been able to see her.

Tom said when he was six he was in the hospital with hepatitis. He was very ill and doesn't remember a lot. His father also had hepatitis and was in the hospital for three months. We asked him if he had worried about his father, but he said he was too sick himself to be aware that his father was sick.

Alan told about his mother having surgery a few years ago. He said he wasn't sure what it was but he was scared when she was gone and she didn't feel well when she came home.

Sean told about his mother and father. His mother had to have her thyroid out and that was very serious because your thyroid gives you energy. She takes medicine every day. His father has an old back injury and he recently hurt it. Now he can hardly get around. Sean was very worried when his mother was sick and he felt sorry for his dad, but he knew he would get better.

Hal told about his mother being very sick in the hospital. They couldn't see her but their father took them to her window and they could look in. There were bars on the window. Everyone joined in the discussion on why there were bars. I told them they were there because the rooms on the first floor face a large open area and the bars are to keep people out.

Bob said it seemed like his mother was sick a very long time, although it was only ten days, and that he was scared because he couldn't see her.

Kelly told about her father's operation and how they sneaked into the hospital to see him. It worries her when her parents are sick.

Karen told about her mother who went to New York for three months to have an operation while her grandmother took care of her and her sister. She was very scared because her mother was gone so long and she was so far away.

We asked them what they worried about and they replied, ". . . they wouldn't get better; who'd take care of them? What would happen?" We asked if they ever worried about their parents dying and they all said they had. After a brief discussion someone asked to play Explode.

Notes from Nueva

DEATH

The group asked questions about Hal's absence. I explained that he had gone to Southern California to attend his grandfather's funeral. The group appeared very curious about the death and wanted to discuss the details of when his grandfather had died, how, where, when the funeral was going to be and how Hal felt. I said that I knew few details but that Hal's grandfather was quite elderly. We proceeded to discuss how Hal might be feeling. Del and Kelly suggested that he might be feeling very sad. Billy and Kay suggested that he might feel relieved if his grandfather had been very old and sick. I asked if they had ever had anyone in their family or someone they know die. Several children in the group had experiences to share.

Terry, who is one of the oldest boys in the group and who has never offered to talk in the group before, told about his grandmother. "Before she died she was sick for a long time. She was little and very skinny and. when you sat down next to her you had to be careful because it hurt her to be jarred. She was very old when she died and we all felt really sad." His tone of voice and demeanor appeared serious and he seemed to be reexperiencing some of the sadness in relation to his grandmother's death.

Art said, "When my grandmother died, we all felt really bad. She lived in Iowa and when we went to visit my grandfather in the summer we were all lonesome for my grandmother."

Del, "My uncle died and everyone felt really bad."

Kristi said, "We had a neighbor who had a seven year old daughter who was dying of cancer. She had seven operations before she died and she was very sick and weak. Everyone felt bad when she died but they were also relieved because she had suffered for so long. It was better that she died. I really felt sad when our dog died. He was my best friend and he had been with our family ever since I was a baby. We grew up together and when he died I cried for a week and I felt like running away from home." She went on to explain how angry she was with her parents because they had to put the dog to sleep. Jim interrupted and said he could never feel that bad about an animal dying—then he quietly said, "I know how it will feel when my mother dies."

Everyone in the room turned to look at him. The group had obviously heard Jim's comment and was somewhat shaken by it. Billy asked him how he knew that. He said, "When my mother went to India it was the saddest day of my life. I didn't think I could stand it—I cried for a week and I never felt so lonely and sad." The other group members wanted to know why his mother had gone to India, how long she would be there, where his father was, did he have any brothers or sisters, where were they, and how long would his parents be gone.

Jim, with sadness apparent in his voice and body movement, told how his parents were missionaries for the church. His father had been in India for one-and-one-half years before his mother left a year ago. They decided not to take him with them because the schools he would go to would be very bad. The only decent schools were English and they hit you with canes; he appeared to be trying to deal with his sense of loss by rationalizing about the schools. Jim went on to say he has one brother who is older than he is and is staying in Denver. He hadn't seen him since June but is really looking forward to seeing him at Christmas. He told Jill, who talks a lot about how she dislikes her sister, that she wouldn't feel that way if she couldn't be with her sister. He used to fight a lot with his brother but now he really missed him and knew how much he loved him. Jim's parents will be gone for one more year and when they come home they are going to have a huge bottle of champagne and a souffle. Everyone in the group was moved by Jim's deep feelings for his family. He had tears in his eyes as did several other children. There was a short silence as the group members appeared to be absorbing what Jim had been saying. Consequently, at this point, it seemed appropriate for the group to review the major feelings of the discussion. I asked the group if they could recall all the different words we had used to describe our feelings about death. We remembered sad, lonely, bad, unhappy and relieved.

I then asked what happens when someone dies and Alan immediately said, "They leave you. They leave you forever." Again the whole group looked at Jim and everyone sat silently for a minute. Jim said in a very soft and saddened voice, "That was it. It was like she died because she went to India and left me and it seemed like forever." There were tears in everyone's eyes.

Notes from Nueva

Alan, Billy, and Kay all told about the times their parents had left them to go on trips and how it had seemed like forever. I asked Alan if he resented his parents at all when they returned from a month in Europe. He said, "No," but then added, "Maybe a little. I was mad at them the next day." I suggested that it was very natural to feel some resentment towards people who leave us, even if they die. Alan said he remembered when he visited his grandfather after his grandmother died and he felt bad that she wasn't there to bake him his favorite cookies he always had before.

At this point, Jim said he felt like he needed to play Explode. Everyone agreed and immediately got up to play. Explode is like a game of tag. I am "It," and when I tag them, they are supposed to explode. We had played this game many times but no one had ever really exploded. There were a few yells, jumping onto the bean bag chairs but no explosion; i.e., real evidence of emotional release.

I tagged Jim first and he ran across the room and dove on a pile of bean bags yelling as loud as he could. Everyone froze for a minute to watch. He was face down, kicking his feet, pounding his fists, yelling. As I tagged each child he or she really exploded for the first time. When all had been tagged, they all wanted to play again. We played two more times. Each time the explosions were greater in intensity. After the third game, I suggested we all sit down quietly for a few minutes. We did some deep breathing exercises to get centered before leaving. The whole group seemed relaxed; before leaving, Jim quietly stated that he was glad he'd talked about his mother and he felt better.

APPENDIX E
Ideas in Support of Self-Science

The following few paragraphs are included not to engage in a weighty discourse regarding psychological theory, but to describe briefly (for instructive purposes) some of the theoretical notions of Kelly and Maslow as they relate to the self-science curriculum. Although the systems may appear in opposition, the authors of self-science believe that aspects of both theories support the foundations of self-science.

Kelly's theory of "Personal Constructs" is basically phenomenological. It is impossible, therefore, to examine the "self" in isolation.

"Self," according to Kelly, must be viewed in the context of its relationship to "non-self" and the phenomena involved in these contexts of examinations. Kelly suggests that we view people as a system of "constructs" in order to facilitate our understanding of human behavior.

"A Construct is a way in which some things are construed as being alike and yet different from others."[1] According to Kelly, one's personal constructs provide the means for viewing situations or events to make them meaningful and predictable. This view of people as predictors of the future allows individuals to exert control over their own future to the extent that they develop a construct system with which they identify self. The system needs to be sufficiently comprehensive to subsume the world around them.[2] From this viewpoint a person is controlled by personal constructs or systems of constructs. The systems, however, are not static as people can learn new constructs (patterns); ones which may rival the old.

The self is only one of a series of major constructs. The self-construct influences numerous other constructs by exerting control over one's behavior, not only when one is alone but also with others. A person's behavior in relation to others is usually a comparison of the constructs observed in their behavior and one's own evolving construct system.

The development of new constructs or the maintenance of old ones is contingent upon several conditions. Validation tends to assure the maintenance of valuable constructs. Approaching constructs in varying contexts which do not involve the self or family members facilitates the development of new constructs. A climate of "experimentation" where new constructs can be "tried on" and the availability of validating data tends to facilitate the development of new and/or additional constructs. The availability and acceptance of validating data allows people to construe from their experiences. People do not seem to learn simply from experience; they learn by successive "construing" of experiences.

Personal construct theory adopts an historical approach which asserts phenomenologically that since one's activities at a given time are influenced by one's perception (perspective) at the moment, the past influences current activities through perceptions. This view is held to exist whether one is perceiving "conscious" or "nonconscious" processes. From this theory comes the belief that both the past and the future affect one's present activities . . . not as they did in the past nor will in the future, but as they influence or color present perceptions. For example, if a young man's history includes a very authoritarian father for whom past reactions were passive compliance, it is likely that the young man's responses to other such figures will be similar (whether appropriate or not). Is the young man destined now to respond in the same way because of "unconscious conflicts" or simple "reinforcement"? We believe not! Rather, his responses are determined by his current perception of authority figures which are a fusion of his past and future. As LeFebre says, "The present is the fusion of my being my future with my being my past."[3]

While Kelly's theory supports a part of the self-science program, the work of Abraham Maslow seems to offer additional support, especially when considered in light of basic human needs. Maslow has developed a schema of the basic needs (in hierarchial order) which motivate action. These needs are (1) the need for physical survival, food, air, water; (2) the need for physical shelter, activity and rest; (3) the need for love; (4) the need for emotional security; (5) the need for belonging; (6) the need for self-actualization, self-esteem and self-knowledge.[4]

Maslow believes that people strive to satisfy all of these needs. One need level cannot be attempted until and unless the preceding need level has been satisfied. A threat to a lower order need will halt or interrupt the attempted satisfaction of a higher order need. The recent economic factors in the United States and their concomitant influences verify Maslow's position. In the past few years in the United States, minimal needs for food and shelter have been assured

1. Kelly, G. H., *The Psychology of Personal Constructs, Vol. I: A Theory of Personality.* Norton, New York, 1955, p. 105.

2. *Ibid.,* p. 127.

3. LeFebre, L., *Psychotherapy Relocated.* Unpublished Manuscript, 1975, Chapter 4, p. 24.

4. Maslow, A. H., *Motivation and Personality.* Harper & Row, New York, 1970.

through many of the social programs. Meeting these basic needs not only tends to satisfy elementary demands, but, additionally, and often equally important, they help to support the requirements for love, belonging, and self-actualization.

The authors of self-science believe it is important to understand one's needs as well as the support systems by which these needs are met. A fundamental goal of education, then, leads more to the need for self-actualization than toward the satisfaction of lower order needs although the lower order needs, too, are beginning to receive attention. Recognition of this need system has resulted in various school-associated food programs aimed at children who are unable to pay attention in school because the students are hungry. Failure to satisfy lower order needs inhibits the ability to satisfy higher order needs.

In Kelly's framework, failure to satisfy any need on the hierarchy represents a threat to the self-construct system. In the formation of new constructs, as he states, ". . . construct is threatening when it is itself an element in a next-higher-order construct which is, in turn, incompatible with other higher-order constructs upon which the person is dependent for his living."[5] "Another effect of introducing threatening elements, and frequently an undesirable one, is the tendency for the traumatic experience to act as further subjective documentation or proof of the client's own maladaptive conceptual framework."[6]

From the work of Kelly, Maslow and others, it seems clear that a non-threatening and supportive environment is necessary for an exploration of one's own personal constructs. Self-Science, therefore, utilizes a series of extended classroom norms or guidelines to achieve an atmosphere conducive to self-exploration.

5. Kelly, G. H., op. cit., p. 166.
6. Ibid., p. 168.

GLOSSARY

approach getting close to—movement towards a goal.

attending paying attention to, listening.

avoidance to withdraw—to keep away.

body talk using parts of the body to communicate non-verbally.

brainstorm a group problem solving technique that involves the spontaneous contribution of ideas from all members of the group.

centered to be in control of oneself.

censor withholding or keeping from the group information, thoughts or feelings.

concentric having a common center.

confidentiality private information that all agree not to share outside the group.

confrontation to face, to encounter—to bring out into the open.

consensus unanimous group agreement.

consequences the result of one's thoughts, feelings or actions.

continuum of awareness a chart that indicates one's understanding of one's thoughts, feelings or actions.

coping to deal with and/or attempt to overcome problems and difficulties.

deliberate careful, thorough consideration—awareness of consequences.

explicit statement clear, direct, non-ambiguous communication.

exploding to let go—to burst out with feelings.

fantasy the process of creating mental images (imagination).

inference skills moving from one proposition, statement or idea considered true to another, whose truth is believed to follow from the former.

inquiry to ask about—to seek information by questioning.

intimate a very close association—a warm friendship.

introspection examination of one's own thoughts and/or feelings.

killer statement a negative statement—an insult.

legitimize to affirm.

metaphor a figure of speech where a word or phrase expressing one kind of object or idea is used in place of another to suggest a likeness between them.

modeling to serve as a pattern—an example for imitation or emulation.

non-verbal communication expressing one's self with little or no language.

pattern a repeated set of thoughts, feelings or actions that characterize an individual.

power control, authority or influence over self and/or others.

reown to take back for oneself descriptions, statements or judgments one has made about an object or person.

resents a statement of what one does not like.

role-play to assume—to pretend to be someone or something else.

self disclosure to open up—to talk about one's self.

self esteem confidence and satisfaction in one's self.

self-science studying self using the scientific process.

to project to describe, make statements or judgments about another that are true of one's self.

values something (a principle or quality or belief) attributed to be desirably worthwhile, important, good, evil, etc.

SELF-SCIENCE CONTRACT

I _____ agree to participate
STUDENT'S NAME

in self-sciencing from now until the end of
the year (or end of semester).

_____
STUDENT'S SIGNATURE

_____
TEACHER'S SIGNATURE

THE TRUMPET

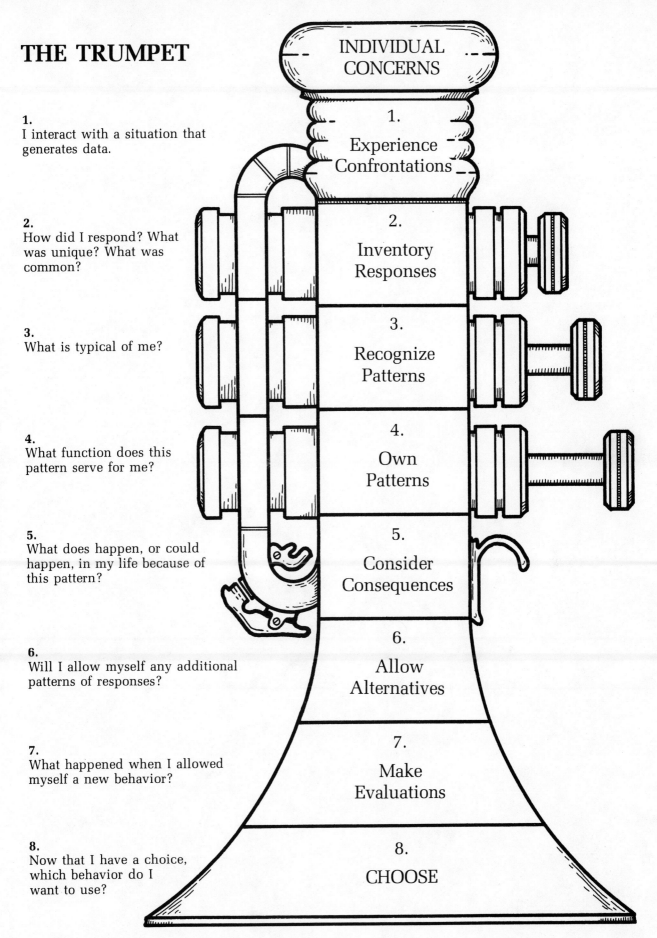

1.
I interact with a situation that generates data.

2.
How did I respond? What was unique? What was common?

3.
What is typical of me?

4.
What function does this pattern serve for me?

5.
What does happen, or could happen, in my life because of this pattern?

6.
Will I allow myself any additional patterns of responses?

7.
What happened when I allowed myself a new behavior?

8.
Now that I have a choice, which behavior do I want to use?

INDIVIDUAL CONCERNS

1. Experience Confrontations

2. Inventory Responses

3. Recognize Patterns

4. Own Patterns

5. Consider Consequences

6. Allow Alternatives

7. Make Evaluations

8. CHOOSE